JOSIE
An East Anglian Childhood Remembered

JOSIE

An East Anglian Childhood Remembered

Joy Wiseman

UNITED WRITERS
Cornwall

UNITED WRITERS PUBLICATIONS LTD
Ailsa, Castle Gate, Penzance, Cornwall.

British Library Cataloguing in Publication Data:
A catalogue record for this book is
available from the British Library.

ISBN 1 85200 068 6

Printed in Great Britain by:
United Writers Publications Ltd.,
Cornwall.

To Rex -
    who probably made someone
    an excellent husband,
and Edwin -
    who probably didn't!

CONTENTS

1

A Gift from God

Josie hesitated at the bottom of the steep flight of stairs. With one hand she clung tightly to her father, with the other she clasped a brown paper bag containing small lead farmyard animals.

Her father had said he had a surprise for her upstairs. She looked up at her father before placing her foot on the stairs. She had her doubts about surprises, hadn't he said exactly the same thing two weeks ago when he had told her that she would be going to spend a couple of weeks with Auntie May?

Josie recalled the despair she had felt at this unexpected announcement. Why was she being sent away when her brother Jimmy was remaining at home? Auntie May lived on the other side of town, so she wouldn't be able to go to school. She wondered what she would do all day alone with her aunt, with no friends to play with.

The thing that had hurt most was the knowledge that Jimmy wasn't being banished.

She had always thought that she was her father's favourite, but this so-called surprise had made her doubt this.

Her father had explained that her mother was not very well and needed a bit of a rest, but as soon as she was better Josie could return home. So she had squared her shoulders and tried not to cry, because only babies cried. All right, she would go to Auntie May she had said, trying not to sound too reluctant as she could see her father was worried. Two bus rides later she had arrived at Auntie May's house accompanied by her brother Jimmy to carry her case and see her safely installed at her aunt's.

Josie was five years old and Jimmy, at ten years old, seemed to her very much the big brother in charge of things. On arrival she was clasped to Auntie May's ample bosom and a kiss planted on her cheek. Josie squirmed unhappily in her aunt's arms, a deeply private child, not given to shows of affection except towards her father whom she adored. When she was at home and relatives visited, if they were the sort to bestow kisses, Josie would disappear into the garden until the danger had passed and the kissing had ceased.

She felt sad when Jimmy left to make the two bus rides home. She sat politely on a chair waiting for her aunt to tell her what to do.

"Perhaps we'll put your clothes away and you can see your bedroom," said her aunt.

Josie had to admit, rather grudgingly, that it was a very nice room, rather superior to her own untidy bedroom at home. There were colouring books and coloured pencils on the bedside table, which Josie realised her aunt must have bought specially for her as she had no children of her own.

The two weeks had gone surprisingly quickly. Each day when she awoke she wondered if her mother was getting any better. Her aunt was rather surprised that Josie never mentioned her mother, but Josie was more worried than she cared to admit about her mother's illness. Her method of coping with this anxiety was to keep her thoughts to herself; she felt if she didn't ask, she couldn't be told her mother had died, and she would never get to go home again.

And now she stood on the landing still clinging to her father's hand as he opened the bedroom door. There in the big bed, propped up with a mountain of pillows, lay her mother. 'She's not dead,' thought Josie thankfully, but what was that wrapped in a white shawl beside her?

"This is your new little brother," said her father.

Her mother smiled. "Come and look at him, Josie," she said, pulling the shawl gently aside.

Josie moved nearer, after being prodded by her father. She gazed at the little red wrinkled face: it was positively the ugliest baby she had ever seen. Why, she wondered, was her mother looking at it so tenderly? She looked at her father, who was making little clucking noises at the infant.

Trying to show some enthusiasm, which was obviously expected of her, she turned her attention once again to the baby. Suddenly the little red face puckered up even more and he emitted an ear-splitting wail.

"There, there," said her mother, gathering up the wailing baby. "Isn't he lovely?" she said after she had rocked him to sleep again.

Josie felt that she wasn't really required to answer this, as her mother was now crooning softly to the baby. Better to keep her thoughts to herself.

Quickly changing the subject she said, "Look at all my farm animals Mum, Auntie May has bought me lots of extra animals and a farmer and his wife." She spread them out on the bed for her mother to look at, but her mother's attention was again attracted by another wail from the baby, who had gone even redder in the face.

"I think he wants changing," said her mother.

"I think we'll go downstairs now Josie, your mother's getting a bit tired," said her father, gathering up the farm animals and returning them to the bag.

Once downstairs away from the wailing infant, her father sat her on his knee.

"Well, what do you think of your new baby brother, Josie?"

Josie hesitated, perhaps her father hadn't noticed what a funny looking little creature he was.

"Where did he come from?" she asked, trying to delay having to express an opinion.

"Doctor brought him," said her father.

Josie's fertile imagination began to work overtime.

The doctor was one of the few people of Josie's acquaintance who owned a car. If the doctor had brought the baby, then obviously he would have brought several samples. Josie imagined the back seat of the doctor's car, with a line of little wrapped bundles. Surely there must have been some who looked like the baby brothers that her friends had. These babies were round and pink, with lovely curls, and they smiled all the time, they didn't wail like this baby her father had picked. She tried to picture the red puckered little face, but the only image she managed to conjure up was a very wrinkled version of her grand-father.

Josie closed her eyes to banish the vision.

"Did you have to pay for him?" she asked.

"Yes, in a way I suppose I did," her father gave a chuckle.

"Can I have my Saturday penny, Dad?" Josie asked, trying to steer the conversation away from the baby.

"Now let me see, you've missed two Saturdays while you've been at Auntie May's, that means you're entitled to thruppence this week."

"Cor! Thanks, Dad," said Josie, pocketing the three large coins, and already sorting out what she wanted to spend them on.

Her Saturday penny was supposed to last the week, but Josie knew she could usually wheedle an extra ha'penny during the week from her father, who usually said, "Don't tell your mother."

The boy next door was named Duncan and he was a couple of months older than Josie. Hailing originally from Scotland, Josie sometimes had difficulty understanding what he said. His mother did not allow him out of his garden so, unless Josie visited him, he was really quite a lonely boy. Josie on the other hand had several friends, but whenever possible she would hang around Jimmy and his friends, hoping to be allowed to join their games. When she tired of being told to 'clear off' she would go to visit Duncan or her very best friend Raymond.

Sometimes when Jimmy and his friends decided to play cricket, first chalking the wicket on a convenient wall, if they found they were one short they would very grudgingly let Josie join them. If she actually made a few runs they might say, "You're not so bad, kid!" This would really make her day, but her moment of glory was usually soon over.

When not worrying her brother, or visiting Duncan, Josie would take her whip and top on to the pavement and press the top into the soft earth at the bottom of one of the trees. Carefully winding the string of the whip around the top and giving it a sharp tug, she would send the top spinning on the hard surface of the pavement. Josie could hold her own when it came to top spinning games, even Jimmy's friends sometimes stopped what they were doing to watch. Skipping was another pastime that didn't require anyone else to join in. Josie would happily chant a skipping rhyme as she hopped up and down.

Five stones, marbles and cigarette cards were all games requiring at least two participants. Josie's favourite of these was cigarette cards, at which she was an acknowledged expert, as many a child losing its entire collection of cards could verify. Whenever someone suggested a game of cards, Josie would bring forth her large pile of 'oddments' and 'twicers' - never, never would she chance losing her 'sets'. Having sorted out a suitable wall with a nice even piece of concrete in front of it, the two protagonists would take it in turn to kneel down and hurl a card at the wall, the object being to cover an opponent's card with your own which then entitled you to all the cards on the ground. Then the whole procedure was repeated until one player had lost all their cards.

Josie gazed into the window of the corner shop at the mouth-watering display of confectionery. A box of sherbet dabs stood next to the liquorice fancies, pipes, shoelaces, catherine wheels with a coloured sweet in the middle. Then a box of the new sensation, bubble-gum, each wrapped in a separate paper and looking like very large toffees. Mother was not at all keen on these, she considered blowing bubbles a very mucky pastime since much of the gum finished on one's face or clothes. This was understandable. Next in line was a box of gob-stoppers, these would change colour as you sucked them, necessitating constant removal from the mouth to check what colour they had become.

In the corner of the window stood a box of wooden tops with brightly coloured stripes and next to them a box of white clay pipes, these were excellent for blowing bubbles and only cost a ha'penny each. Josie had carelessly dropped the last one, shattering it into small pieces, and she thought she might invest a ha'penny of her thruppence in buying a replacement. Blowing bubbles could be good fun. If you blew very carefully, you could produce an enormous sparkling jewel coloured bubble, which would float away until it burst in a shower of tiny droplets.

On a shelf around the top of the window stood rows of large glass jars containing bull's-eyes, clove balls, pear drops, jelly babies, dolly mixtures, chocolate drops, acid drops, spearmint balls, and aniseed balls. As well as this dazzling display of boiled sweets, there was toffee in a large block, broken up with a hammer by the shop-keeper.

On the counter stood boxes of various sorts of chocolate bars, the cheapest of these cost a penny, so were seldom bought by the children. Another favourite with both Josie and Jimmy was brown sugar. The shop-keeper would take a sheet of blue sugar-paper and twist it into a funnel shape, turning over the end to form a bag, this he would fill with brown sugar which was stored in a barrel with a scoop for ladling it out. A bag of sugar would last a whole afternoon if you just wet your finger, dipped it in the bag and sucked it.

Josie finally settled for a hap'orth of brown sugar, a hap'orth of aniseed balls and a clay pipe.

She carefully carried her purchases into the back garden and sat on the doorstep to concentrate on her bag of sugar. When Jimmy appeared she offered him the bag of aniseed balls.

"Like a sweet, Jimmy?" she asked.

Jimmy helped himself to two.

"What's this in aid of?" he asked suspiciously.

"Nothing, nothing," Josie said quickly. "It's nice to be home again."

"I thought you had a good time at Auntie May's!"

"I did, much better than I thought - er - Jimmy, would you make me a cup of soap-suds so I can use my bubble pipe?"

"I knew you wanted something, it's just bribery," said Jimmy. "Oh! all right, I'll make you some soap-suds, anything to keep you quiet for a little while," he grumbled.

Settling herself more comfortably on the hard concrete step, she blew the most beautifully coloured bubble she had ever seen; carefully blowing just a little at a time the bubble grew bigger and bigger, until she was suddenly distracted by a voice from the other side of the garden fence.

"Josie, I hear you've a new wee bairn."

The bubble burst. "Blow you, Duncan!" shouted Josie. "Look what you've gone and made me do."

"Wa' did I do?" said Duncan in alarm.

"I had a beautiful bubble, best I've ever had and you made me burst it."

"Sorry Josie."

Somewhat disgruntled, Josie made her way to the fence. "Yes, we've got a new brother," she said, not really wishing to enter into any discussion about the baby.

"My Mam says you found him under a gooseberry bush!"

"Don't be so silly," said Josie, indignantly. "The doctor brought him; anyway we haven't got a gooseberry bush, we've only got currants. Jimmy, Jimmy!" she yelled, "Come here."

"What is it now?" asked Jimmy. "I thought I'd got rid of you for a little while."

"It's him," said Josie. "He says his mother told him we found the baby under a gooseberry bush. That can't be true, can it?"

"My Mam says . . ." began Duncan.

"I don't care what your Mam says, my Dad says the doctor brought him, so there, and we had to pay for him," she added importantly.

Although she wouldn't admit it, Josie was becoming a bit confused. It seemed to her that she had heard the gooseberry bush story before, but what her Dad had said about the doctor seemed to make better sense. After all, babies couldn't just be left under bushes, that would mean anyone could take them, and what if it rained, or worse still, snowed, surely they would die of cold. Josie looked at Jimmy for support, but Jimmy just turned pink and looked embarrassed.

"Oh shut up, Josie!" he said grumpily. "Go and blow bubbles. I haven't got time to answer silly questions!"

With that, Jimmy beat a hasty retreat.

Duncan, trying to get back in Josie's good books, said, "I 'spect I'll see him soon, I'll tell my Mam what your Dad said."

"OK!" said Josie, wandering away. "I'm going to blow bubbles or my soap-suds will all be spoilt."

As she sat once again on the door-step she felt there was something here she didn't quite understand. She thought about this doubtful situation regarding the supply and delivery of infants. She felt sure her father would never be untruthful. What ought she to do?

Josie blew a few more bubbles and carried on thinking. Suddenly, out of the blue, came the answer. She would consult her Sunday School teacher, Miss Lanham. That was it, tomorrow she would ask Miss Lanham about babies. Miss Lanham was sure to know, and in the unlikely event that she didn't, Josie was sure she would ask the 'Lord' for help. Josie believed that Miss Lanham had a direct line to the 'Lord'; many a time she had said she had asked the 'Lord' for help and had received what she called 'divine guidance'! Yes, undoubtedly, this was definitely a case for 'divine guidance'. Having temporarily solved the problem, Josie was able to concentrate on blowing bubbles and

15

eating aniseed balls and sugar.

The next day being Sunday, Josie and Jimmy, attired in their Sunday clothes, left for Sunday School at the little chapel a few streets away. As they turned the corner into the next road Josie spotted Miss Lanham walking ahead of them.

"There's Miss Lanham, I'll catch up with her," said Josie.

What a heaven sent chance to have a private word with Miss Lanham. She had been scheming how she was going to ask Miss Lanham about babies, she didn't feel it would be right to ask in front of the class.

"Miss Lanham!" said Josie, a little breathless from running.

"Hello, Josie, are you making your way to Sunday School?"

"Yes Miss, please Miss I want to ask you something. I thought you'd be bound to know the answer, you being in touch with the Lord and all!"

"What is it Josie? I hope I can help you."

"Well Miss, do babies come from the doctor, or do you find them under gooseberry bushes like Duncan's mum says?"

Miss Lanham stopped in her tracks, her face went a delicate shade of pink, and her lips pursed slightly.

"Why do you ask, Josie?"

"Well, you see Miss, we've got a new baby and I wanted to know where he came from."

"You've got a new brother. How nice Josie. You know all babies are gifts from God and you must help to take care of him."

"You mean he came from the Lord, not the doctor like my dad told me?" Josie sounded astonished.

Miss Lanham fell silent and walked a little faster.

"You mean like the virgin Mary?" persisted Josie (this being one of her favourite bible stories). Josie had never quite seen her mother in the role of Mary.

"Well, not exactly," said Miss Lanham, feeling very relieved that the chapel door was now in sight.

Josie's imagination had taken over by this time. She tried to picture the scene. Perhaps her mother had had a visit from an angel. She would have a better look at the baby when she got home, she hadn't really looked at him very closely. Perhaps he had a halo and she hadn't noticed it.

Josie, deep in thought, entered the chapel at Miss Lanham's side, she made her way to the front row where the youngest children sat. The first two hymns went by in a flash with Josie barely conscious of what they were singing. They followed a set pattern at the chapel. After the first two hymns they broke into five separate groups, to cover the ages from five to twelve, Josie being in the younger group of five and six year olds.

Miss Lanham would then read the group a biblical story, not actually using a bible, but a colourfully illustrated book called *Bible Stories for the Very Young*. Today Josie hoped it might be the 'Birth of the Baby Jesus' which came at the beginning of the book. There was a lovely picture which Miss Lanham would hold up for them to see of Mary and Joseph and the animals in the stable, with the baby Jesus in the manger. However, Miss Lanham started on a spirited rendition of the parable of the Prodigal Son. Josie listened enthralled as she always did when Miss Lanham was in full flight. She sighed as the story came to an end.

"Any questions children?" asked Miss Lanham.

The children prattled on about how lovely it was when the Prodigal Son returned. Josie said not a word, and appeared to be deep in thought.

"You're unusually quiet Josie," said Miss Lanham. "Don't you have a question?"

"Well," said Josie thoughtfully, "I don't think it was very fair to the other brother, the one who stayed at home with his father and didn't go and waste all his - what was his money called, Miss Lanham?" asked Josie.

"His inheritance, dear."

"That's right, his inheritance, why didn't his father kill the fatted calf for him, after all he was the good one."

After the story and question session was at an end, the Superintendent made his announcements. Today he gave details of the forthcoming Sunday School outing to take place in two weeks time.

"We'll be going by train to Mundesley, leaving City Station at 9 o'clock sharp. We will picnic on the beach at dinner-time, will you all please bring sandwiches. At 4.30 we will assemble on the promenade and march to the Church Hall, where we will have a strawberry tea. There's one other thing to say, children, please note only those children here today will go on the outing, anyone turning up for the first time next week will be excluded. I'm afraid we usually find our numbers suddenly increase before the summer outing and the Christmas party." There was a murmur of agreement from the teachers. "Now we will sing hymn number 25 in the red hymn books."

When they had finished singing he said, "That's all for today children, thank you for coming and don't forget to come next week or you'll be disqualified from the outing."

Everyone made a dash for the door. Josie looked around for Jimmy, should she tell him what Miss Lanham had said about the baby? No, perhaps she wouldn't, he'd probably say she was being silly and Miss Lanham didn't know a thing anyway.

"How was Sunday School?" asked her father when she arrived home.

"Miss Lanham says the baby is a gift from the 'Lord', all babies are gifts from the 'Lord' she says."

"Oh! is that what she says, she probably thinks all marriages are made in heaven too, typical spinster."

"What's a spinster, Dad?"

"An unmarried lady."

"Miss Lanham is an unmarried lady?" Josie seemed surprised.

"Of course she is or she wouldn't be a Miss, would she?"

"Oh, you mean she'd be a Mrs," said Josie. "I never thought of that. She's in touch with the 'Lord' you know Dad."

"Good for her then," Mr Brown seemed unimpressed. "Josie, you can give me a hand to get tea ready."

"Can I take Mum's tea up to her?"

"You can take the sandwiches but I'll carry the tea."

This arrangement suited Josie perfectly, all she wanted was a quick look at the baby's head. As she dashed noisily upstairs, her mother said, "Steady Josie, don't be so noisy, you'll wake the baby."

"Can I see him?" asked Josie moving closer to the bed.

Her mother felt pleased at this request as she thought Josie had been less than enthusiastic in her first reaction to the new addition to the family; she hoped this wasn't a sign that Josie was going to be jealous of the baby. Josie moved the shawl away from the baby's head. No, there was definitely no halo, there wasn't even any hair. So much for Miss Lanham's information, thought Josie. The baby stirred in his sleep so Josie hastily replaced the shawl.

A banging door announced Jimmy's arrival home.

"Look at the state of your hands, go and wash them before you sit down to tea," said his father.

"Coo, what have you been doing?" asked Josie, eyeing Jimmy's filthy hands.

"I did a bit of whittling that's all. Pete had some bits of elder-berry so we made a couple of pop-guns. Tomorrow we're going to collect some acorns."

"Can I come?" asked Josie, almost before he had finished.

"No, you can't, we're going on our bikes."

"When am I going to get a bike, Dad?" pleaded Josie.

"When you're older and I'm richer, remember we've an extra mouth to feed now."

If having an extra mouth to feed was going to prolong her wait for a much desired bike, Josie began to feel even less enthusiastic about the new baby.

2

The Sunday School Outing

The day of the Sunday School outing dawned fair and fine. The children were awake early, eager to be off on the great adventure, with a bag of toffees to eat on the train and sixpence each to spend.

"A whole sixpence," said Josie who seldom saw so much money all at one time. Jimmy had his instructions to keep an eye on his sister and make sure she didn't lose her money.

On arrival at City Station they found most of the Sunday School membership and teachers assembled. When the train pulled in they moved forward in orderly ranks and filed into the carriages. The massive steam engine was a lovely sight, every few moments it belched out a cloud of steam.

The children settled in their carriages to enjoy the journey. For many of them this would be their only visit to the seaside until next year's outing. Josie and Jimmy were luckier than many of their friends as they always had a week at the seaside, the first week in August when their father had his annual holiday from the factory where he worked.

The train sped on, it seemed to the children that they were travelling at a tremendous speed as trees and telegraph posts whizzed by and the wheels went clickety-click as they went over the points. Those who were able to get near a window hung their heads out whenever there was a bend in the track. This enabled them to get a glimpse of the huge lumbering engine ahead, until clouds of black smoke and cinder dust got in their eyes. The patrolling teachers were called to administer first aid to the victims, and admonish them for hanging out of the window in the first place.

When, at last, the train pulled into Mundesley station, Miss Lanham called to them.

"Make sure you leave the carriages tidy, I do not want to find sweet papers or orange peel on the floors. Right, away we go then," she said as the children hastily gathered up the litter.

They marched to the barrier and were ushered through in twos to line up on the other side.

At last, reaching the beach, they broke ranks and rushed down the steeply sloping pathway to hurl themselves on to the sand. Called to order by the Superintendent, they lined up again on the promenade.

"You can do as you please from now until four-thirty, when we shall leave to go to the Church Hall for our tea. The teachers will place flags in the sand to indicate the area in which you can play. If you wish to paddle, you may do so. On no account are you to go out of the marked area and no one is to swim. You understand, NO ONE IS TO SWIM, the sea can be quite treacherous and we don't want any accidents."

The children jumped joyously from the promenade onto the beach, all claiming their own spot within the marked out area. Jimmy and his pals Peter and William found a quiet stretch of sand and proceeded to dig a large hole. Josie hung about watching as the boys spread their towels out in the bottom of the hole and, removing their shirts, settled down to a spot of sun-bathing. They ignored Josie who wandered off in search of Miss Lanham and the members of her class.

By four-thirty the younger ones were beginning to tire and were quite relieved when everyone had assembled ready to move off to the Church Hall for tea.

The Superintendent asked the teachers to count their own class. All were complete except for Jimmy's class. Mr Briggs reported three missing: James, Peter and William.

"When were they last seen?" enquired the Superintendent.

"I saw them in the sea, Sir," said one boy.

"Climbing on a groyne a long way out," chorused a couple of girls. "We told them they'd cop it if they fell in."

"You said it was dangerous, didn't you, Sir?"

Panic was beginning to spread among the children as the

teachers got into a huddle to decide their next move.

Mr Briggs appeared beside Josie.

"Have you seen your brother?" he asked.

Josie was beginning to get a bit tearful.

"Not for a long time," she said. "I saw him in his hole with Peter and Willy, then I went with Miss Lanham."

The teachers conferred in hushed whispers.

"All right children, get into twos please and follow Mr Dugdale."

"What about my brother?" wailed Josie, tugging at Miss Lanham's arm.

"I think he's drowned," said one of the children, dramatically.

Josie burst into tears.

"He's not Miss, is he Miss?" she asked between jobs.

"Now Josie, you come with me, the Superintendent and Mr Briggs are going off to look for the boys. Miss Lanham placed an arm round Josie's shoulders.

"Come along dear, I'm sure they'll find them, I expect they've just gone off to the shops."

The 'crocodile' made its way up the slope and turned into the main thoroughfare. A little further along was a large lawned area with flower beds and a little wooden open-fronted shelter in which, huddled together, sat three very wet, shame-faced boys. Josie was first to spot them.

"Jimmy! There's Jimmy!" she shouted, dropping Miss Lanham's hand as she raced toward the shelter, tears of relief streaming down her face. Her first instinct was to throw her arms around Jimmy but she stopped abruptly as she realised this would acutely embarrass him. Instead she stamped her foot in frustration and fury, "I'm going to tell Dad," she wailed.

Miss Lanham, having reached the shelter, added her bit.

"I'm extremely angry with you. What have you been doing? You know you are prohibited from this area."

"Sorry Miss!" chorused the boys.

"We fell in Miss," said Peter. "We was soaked, our shoes and socks and clothes are still soaking."

"We were trying to dry out in the sun," said Jimmy. "We thought we could get dry before we had to go for tea, then no one would know."

On reaching their destination the children were seated on the grass. Plates of strawberries and bread and butter were passed around. The miscreants were called into the Hall by the Superintendent, eventually emerging wrapped in blankets, looking very chastened.

Josie, comforted by Miss Lanham, had dried her tears; she was beginning to feel rather important at receiving all this attention.

After tea was over the children played games on the lawn, then made their way to the station for the return journey home.

Jimmy searched for Josie once they were on the train. Finding her at last, he pulled her into the corridor.

"Josie, don't tell Dad!" he pleaded.

"Yes, I will. Everyone thought you were drowned. I thought you were all drowned," said Josie, passionately. "You and Pete and Willy."

"Please Josie, I'll give you two of my sticks of rock and I'll let you have a ride on my bike."

Josie brightened.

"Three sticks of rock and a ride," she said with a sly smile.

At the end of their journey the train pulled in to a platform lined with parents. Jimmy took Josie's hand and walked toward their father.

"Don't forget Josie, you promised," he whispered.

"Hello!" said their father. "Had a good time children?"

"Yes, fine," said Jimmy quickly.

"Has Josie been a good girl?"

"Oh yes, Dad, she's been very good," said Jimmy.

Come along then, say goodbye to your friends and let's get home."

They boarded the bus which took them most of the way home.

"I've got a surprise for you when you get home," said their father as they took their seats.

Not another surprise thought Josie. I wonder what it is this time, surely not another baby as soon as I leave home for a few minutes.

"Where's the surprise?" asked Josie as soon as they entered the house.

"In the front room, come and look," said her father.

The front room was the holy of holies, only used at Christmas or when special visitors were being entertained. It was swept and dusted every week, whether or not it had been used during the previous seven days. It was the only room in the house which had a carpet; usually outdoor shoes had to be removed and slippers put on before anyone was allowed to enter. In his excitement, Mr Brown forgot his wife's strict rule about this and the children dashed in trailing sand behind them.

"Where's the surprise? . . . Oh! look!" said Josie, stopping in her tracks.

"There, what about that?" said her father as Josie gazed at the shiny piano. "You're both going to have lessons."

This announcement was greeted with whoops of joy from Josie, who skipped up and down in her excitement. Jimmy uttered a long, mournful sigh.

"Do I have to, Dad?" he asked.

"Yes you do, it's your mother's idea, she says all children have lessons these days."

In the months that followed, the piano was going to prove to be more of a problem than an asset. Josie, though wildly enthusiastic, was completely lacking in talent, her short, stubby fingers were just not suited to playing the piano, her teacher said. It was such a shame as she had seldom had a more conscientious pupil. Jimmy, on the other hand, in the opinion of his teacher, showed a lot of talent, but absolutely no dedication. After a couple of years of sheer frustration for Josie and misery for Jimmy, the whole project was abandoned. The piano was left in a lonely state standing in the corner of the front room. Although it had proved to be a complete 'white elephant' it had to be retained, as everyone who was anyone had a piano in the parlour.

After tea their father informed them that there would be no seaside holiday this year as their mother was not really up to it and the baby was very frail. The children were disappointed, but accepted their father's explanation.

"You can have three weeks with Grandma in the country at the end of the school holidays if you wish," said their father, trying to soften the blow.

"Oh, lovely!" sighed Josie, she enjoyed staying with Grandma as much as going to the seaside.

"I don't think your mother and the baby will be well enough to go to Grandma's," said their father.

"You mean we're going on our own?" asked Jimmy.

"Yes, that will be all right, won't it?"

"All right with me," said Jimmy. "But I've got friends in the village and I don't want to cart her around with me all the time. She usually stays with Mum and Grandma."

"I can stay with Grandma when you go with your friends," said Josie. "Anyway, I've got a friend at the farm now, I played with her last time we went to Grandma's so I don't need you." Josie was already remembering the fun she had in the country. It would be harvest time and the farmer always allowed her and Jimmy to ride on the hay-cart when it had finished for the day and was making its way back to the farm. Once the reaping was finished and there was nothing left but stubble, she would go with Grandma to gather up all the grains of corn left after the men had finished threshing. Grandma would feed this to her chickens.

School was finished until September, the neighbourhood's child population settled to summer games and outings. On the streets a new phenomenon had appeared. Wall's had introduced tricycles selling their ice-cream. These vehicles were painted navy blue and white and their vendors wore navy caps with navy and white checked bands, with the slogan 'Stop me and buy one' painted on the front of the tricycle. The ice-cream they sold was totally new, triangular in shape, encased in a checked navy and white cardboard cover. There was a choice of water-ice or cream-ice in various fruit flavours. These ices cost one penny, but the ice-cream seller would obligingly cut one in half for a ha'penny.

With three weeks of the summer holiday left before they had to return to school, the children, accompanied by their father, made their way to their Grandma's. As the bus stopped the children scrambled out and made their way across the field and past the village pond. Josie ran ahead, she could see her Grandma standing at her garden gate.

"Grandma we've come, for three whole weeks, Mum can't come 'cos of the baby," babbled Josie excitedly, skipping up the path and in at the little front door. Grandma's house had a special smell, made up of polish, cake baking and apple storing. Josie wouldn't have been able to isolate the segments producing the smell, she just knew it was a lovely homely smell that seemed to be exclusive to Grandma's house.

Her first action was always to dash into the stone floored scullery, pick up the ladle and pour out a glass of ice-cold well water from the bucket standing on the table. This was the best

b

water in the world, no other water ever tasted like this.

While they stayed at Grandma's, getting the water from the well at the top of the garden was one of Jimmy's jobs. Josie was allowed to help, Jimmy would let her hook the bucket on to the chain then he would turn the handle to lower it into the well. When it landed at the bottom there was a loud splash. Josie was afraid to look down the well as it seemed an enormous way down judging by the length of time it took to reach the bottom. Jimmy turned the handle to winch it up again when it was full.

The little cottage had no running water and no electricity but this never seemed to bother Grandma. The toilet, referred to as the 'bog' or the 'lavy' was at the bottom of the garden, quite a way from the house. Josie only used it from dire necessity, usually as she sat on the wooden construction she would spot a spider or a beetle running around, and she would watch its progress in horrified silence in case it ran towards her.

At six-thirty the bus left to go back to town, father said his goodbye and bade the children behave themselves.

"Bye bye Dad!" yelled Josie, frantically waving her hand as the bus disappeared from view.

Suddenly she felt very alone with only Jimmy to keep her company.

When they returned to the house Grandma said, "I'm going to get the lamps ready before it gets dark, would you like to help me, Josie?"

Josie had seen her Grandma prepare the lamps before so she knew exactly how it was done. First the shade was carefully removed, then the glass funnel which contained the flame. Tonight it was time to trim the wick, an operation which took place about once a week. Carefully trimming away the black bit with her scissors, Grandma was finally satisfied with her efforts, then she put the whole thing back together again.

"Don't you miss not having electric lights, Grandma?"

"Not really, I've never had them you see, and what you've never had you never miss."

Josie wasn't really sure about Grandma's reasoning, after all she'd never had a bike but that didn't mean she didn't miss it!

"I think it's nearly time you went to bed," said Grandma.

"Just let me see you light the lamp Grandma," said Josie, trying to postpone going to bed for as long as she could.

26

"I'll light the lamp now, it's getting dusk and we'll get you a candle ready to take upstairs."

"Can I keep it alight when I'm in bed? I don't like being in the dark."

Josie never minded being in the dark at home, but in Grandma's bedroom she preferred to keep a candle burning. This would be the first time she had been alone in the bedroom, usually her mother shared this room with her. She hadn't really appreciated the fact that she would be on her own when she had been so keen to visit Grandma. She was beginning to wonder if it had been such a good idea after all as she made her way up the steep little staircase behind her grandmother, who carried the flickering candle which cast strange sinister shadows on the wall.

Grandma helped her to undress and get into the big, soft bed - she wished her mother was there to share it with her. She lay quite still watching the shadows in the corners where the faint light from the candle failed to reach. She thought about her Mum and Dad and her poor delicate little brother. She remembered she hadn't said her prayers, but she felt afraid to get out of bed and into the shadowy darkness. "I wonder if the 'Lord' would mind if I didn't kneel down," she whispered to herself. Perhaps it was permissible at a time like this.

"Please bless Mum and Dad and baby John," she began, "and I suppose you could include Jimmy even though he is a pig to me. Bless Duncan and Raymond and Mary at the farm, and specially Grandma and make her life a bit easier. Perhaps you could send her a Grandpa to do the heavy work for her. My other Grandmother has a Grandad and he digs the garden and gets the coal in, and please Lord make me not afraid of the dark."

Her prayers completed she buried her face in the pillow and tried to sleep. She was still restless when she heard Jimmy come clattering upstairs past her door and up the next flight of stairs to his bedroom in the attic. It was awfully dark up there, she was glad it was Jimmy and not her sleeping in the attic.

A little later Grandma entered the room.

"What, not asleep yet Josie?"

"I can't get to sleep Grandma, I don't like being on my own."

"But you're on your own when you're at home."

"I know," said Josie, "but it's my room and it's not like this. I'm afraid of that big cupboard, someone might be hiding in it."

"Don't be silly, Josie," said Grandma, sitting on the edge of the bed. "Who'd want to hide in a cupboard?"

"I don't know," said Josie, beginning to cry. "I want to go home to Mum."

Grandma got up from the bed and went over to the cupboard. Opening the door she said, "Look Josie, you can get out of bed and see for yourself, there's no one in there!"

She shone the candle into the interior to assure Josie that it was completely empty apart from her own clothes hanging from the rail.

"I thought you liked staying with me."

"I do," wailed Josie, "but I don't like being on my own."

"Well, would you like me to sleep in this bed with you?"

"Oh yes, Grandma, I'd be all right then, I wouldn't even need a candle."

"All right Josie, I'll just clear up downstairs and then I'll come to bed," said Grandma, tucking her in.

By the time she came back again Josie was sound asleep, her tears were still wet on her cheeks, her black hair spread out on her pillow and one chubby thumb stuck in her mouth.

The weeks passed very quickly. Jimmy spent most of his time with his friends in the village, fitting in the jobs he had promised to do for Grandma, and having as little as possible to do with his sister. Josie told herself that she didn't care and anyway she was learning a lot from her grandmother.

She got into the habit of getting up early in the morning as soon as her Grandma got up. As soon as they were washed and dressed she accompanied her to the field where mushrooms grew. Grandma seemed to know which tree would have the best crop of mushrooms growing under it. At first Josie had hung back, reluctant to climb the gate into the field. When asked what was wrong she had confided to her Grandma that she was afraid of the cows grazing in the field.

"There's no need to be afraid of cows," said her Grandma.

"What if one's a bull?" said Josie. "I don't know which are cows and which are bulls."

Grandma laughed.

"What a funny little girl you are, I wouldn't bring you into a field where there was a bull. Anyway, the farmer hasn't got any bulls at all at the moment."

Somewhat reassured, Josie now entered the field, but she still gave the cattle a wide berth and kept a wary eye on them as she gathered mushrooms.

While Jimmy was busy with the village boys Josie teamed up with her friend Mary from the farm. Having spent the morning lazing in the orchard Mary confided shyly.

"I like your brother, Josie."

"Do you? Well I can't stand him, anyway he doesn't like girls."

Mary looked disappointed, sighed loudly and returned to her comic.

"I wish I could stay here for ever," said Josie. "I wish I lived in the country like you, Mary."

"But you've got all the lovely shops and the pictures and everything."

"Well, I s'pose the shops are quite nice, but I've never been to the pictures. Jimmy goes on Saturday afternoons but he won't take me, but then he won't take me anywhere if he can help it. He's rotten my brother."

"I don't think he is,'" said Mary, blushing. Then, changing the subject to cover her embarrassment, she said, "Two of our pigs have got litters, do you want to see them?"

Josie looked puzzled.

"What's litters, Mary?"

"Babies, of course," Mary sounded a bit scornful.

"Oh! baby pigs. Yes please," said Josie.

Mary led the way out of the orchard and across the lane to the farm. There were three pigsties surrounded by a wire netting enclosure and as the girls peered through the netting they could see two large fat pink pigs. One had seven babies and the other eight. Most of the babies were pink, but a few had the odd black spot, and each had a minute curly tail.

"Aren't they lovely," breathed Josie, her nose close to the netting.

"Would you like to see my Dad's ferrets?" asked Mary when, at last, they got tired of watching the pigs. "But you mustn't put your fingers anywhere near 'cos they bite."

The ferrets were in a little hutch with a wire netting front, they darted about with such speed it was difficult to see them clearly. They were long and thin and had beautiful ginger coloured fur, their tiny faces were quite pretty and they had bright beady little eyes.

"What do you do with them?" enquired Josie when she had watched them for quite a while. "Are they pets like dogs and cats?"

"'Course not, Dad puts them down the rabbit holes on a long lead and they chase the rabbits out."

"Does the rabbit run away then?"

"Not if Dad can help it, he's waiting to hit it over the head, then we have it for dinner."

Josie wondered how Mary could say something so gruesome in such a matter of fact way, it seemed so cruel to treat poor little furry rabbits like that.

When Jimmy came home for his dinner Josie greeted him.

"I've been to the farm to see the baby pigs and the ferrets with Mary. She thinks you're lovely," she sniggered. Jimmy turned bright red. Grandma laughed.

"Oh! dear, Jimmy, you've got a follower."

"Don't be silly, she's only a kid," growled Jimmy, looking even more uncomfortable.

Despite Jimmy's protests, however, Josie noted that he suddenly started to volunteer to fetch the milk from the farm when previously he had left this job to his Grandma and Josie. He always slicked down his hair, pulled up his socks and glanced at himself in the mirror before he set off.

After a very busy day with Mary, Josie was willing to go to bed as soon as her Grandma suggested it. After Grandma had gone downstairs again Josie slipped out of bed to say her prayers. She had gradually lost her fear of the dark, but she didn't like to say her prayers while her Grandma was in the room; her prayers, she felt, were her own private concern. She had her usual lengthy conversation with the Lord and made her requests for blessings. Then she added, by way of a postscript, a plea for the rabbits. "Do you know what they do with those ferrets Lord? I thought if I had a word with you, well perhaps you could think of something. Perhaps you could make it so they had an extra hole then they could run away." Josie giggled as she had a vision of the ferret down one hole and Mary's father with his stick at the other and the little rabbit running out of the third hole and belting off down the field. Josie tried to stifle her giggles, one didn't giggle when one talked to the Lord. Saying one's prayers was supposed to be a serious occupation, Miss Lanham said so. Josie apologised to the Lord and got back into bed.

Like all good things the holiday came to an end and it seemed no time at all before their father was waiting for them to pack their cases and take the bus home again. Josie dragged her feet as she walked across the field and past the pond. Jimmy and his father walked briskly ahead.

"Come on Josie, get a move on or we'll miss the bus."

"Goodbye pond, goodbye farm, goodbye Mary, goodbye Grandma," said Josie sadly to herself. She felt she could even squeeze out a tear if she tried hard enough.

"Come on Josie, stop dragging your feet, there's a good girl," called her father.

Josie picked up her heels and ran to catch up with her father and brother.

"I was just saying goodbye, that's all," she said.

3

Winter

The long hot summer was drawing to a close, already there was a nip in the air in the evening. The fish and chip shop began to get more trade than the ice-cream vendor. Following their return from holiday, Josie and Jimmy were sharing an unusually amicable period. With a penny each they made their way to the fish and chip shop. Standing patiently in line until they reached the counter, Jimmy, who was just tall enough to see over the top, ordered his penn'orth of chips.

"Who's next then?" enquired the fish-man, peering over the counter.

"She wants a penn'orth too," said Jimmy. Taking his packet of chips further down the counter, he coated them generously with salt and vinegar.

"They're starting fritters next week," said Jimmy. (Fritters were made from slices of large potatoes, coated with batter and fried.)

"If I can manage to save a ha'penny we could get some and have half each."

"All right if you pay your half," said Jimmy.

"It's easier for you Jimmy, you get thruppence but I only get a penny."

"No you don't, 'cos you usually scrounge something during the week off Dad. Anyway, it's our turn to go and see Auntie Lil tomorrow and she's usually good for thruppence at least."

"Lovely, we might save enough for two bags of fritters then."

Sunday mornings were always taken up with visits to either

Auntie Lil or Auntie Maud or their Granny and Grandad. They all lived within walking distance of the children's home so they were able to visit on their own.

Visiting Auntie May was more difficult as she lived the other side of town, therefore these visits were carried out on Sunday evenings with their parents. Although the least profitable from a money point of view there were other attractions in visits to their grandparents. Grandad kept rabbits and chickens in the back garden, and bred canaries in the back bedroom. You could hear the birds as soon as you entered the house, all trying to outdo one another with the volume of their song. It was Grandad's dream to breed a perfect bright orange bird. Each new batch of eggs was watched over with great anxiety. Norwich canaries are famous the world over for their beautiful colour and glorious song. The shelves around the canaries' room were crowded with trophies bearing the inscription 'Best in Show'.

The weather got colder day by day. November brought heavy frosts. Jimmy had to take Josie to school each day. As he had to pass her school gate on the way to his own, there was no way he could get out of this chore. As they walked along they noticed on most of the privet hedges beautifully constructed spiders webs all silver and sparkling with a coating of frost. They found that by breaking off a twig and bending it into a shape like a fan they could gather the fairy-like webs, until eventually the whole thing was criss-crossed with threads of gossamer fineness which sparkled like jewels. After they had made themselves late for school a couple of times and Jimmy had been threatened with the cane, he decided that enough was enough and he pulled Josie well away from the hedges and managed to get her to school on time.

The children were waiting anxiously for November 5th to arrive, they had been collecting fireworks for the past month. Any extra money that came their way was spent on fireworks instead of sweets.

By the time Guy Fawkes night arrived the children, with the help of their father, had built a large bonfire at the bottom of the garden. Their mother contributed by helping them to make a guy. He was dressed in their father's old clothes, stuffed with straw, with a paper mask for a face and discarded trilby on his head.

When their father put a match to the fire the flames leaped up, fanned by the wind, and quickly reached the figure sitting on the top. The boys cheered.

Josie stayed close by her father; though she didn't like to admit it, she never really liked it when the figure at the top began to burn. She had heard the story of the gunpowder plot and she supposed Guy Fawkes was a very bad man, but that didn't seem to make the situation any more bearable as the flames began to flicker around him.

Once the fire was burning well father put large potatoes into the embers to cook. Mother made cups of hot cocoa.

Josie limited herself to holding sparklers as she never really felt she trusted the fireworks marked 'Can be held in the hand'. They were the same shape and colour as Jimmy's bangers.

As the fire died down the children huddled nearer for warmth. The smell of smoke would cling to their clothing for days afterwards, but this didn't really matter in the general feeling of happiness and well-being that being together with family and friends could bring.

Josie had noticed that baby John did not seem to be making very much progress. When she asked her mother why he didn't seem to get much bigger, she knew by the way her mother looked, that she was quite worried about him. He often cried and coughed during the night and Josie would hear her mother trying to pacify him. One night Josie was awakened by the baby making a most awful noise. She lay awake listening, she could hear her parents talking in hushed voices, the baby seemed to be gasping for breath. Suddenly she heard the noise of her father going rapidly downstairs, then the sound of the front door shutting and the shuffling as he ran down the gravel path.

Josie felt panic rising; where had her father gone so late at night? She crept into her parents' bedroom, her mother was cradling the baby in here arms as she walked up and down the room.

"Mummy, what's wrong, is the baby ill?"

"I think he's very ill, Dad has gone to fetch the doctor."

Josie burst into tears.

"He's not going to die is he?"

Jimmy, hearing the commotion, appeared at the door.

"Jimmy, get your sister back to bed there's a good boy, your Dad has gone to fetch the doctor, I think the baby has croup."

The baby was racked with another burst of coughing. Josie,

still crying quietly, was led back to bed.

"Don't cry Josie, he'll be all right when the doctor gets here."

"Will he really Jimmy, you promise?"

" 'Course he will, now go back to sleep, I'll leave the light on," he said as he went back to see if he could help his mother.

Josie, unable to sleep, could still hear the baby coughing. Perhaps it's my fault, she thought, I never really loved him like I should. I can even remember telling my friends that he wasn't really my brother. Perhaps God is punishing me for behaving like Judas in the Bible story. Josie got out of bed and knelt down beside her bed.

"Lord, please help baby John to get better. I promise I'll love him and even take him for walks in his pram if you'll just get the doctor to come quickly and make him well, please don't let him die. Thank you Lord," said Josie through her tears.

She lay quietly, still crying to herself, when she heard her father return with the doctor. There was murmur of voices on the landing, but she couldn't hear what they were saying. After the doctor had entered the bedroom the baby's laboured breathing seemed to improve.

"He should be all right now," said the doctor as he came out of the room. "I'll call again in the morning."

When her father put his head round the door to check that she was all right, Josie was still crying.

"Don't cry Josie, your brother is going to be all right now that the doctor has been. You've got to get some sleep, you have to go to school in the morning."

"Do you think it's all my fault?" sobbed Josie.

"What do you mean, your fault?"

"The Lord is punishing me for being a Judas."

"For being a what?"

"A Judas, you know, like in the Bible story, he denied Jesus. Well, I denied baby John was my brother."

"Don't be silly Josie, it's no one's fault, the baby has just had a bad start that's all, he'll pick up soon."

"Did the doctor say so?"

"Yes - now dry your tears and try to go to sleep. Listen, the baby has stopped coughing now!"

Indeed, as Josie listened, her father was right.

When she awoke next morning her first thought was that all

was quiet, there was no sound from baby John. Was he all right, or had he died in the night? Josie reluctantly got out of her warm bed, pulled on her dressing gown, went to the window and pulled back the curtains. The window was covered in a beautiful frosted pattern of spirals of fern-like shapes. Josie scraped a hole with her finger and looked out. Everywhere was white, the familiar landscape was covered in snow, untouched, sparkling white snow, not even one single footprint could be seen.

"How lovely!" sighed Josie, she loved snow, there hadn't been any last winter, but she could remember seeing it the year before.

"It's like fairyland," thought Josie, just like on the Christmas cards.

She dashed into Jimmy's bedroom.

"Snow!" she yelled. "Snow!" She was shaking him to wake him up.

"All right, all right, hold on a minute and stop shouting or you'll wake the baby."

Josie had momentarily forgotten about the baby in her excitement over the snow.

"How is he?" asked Josie, calming down.

"I don't know but we can go and find out if you stop making so much noise."

They walked along the corridor to their parents' room. Their mother was sleeping, having had very little sleep all night, their father was bending over the baby's cot.

"Is he all right?" whispered Jimmy.

"Much better," said his father. "You're up early."

"Josie found it had snowed in the night so she's really going potty," said Jimmy.

"It's lovely Dad, you look out of the window. Is the baby really better?"

"Well, he's certainly much better than he was last night. The doctor's coming in this morning so I shan't go to work until after dinner. It would help if you could both get yourselves ready for school. I'll come and get your breakfast when you're dressed."

The comment "It looks like being a white Christmas!" could be heard time and time again as people bustled about doing last minute Christmas shopping. The first fall of snow had lasted for about a week, until it had finally turned into a grey slushy mess which froze over every night and turned back into slush and water by day. Eventually most of the water had cleared. When, overnight, there was another very heavy fall of snow, Josie was delighted. Jimmy was quite upset because his old sledge had finally fallen to pieces and no amount of nails and hammering could put it together again.

Baby John seemed to be making much better progress now, his little cheeks grew rosier each day. Their mother looked much better, she had lost her anxious look. Their father laughed and joked again.

"We're doing a nativity play at school," Josie informed her mother. "I'm an angel, could you make me some wings by Friday, they've given me some white robes from the stock they've got at school but they said to ask our Mums to make the wings. Then, on the following Friday, when we break up for Christmas, you can come in the afternoon and see the play. You could bring the baby," said Josie tentatively.

It was only about a month ago when Josie would have died at the suggestion of bringing the baby anywhere near her school.

Josie spent her evenings practising the carols she was to sing with the angelic choir of fifteen pint-sized angels from Class 5. At last, the great day arrived. The mothers turned up in droves to witness the nativity play. It was the culmination of months of hard work by the teaching staff.

The audience were seated and a hush descended on the assembly hall. The curtains on the minute stage were pulled aside. Mary and Joseph had centre stage, the baby Jesus (a large baby doll) was lying in the straw filled manger. Behind them stood the heavenly choir, each painstakingly made wing in place, each halo at the correct angle. The nativity story began to unfold accompanied by "Oh's!" and "Ah's!" from the audience when they recognised their particular offspring.

At last it was time for the choir to perform. It was becoming obvious that the choir was a little large for the size of the stage. The little angels jostled for position, elbowing each other in the process. The back line, standing on a bench to enable them to be seen, were visibly tottering a bit. The teacher playing the piano struck up 'Away in a Manger', the heavenly choir broke into song. Still determined to be seen as well as heard, the pushing and shoving reached a climax. Suddenly the bench overturned, throwing its complement of angels into the front row, who in turn collapsed into the manger. Baby Jesus took to the air, his swaddling clothes in disarray. Mary and Joseph dropped gracefully into the laps of two large mothers sitting in the front row. Pandemonium reigned, the angels clinging to their parents. Joseph and Mary, also in tears, rescued the now naked baby Jesus from the pile of straw that had been his manger.

Teachers apologised to the parents, reprimanded the back row angels, rearranged the stage and cajoled the tearful cast into making another start on the nativity. This time the choir, with torn and tattered wings and halos slightly awry, got through their repertoire without further mishap.

When she was not singing carols, Josie was writing notes to Father Christmas and posting them up the chimney, much to the amusement of her mother and father and the disdain of her brother. Whenever Josie mentioned Father Christmas to Jimmy, he growled, "That's kid's stuff."

Josie could not persuade him to enlarge upon this. Threatened with dire consequences, he had strict instructions from his father that he was not to tell Josie there was no Santa Claus.

After Josie had enlisted her mother's help for about the sixth time with regard to the spelling of her numerous requests to Father Christmas, she suddenly had a bright idea. She remembered that during the summer, whilst staying in the country at Grandma's, she had requested God to help by finding a Grandad for her, to get the coal in and fetch the water from the well. There had, as yet, been no response from the Lord. "I suppose he is always very busy with such a lot of people to look after," mused Josie. However, she could see no reason why she should not bring in reinforcements in the form of Father Christmas. She could send him a note explaining about Grandma and about the Lord being so busy.

For the next couple of evenings, Josie slowly transferred her request to paper, with the help of her mother, who tried to suppress a smile, not wishing to deter Josie in her earnest endeavour to be of assistance to her Grandma in her hour of need. Finally the request was neatly written out by her mother and Josie proudly signed 'love from Josie', slightly askew, but legible at the bottom.

Having posted her request up the chimney Josie settled to await results; with two such powerful agents as God and Father

Christmas, she felt sure her Grandma wouldn't have long to wait.

On the Saturday before Christmas their father arrived home carrying a large fir tree. This was planted in an old garden bucket and carried into the front room. In the afternoon he lit the fire and by the evening the little room was warm as toast. All the family assembled to trim the tree.

The children had been collecting chocolate novelties for the past month. With great self-control they had managed to eat only one each. Dad had brought home sugar mice and this year there were also pink and white sugar pigs wrapped in cellophane and bundles of oblong shaped chocolate discs wrapped in various coloured silver paper. But, best of all, were the bags of golden coins looking so realistic, it seemed a shame to eat them.

The fairy for the top of the tree was very old, having been bought for Jimmy's first Christmas. It was, however, in pristine condition, even the muslin wings were in perfect order.

The children were allowed a fairly free hand with decorating the tree. Their father fixed the fairy on the top, as neither child could reach to do this. Then he left them to complete the decorating, only returning when the arguments as to what should go where got too heated. At the end of it all, with the streamers and balloons in place and 'Happy Christmas to all' pinned over the mirror above the fireplace, their mother appeared with steaming cups of cocoa. Taking as long as possible to drink her cocoa, Josie went reluctantly to bed, to be followed by Jimmy an hour later. The excitement of Christmas was beginning to take hold and they both found it difficult to sleep, in spite of being exhausted.

This year Jimmy was asking for a new sledge and hoping that the snow would last if he was lucky enough to receive his request. His second choice was for roller-skates. Josie wanted a bike which she was pretty sure she wouldn't get as her father thought she was still too young to be trusted with one. She had doubts about her second choice of a doll's-house complete with furniture; perhaps this was a bit expensive for her parents to manage, especially with baby John to buy for this year.

Unknown to the children, their father had a friend who was quite accomplished at woodwork. He had produced a really beautiful sledge, big enough to carry at least two in comfort, upholstered in red leather it was totally unique. He had also made a beautiful doll's-house for Josie, it contained miniature versions of everything one would find in a house. Josie's mother had been busy for weeks in the evenings, after the children were in bed, dressing a family of tiny dolls to occupy the doll's-house. Harry, Dad's carpenter friend, had agreed to store the presents until Christmas Eve, this would solve the impossible problem of where to hide such large items from prying eyes.

With a whole week to go before the great day arrived, the children busied themselves collecting as much money as possible from various relations and friends of the family. They pooled their resources and bought a box of chocolates for their mother and a packet of Players cigarettes for their father; they knew these were his favourite brand, although when he was short of money he had to make do with Woodbines.

It was Josie's great ambition to be able to buy her father a box of cigars like she had seen in the window of the high class tobacconist in the city. The boxes were made of wood with a colourful picture on the front and lettering in gold. In the window they had an open box on display, the fat brown cigars all had gold bands around them. This, to Josie, seemed to be the height of luxury. Her father usually had one cigar on Christmas Day. She sighed as she thought how pleased her father would be when she was old enough and rich enough to buy him a whole box of cigars for Christmas.

They consulted their mother about what they should buy for baby John. As she knew their resources were somewhat limited, she suggested a rattle which could be from both of them.

On Saturday, which was the last one before Christmas, they made a family visit into the city to do their last minute shopping. This trip was a special treat organised each year so that the children could see the Christmas lights. The snow was thick, the air frosty, but a watery sun was breaking through when they left home. John was left with Jessie, the girl who lived next-door, as his mother thought he was too young to spend such a long time in the cold. The children were delighted with the festive look of all the big shops and the coloured lights and Christmas trees added to their enjoyment. The last port of call was always the big Woolworths store, where they were allowed to pick a quarter pound of sweets each from the vast range displayed: this took quite a long time as they walked up and down the mouthwatering displays before finally making their choice. Then up one flight of stairs to the cafeteria for tea and cakes.

Then out into the cold frosty air and up to the market to buy fruit. The market looked very festive with its bright striped awnings. At the side the old Guildhall was aglow with light streaming through the lattice windows on to the stalls and pavement below. At the front of the market Santa Claus had his pitch with a sack full of lucky dips. Dad fished in his pocket for money to pay for two lucky dips for the children.

"What do you want Father Christmas to bring you?" he asked Jimmy.

"Sledge or skates please," said Jimmy with a grin, but Josie became shy and tongue-tied when Santa Claus bent to talk to her. Clinging tightly to her father's hand, she eventually managed to stammer that she was hoping for a doll's-house.

All the shopping completed, they joined the queue at the bus stop. This special trip always seemed to the children to be the beginning of Christmas. Tomorrow would be taken up with the Sunday School party where there would be tea and party games. Tired and happy the children arrived home and after tea and a hot bath, with a kiss for baby John, the children fell into bed, not even requesting a story or a glass of water to postpone the inevitable as they usually did.

"Night night, Josie!" said Jimmy. "Christmas is great this year, we've got the party tomorrow then one more day then Christmas - wonder if I'll get a sledge."

"Wonder if I'll get a doll's-house," said Josie. "Do you think it might be too expensive Jimmy?"

"Well, there's the baby extra this year remember, so don't be too disappointed will you if you don't get it."

"No, of course not," said Josie doubtfully, knowing that she would actually be very disappointed if she didn't.

"Come on children, stop that chattering and go to sleep."

"Night night Dad, we've had a lovely day," said Josie.

Sunday morning was bright and crisp, there had been another fall of snow during the night.

After lunch her mother brushed Josie's black hair until it shone, tying a red ribbon on it to match her party dress. Jimmy was already wearing his Sunday suit. He had to admit, his scruffy little sister could look quite nice when she tried, he even felt quite proud to escort her to the party. His friends, Peter and Willy, remarked on how nice she looked. Josie was positively preening herself by the time they arrived at the chapel for the party. This was her first experience of admiration from the opposite sex and she decided she liked it, perhaps it would pay to take more trouble with her appearance in future.

The children were welcomed by the Superintendent. They played the usual party games of 'Squeak Piggy Squeak', amid screams and giggles from the girls. A very large boy was blind-folded; after passing round the circle of seated children, he sat on Josie's lap and almost squashed her, but she still managed a stifled grunt and he didn't guess who she was, so he had to try again. Next time he sat on Willy's lap, who he guessed straight-away, this meant Willy was now piggy.

Whilst the children were playing games, the helpers were busy arranging the party tea - sandwiches, cakes, jelly and blanc-mange. The chocolate blancmange had been made in moulds which were shaped like rabbits and they were sitting on a bed of green jelly. The children each found a place at the table.

"Doesn't it all look lovely?" said Josie as she pulled a cracker with Pete, who was sitting beside her. Willy had fought to get the chair on the other side.

"I thought you couldn't stand her," Jimmy whispered to Pete between mouthfuls of meat-paste sandwiches. "Just 'cos she's got her best red dress on and a ribbon in her hair you seem to be all of a dither, and Willy's just as bad."

"Shut up and eat your tea," said Pete rudely. Then, smiling at Josie, he handed her a sandwich.

"He's looking after you isn't he?" remarked the lady who was dishing out the jelly. "Is he your brother?"

"No, my brother's over there," said Josie.

"Oh, is he your little boyfriend then?"

Josie blushed. "I didn't think he liked me really, he used to say I was a nuisance, so did Willy and my brother Jimmy."

"Perhaps it's your lovely red velvet dress."

"My Mum made it for me," said Josie proudly.

"She's a clever Mum," said the helper.

I suppose she is quite clever thought Josie, it was funny but she never really gave her mother much thought, she was always so busy extolling the virtues of her father. I'll tell her how everyone liked my dress when I get home, she'll be pleased about that, vowed Josie.

After tea was over there were more party games. 'Musical Chairs' proved to be very rough and noisy. Willy made sure Josie got a chair each time and she stayed in the game until the last six children and five chairs were left. Willy, Pete and Jimmy were all out by this time, so without them to help her, Josie found she was the one without a chair next time.

"Well done Josie!" said the boys.

"You stayed in longer than any of us," said Willy.

"Only 'cos you helped her," said Jimmy.

Willy just grinned. "I think it's 'Postman's Knock' next. I'll choose Josie if I get the chance."

"Oh, I hope I don't get any blooming girls," said Jimmy.

When the last game was over the superintendent rose to his feet and said, "Well, children, I hope you have enjoyed the party."

There was a roar of approval from the children.

"We will end," he continued when the din had died down, "by singing 'Away in a Manger', then when you have got your coats and hats on you can collect your bag of sweets and an orange to take home with you. Have a happy Christmas and I hope you will all be here again next Sunday."

The children responded enthusiastically, the boys shouting themselves hoarse. There was a mad dash to the cloakroom to collect hats and coats. Near the exit door was a large box containing bags of assorted sweets, and at the opposite side was an opened wooden crate containing oranges, all wrapped in individual paper wrappers, with an exotic picture and 'Produce of Spain' written on them. Christmas was a time for oranges, some of the less well off children seldom saw an orange except at Christmas. As the children passed out of the door they were each given an orange and a bag of sweets.

When the children were finally tucked up for the night, their parents settled down to sort out yet more last-minute preparations for Christmas.

Josie lay awake for ages it was exciting being admired instead of rebuked by Jimmy's friends, she decided she liked older boys. Duncan and Raymond paled into insignificance, they seemed so juvenile compared with Jimmy's friends. Just kids thought Josie, feeling very superior. If all the parties were as good as the Sunday School party, then this should be the best Christmas ever.

4

Christmas

Christmas Eve at last, it had seemed such a long time coming. Now with a pillow-case and a sock attached to the foot of each bed the children were trying hard to sleep. Jimmy, having had a very busy day, was tired and soon fell asleep, he knew that eventually his father would creep into the room to fill the pillow-case with presents and the sock with nuts, dates, sweets and an orange.

Josie, on the other hand, still believed that an old gentleman with a white beard and red clothes would come down the chimney to fill her pillow-case, but he would do this only if she was asleep.

Josie closed her eyes and turned her face into her pillow. How could she make herself go to sleep? The excitement of the last few days all helped to make this impossible. She strained her ears to hear any sound of movement, but all was strangely quiet.

Her father had placed a mince-pie and a glass of port-wine on the table beside the Christmas tree in the front room, so this was obviously where he was expected to descend.

The time passed very slowly as Josie tossed and turned. Downstairs her parents were very busy, all the presents had been sorted and placed in two pillow-cases identical to the ones at the foot of the children's beds. Jimmy's sledge and Josie's doll's-house would have to be carried upstairs separately. They would wait until they wanted to go to bed themselves before doing this as they knew the children were too excited to be able to get to sleep very quickly.

At eleven thirty Mr Brown made his way up to Jimmy's room

carrying the pillow-case. Groping around in the dark he found the empty pillow-case and sock and removed them, placing the full ones carefully at the foot of the bed without disturbing Jimmy who was snoring slightly - whether genuinely asleep or not his father didn't wait to find out. Leaving the door ajar, he picked up the sledge which he had already placed on the landing and stood it up on end resting on the chest of drawers so that Jimmy would see it as soon as he awoke, if indeed he was actually asleep. Jimmy slumbered on unaware of all this activity.

Josie, laying very still with her eyes tightly closed, had heard the sounds of footsteps on the stairs, they had passed her door a couple of times but her door had remained closed. She could feel her heart beating fast at the sound of her door handle being turned. Don't move, she kept telling herself, he won't be able to tell that you're awake. She dared not try to take a squint at him in case she gave herself away; if he knew she was awake that would mean no presents. Josie held her breath, she felt the weight of something being placed at the foot of her bed. The footsteps plodded back towards the door, then the sound of feet going downstairs. Josie opened up one eye and peered into the darkness. By the faint light coming from the landing she was able to distinguish a full pillow-case at the end of the bed. Her door was still slightly ajar and once again there was a foot-fall on the stairs. Josie closed her eyes tightly again. If only she dared look she would be able to tell Jimmy that she had actually seen Father Christmas, but her fear of losing all her presents outweighed her desire to see the provider of all these good things.

Her eyes remained closed as her father, staggering a bit under the weight, deposited the doll's-house next to the bed. Carefully closing the door, he made his way downstairs again.

"Josie's sound asleep," he informed his wife. "I'm not too sure about Jimmy. Does he usually snore?"

"Well, he does sometimes," said Mrs Brown. "I thought Josie would be the one who would be a problem, she's been so excited for the past few days."

Josie listened carefully to hear when her parents came upstairs to bed. She had opened her eyes and, by the faint light of the street lamp shining through her window, could make out the bulging pillow-case and, if her eyes were not playing tricks, the outline of the longed for doll's-house on the floor beside her bed.

She dared not get out of bed to look. She had decided to wait until her parents had gone to sleep then she could creep out and wake Jimmy and they could look at their presents together as they had done last year. If they were quiet they needn't disturb their parents until morning.

Josie snuggled down under the soft blankets quite prepared to bide her time, happy in the knowledge that Father Christmas had delivered her heart's desire even if she hadn't seen him. Still dreaming of her doll's-house she dropped off to sleep.

Waking some hours later to a silent house and the faint light of dawn beginning to spread around the room - there was her doll's-house. She climbed out of bed and sat on the floor to explore the inside.

"Oh! it's lovely," she sighed.

Then Josie crept past her parents bedroom door and got safely to Jimmy's room. Quietly opening the door she peered tentatively inside, it was much darker than her room. Without waiting for her eyes to become adjusted to the lack of light, she stepped into the room, colliding with the upturned sledge which fell with a clatter on to her bare feet. "Ow!" yelled Josie, jumping up and down.

"What's up?" asked Jimmy, waking from a deep sleep. "Josie what the heck are you doing?"

"My foot," cried Josie. "You've got your sledge all right, it's just fallen on my foot!"

"If you've broken anything I'll kill you," said Jimmy unsympathetically.

Getting out of bed and putting on the light he examined his sledge for damage. His father's head appeared at the door.

"What on earth are you doing making all this noise? You'll wake the entire neighbourhood."

"Sorry Dad, it's Josie, she walked into my sledge and it fell on her foot. Boy! what a super sledge Dad, I've never seen one as good as this."

"Are you hurt Josie?" asked her father, bending to look at her foot.

"I've seen my doll's-house Dad, it's lovely," said Josie, the pain in her foot forgotten.

"Do you know what time it is?" asked Dad. "It's half past four, it's much too early to get up, you must go back to sleep."

"Can't we open the rest of our presents?" pleaded Josie.

"All right, but don't make any noise, I don't know how the baby has managed to stay asleep, if you wake him you'll catch it, both of you!"

Josie and Jimmy spent the next half an hour unwrapping the parcels and trying hard not to make any noise, they limited their enthusiasm to excited whispers. As Josie unwrapped a small parcel she went into raptures over two small closed shells.

"Jimmy, they're my favourites."

"Coo! they're only cheap old things," replied Jimmy.

"But they're beautiful, when you put them in a glass of water lovely coloured flowers come out as they open."

Jimmy grinned, "They're clever, these Chinese."

"What a lovely lot of presents," said Josie as she pulled a blanket from the bed and wrapped it around their legs as they sat on the floor.

"That's better," said Jimmy, tucking the blanket under his feet. He hadn't realised how cold he had got sitting on the floor.

"I saw him," lied Josie.

"You saw Father Christmas you mean?"

"Yes, I saw him 'cos I wasn't asleep and I opened my eyes."

"What did he look like?" asked Jimmy with a grin.

"He was very old but he had a lovely face and soft silky white whiskers," said Josie, giving reign to her imagination.

"You didn't see the reindeer I suppose?"

" 'Course not, he left them on the roof didn't he? They wouldn't get down the chimney would they? Don't be so silly Jimmy!"

"I'm getting tired and cold," said Jimmy. "You go back to your room now, you can leave your presents here until morning."

When she was back in bed Josie propped herself up on her pillows so she could still see her doll's-house. 'It's Christmas!' she thought as her eyes finally closed in sleep.

The great day was here at last. The children, having been awake most of the night, were both sound asleep when their parents arose.

"Better leave them for a bit, I expect they're tired out," said Mrs Brown.

After having breakfast and bathing the baby, there were sounds of movement from upstairs and a sudden rush of feet upon the stairs as the children descended, each clutching as many presents as they could carry. Their happy chatter filled the house.

"Now, calm down a bit you two!" said their father. "I suggest you have breakfast and get washed and dressed, then I'll help you to get all your presents down into the front room. I've got a good fire going so it's nice and warm in there."

After carrying their presents downstairs with the help of their father, the children settled down on the front room carpet in front of the fire.

Josie immediately knelt down in front of her doll's-house and started to rearrange the dolls.

"It's time you got up," she told them, placing them on chairs in the dining-room.

"Josie, you talk to them as if they're real people, not silly old dolls."

"They're not silly. I'll tell Mum you said they were silly, I bet she spent no end of time making their little clothes."

"'Yes I expect she did," agreed Jimmy, not wanting to offend his mother on today of all days.

Josie was so completely absorbed that Jimmy's remarks had no effect on her at all; today was Christmas, she even felt kindly disposed to Jimmy, no matter what horrible remarks he made.

By mid-morning Grannie and Grandad had arrived, they were to stay until evening. Auntie May and Uncle Walter were expected to arrive in time for tea in the afternoon, they too would stay for the evening, playing cards until the last bus home.

Jimmy was anxious to get out into the snow for a trial run with his new sledge. His friends, Pete and Willy, had already called to see if he could come out. His father promised him that, once dinner was over, he could go out with his sledge, but until then he and Josie were to keep the grandparents entertained while he and their mother were busy preparing lunch.

Jimmy was rather surprised that Josie hadn't made her usual plea to come with him. Josie, however, was quite happy surrounded by adults who made a great fuss of her, she was even quite relieved that Jimmy would be absent for the afternoon, she felt there would be enough competition from baby John.

Jimmy settled himself more comfortably in the armchair, kicked off his slippers and stretched his toes toward the fire; by lunchtime he was half way through his 'Magnet' annual.

Baby John was wearing his new blue romper-suit, which

matched his eyes. Josie thought he was really beginning to look quite pretty, his white-blond hair was beginning to curl and he had a mischievous grin which was quite endearing. Grannie was quite entranced, and, rocking him gently on her knee, she crooned 'Ride a cock-horse to Banbury Cross' as John gurgled and giggled.

When the call came to say dinner was ready they all made their way to the living-room. Grandad carried John and placed him in his high chair. The table was a sight to behold. The cloth was bright-red and used only at Christmas and for parties. The crackers were red and gold. The 'blue dawn' crockery contrasted beautifully with the table cloth, the best cutlery sparkled.

At the head of the table was an enormous turkey roasted to a golden brown. Father was brandishing a large carving knife, anxiously waiting for everyone to be seated so he could begin carving the turkey.

Once the first course was finished, father disappeared into the kitchen, returning carrying a large round flaming Christmas pudding.

"It's on fire!" said Josie in alarm as the blue flames licked around the pudding.

"It's supposed to be," said Jimmy, as his father cut the pudding into portions.

"I've got a thruppenny bit," yelled Josie. "Look Dad," as she dug the little silver coin out of her pudding.

One by one everyone except Jimmy found threepenny pieces in their helping of pudding. Jimmy looked very disappointed.

"I can't understand it," said Dad, "I made sure I spread them round evenly and no one's got two. You'd better have another piece of pudding if you can eat it."

"I can eat it," said Jimmy, determined to get his share of the spoils. There was a metallic click as the pudding touched the plate.

"You've got one now Jimmy, I can hear it," said Josie.

Dinner over at last, the grandparents insisted on helping with the clearing away and washing up. Dad was supervising things in the kitchen. Mother had been told to have a rest and eventually came downstairs having changed into her best dress. Grandma made tea for everyone and served it in the front room.

Jimmy left with Willy and Pete to find a suitable hill for

c

sledging. Eventually both Grannie and Grandad dozed off, and baby John, also sound asleep, was on Grannie's lap.

This was surely a day to remember! Josie looked over baby John's blond curls to her Grannie's soft, pink, sleeping face, so different from her other Grandma's brown, lined one.

"I wonder what Grandma in the country is doing, Dad," said Josie, a little sadly.

"Josie, you worry about your Grandma don't you?"

"Yes, I worry 'cos she's got no Grandpa to look after her. Is she all alone today?"

"No, of course she isn't, if she was she would have come to stay with us. She prefers to stay at home and have her friends to dinner."

"Her friends?" asked Josie, surprised that her Grandma had friends, she always seemed to be too busy to have time for friends.

"I asked God and Father Christmas to bring her a Grandad," she confided.

"Don't you think you should check that she really wants a Grandad before you put in these requests?" her father asked, concealing a grin.

The family were still slumbering when Auntie May and Uncle Walter arrived. Jimmy returned with his friends, all were very enthusiastic about Jimmy's new sledge. The boys said 'hello' to everyone and stayed to chat for a bit before going home for their tea. Josie felt inexplicably shy in the presence of Pete and Willy and sat tight on her father's lap, merely saying a curt 'hello' to the boys.

Christmas night belonged to the grown-ups, they settled in the living-room, with an ample supply of beer and spirits, to play cards.

The children pleaded to be allowed to stay up, although they were both tired out by this time.

"Oh, let them stay up a little while," said Grannie. "After all, it is Christmas."

"All right, you can have a little longer, but you will have to amuse yourselves in the front room," said their father.

The children, with whoops of joy, settled in the front room organising their own game of 'snap', followed by 'snakes and ladders'. Josie, by this time, was really struggling to stay awake.

Jimmy watched as her eyelids dropped, he pushed a cushion under her head, she snuggled down with a sigh and within minutes was asleep.

Jimmy wondered if he could manage a bar of chocolate from his selection-box but decided he already felt a bit queasy so perhaps it wasn't a good idea. He settled himself comfortably in an armchair and picked up his book. After reading a couple of pages he also began to get drowsy. When their mother came to tell the children to start getting ready for bed she found them both soundly sleeping. Shaking them gently awake they were willing to go to bed with no further protests, stopping only to say 'good-night' to the relations.

The fair, which had arrived in town several days before Christmas, got into full swing on Boxing Day. Located in the Agricultural Hall and the adjoining cattle market, it stretched up toward the Norman Castle. The carousels, dodgems, cake walks and side-shows were out in the open on the cattle market, whilst under cover in the Agricultural Hall were stalls selling sweets, novelties and food.

One stall which Josie always loved to visit sold nothing but brightly coloured birds attached by string to a piece of cane. When you swished the cane through the air the bird on its string made a lovely whirring noise and its tail rotated. Josie had never quite fathomed out what caused this to happen, but she knew that the visit to the fair wouldn't be complete without a bird-on-a-stick to take home.

When the children awoke on Boxing morning they were up and washed and dressed in record time knowing that their father had promised them a visit to the fair. After breakfast was over they all dressed in their warmest clothes. A gentle snow was falling, covering the earth in a new coat of sparkling white. Luckily the bus which stopped at the end of the road also stopped outside the Agricultural Hall, so there was no long walk in the snow to get there.

Once they were safely on the bus Josie enjoyed the snow covered scenery as they sped along toward the fair. Although Jimmy was old enough now to venture into the centre of the city on occasions for visits to the shops or the cinemas, Josie seldom went this far. Alighting from the bus she skipped along at her father's side, up the flight of stone steps and into the hall.

After a quick look around the stalls they went out of the door at the back and into the fair proper. The noise from the steam organs was quite deafening, each playing a different tune. There was something special about this kind of mechanically produced music, it had the effect of almost forcing one to dance.

There was a great hubbub of voices as everyone tried to make themselves heard above the cacophony of sound, of music and the raucous voices of the barkers in the various side shows.

"I'm going on the dodgems Dad, I've got the money," said Jimmy.

"Come on then, my maid," said Mr Brown, taking his daughter's hand. "Let's have a try on the hoopla stall, though I reckon it's a swindle anyway."

"Why is it a swindle Dad? We might win that lovely gold watch."

"It's a swindle," said Mr Brown, "because if you look at the size of the stand which has the watch, it's as big as the hoop, so it's almost impossible to get the hoop over and make it lay flat. That's what you have to do to win, so try for the smaller prizes where the stands are not so large, at least there you might have a chance of winning."

Josie could see the logic of her father's argument, but she still thought how lovely it would be to win the watch.

She paid her money for five hoops dutifully hurtling the first three at the smaller prizes. The other two she aimed toward the coveted watch, one actually struck the stand and bounced off.

"Never mind," said her Dad.

"Hard luck missie," said the stall holder.

"Here you are for a good try," said the stall holder's lady assistant handing Josie a small box of toffees.

"Oh thank you," smiled Josie, looking as pleased as if she'd won the watch.

"Coo, Dad, wasn't that nice of the lady to give me a prize."

"Very nice, I expect she thought you tried hard," said her father. "Let's go and look for Jimmy shall we?"

When they reached the dodgems they could see Jimmy still bashing his way around. Mr Brown had a distinct suspicion that Jimmy must be on at least his second and possibly his third ride. Catching sight of Josie and his father he waved cheerfully, then reluctantly climbed out as the ride came to an end.

"I won a prize," boasted Josie, holding up her box of toffees. "You can share them when we get home."

"Let's have a go at rolling the pennies," said Jimmy, sorting out all the pennies from his pocket.

"I've got seven pennies," said Josie.

Josie and Jimmy rolled down their pennies, sometimes winning small amounts, which were paid out in pennies, thus tempting the winner to continue playing. They followed the usual pattern, very few punters quit when they are ahead and, sure enough, they didn't stop until Josie's seven pence and Jimmy's six pence were gone. As they walked around to look at the other stalls they passed a boxing booth.

"You'd like to go in there, wouldn't you Dad?" asked Josie, as she watched the boxers standing outside the booth flexing their muscles and looking fierce.

"Walk up, walk up!" yelled the barker. "A pound to anyone who can last a round with one of the lads. You look a likely contender son," he said as he singled out a big curly-haired, freckle-faced young man standing at the front of the crowd. "Would you like to try your luck? Last a round and you win a pound!" boomed the barker.

The young man looked rather embarrassed as his friends egged him on.

"Which one?" he asked, eyeing the three pugilists who were now giving an exhibition of shadow boxing.

"Me," said the largest, roughest one, saluting with his boxing glove.

"No thanks," said the freckled young man beating a hasty retreat followed by his jeering friends.

"Why don't you fight him Dad?" asked Josie.

"Me? He'd murder me," said her father.

"But you're brave, you won a medal in the war," insisted Josie.

"That's not quite the same thing," explained her father.

"He's a lot bigger than you," said Jimmy. "Don't take any notice of her, it's only 'cos Miss Lanham told her about David and Goliath!" This remark brought a giggle from those standing near.

"Why don't you try the darts Dad?" said Josie, admiring the display of prizes on the next stall.

"OK, let's have a try then," said Mr Brown, thankfully leaving the boxing booth.

"Hard luck sir," said the stall-holder. "Double top, and you'd have won."

"All right, I'll have one more try then," said Mr Brown. With five darts gone, Mr Brown totted up his score.

"Just double top," he said, aiming his last dart. "Got it! What about that then?"

Josie jumped up and down with excitement.

"Dad's won," she pulled on Jimmy's arm.

"Well done sir, slab of chocolate, tin of toffees, or small teddy bear?"

"Have the teddy for baby John," said Josie.

They walked on until they came to the end of the stalls.

"I'll buy you both a bag of roast chestnuts," he said as they reached the barrow with the glowing brazier. The children stamped their feet and warmed their hands near the brazier as their father purchased the nuts.

For a little while silence reigned as they shelled and ate the chestnuts.

"Do you think I could go on the cake-walk?" asked Jimmy.

"I don't see why not, would you like to go with Jimmy?" Mr Brown asked Josie.

"No, I don't like it, I'd rather stay with you."

"Oh, come on Josie, I'll keep hold of you," said Jimmy.

"Don't make her if she doesn't want to," said his Dad. "You can go, we'll watch, won't we Josie?"

Jimmy staggered off the cake-walk, his legs still seemed to want to keep in time with the rhythm of the music.

"Great!" enthused Jimmy as he joined his father and sister. "You should have come on it Josie."

"I think we'll have to start thinking of going home Jimmy, it's nearly dinner-time."

"Oh, what a shame, I wanted to go on the roundabout and on that new thing where the carriages go round and round and up and down like the waves in the sea."

"Makes me feel ill to watch it," said his father. "Well, look Jimmy, it's either a ride on that or sweets to take home!"

"I've still got plenty of sweets and chocolate from Christmas. I'd rather have the ride please Dad."

"If I leave you to have a ride on this new thing, will you

promise to come straight to the hall when you've finished then I can get Josie her bird and fair rock."

"Yes Dad, I'll see you in the hall then."

Mr Brown handed Jimmy the money to pay for his ride, then, taking Josie's hand, they made their way to the hall. Josie chose a beautiful blue bird on a stick. Her father got two quarters of fair rock, one for each child, and a bag of Pontefract cakes which were his wife's favourite. With the teddy for the baby everyone should be satisfied thought Mr Brown.

The rest of the Christmas holidays passed very quickly. Mr Brown returned to work on the day following Boxing Day. The children had the rest of the week before they were due back at school. Jimmy spent all his time happily in the snow with his sledge and his two friends Pete and Willy. They took Josie with them on their first expedition after Christmas. After about an hour Josie was crying because her hands and feet were frozen. Feeling very annoyed, Jimmy had to take her home again. The boys' admiration for Josie took a severe blow and they were back to considering her a confounded nuisance.

As Josie returned to the warmth and comfort of home she vowed to spend the rest of the holiday with her mother and baby John. She didn't care tuppence for those silly boys! Poor Josie, her moment of Christmas glory seemed to have evaporated the moment she took off her glamorous red velvet dress. She felt, however, that maybe things might improve again as there were still a number of parties to which she had invitations during the next month or so, when she could bring out her dress again.

While the boys were out in the snow Josie helped her mother with the planning for both her own and Jimmy's party. They made lists of games to play and another list of the food each would have. The lists of friends to be invited had already been compiled by her mother and father and Josie had already given verbal invitations to the children on her list.

It was the custom at all children's parties for each child to be given a small gift at the end of the party. Josie was to accompany her mother to the big Woolworths store in the centre of the city later in the week to pick something for each child on her list.

The gifts were items like pencil cases, pencil boxes, pen knives, clockwork toys, boxes of coloured pencils or wax crayons. The gifts varied from party to party according to the finances of the parents. It would be a talking point with the children who could be quite cruel in their comparison of the presents received.

With the Christmas festivities at an end and the dreary months of January and February behind them, the children had begun to look forward to spring, not that there was really much sign of it yet. The snow still covered the ground, it had cleared several times and then after a few days there was another heavy fall.

The papers reported that it was the worst winter for fifteen years. Even the boys were getting heartily sick of it. Each time it cleared it left a slushy mess behind, which seemed to seep through everything except 'wellies'. Josie declared that she felt like she had been wearing her boots forever. March was dreadfully cold and windy but the last of the snow had disappeared. The boys had begun to mourn the loss, completely forgetting their previous moans about it.

Easter came and went, the children received Easter eggs from all the relatives. Josie made short work of her pile of eggs, saving till last the beautiful eggs made entirely of marzipan decorated with sugar flowers. They seemed much too pretty to eat.

5

Empire Day

Back at school after the Easter break the children started to prepare for Empire Day on May 24th. At Josie's school they were having a pageant, with children dressed in the clothes of the countries of the British Empire. Josie was thrilled to be chosen to wear an Indian sari. Her teacher, Miss Chamberlin, said, with her dark colouring and large brown eyes, she seemed the most suitable choice to represent India.

Each country had one boy and one girl in national costume. The boy chosen for India was, like Josie, very dark with thick black hair and flashing eyes. Josie had admired him from afar for some time. He had joined the class half way through the term, having recently moved into the area. He was to wear baggy silk trousers, a brocade coat and a turban.

When the great day arrived the pageant paraded around the playground, then into the assembly hall to the accompaniment of 'Land of Hope and Glory' played on the piano with great enthusiasm by one of the teachers. The rest of the school were seated on the floor in neat rows. At the front of the hall was a large stage. The procession wound its way round the hall and came to a stop in front of the stage.

On the stage were two children from the top class, a girl dressed as Britannia and a boy looking splendid as John Bull. Sitting on chairs in the centre of the stage was the Lord Mayor, the Lady Mayoress and the Headmaster. The Mayor wore a wonderful robe edged with fur, on his head was a tricorn hat, around his neck a magnificent golden chain. The Mayoress was a vision in blue, but she paled into insignificance beside her colourful husband.

"Thank you children for this wonderful pageant," said the Mayor, "I am sure you and your teachers have all worked very hard to produce such a splendid display."

The children clapped, the Major continued his speech.

"I expect you all know about the British Empire, don't you?" he asked.

"Yes," yelled the children with one voice, although the younger ones, like Josie, had only a very vague idea. Josie knew it was the pink bits on the map, of which there were a great number. The children's costumes each represented one of these countries and the King was King over all of them. As Josie daydreamed about India the Mayor continued:

"As I see you all sitting here today I realise that you are all heirs to this great empire and I hope you will all do it justice just as your fathers and grandfathers have done before you."

Josie made a mental note to ask her father what he had done about the Empire.

"Because I am so pleased with your efforts children," said the Mayor, "I am going to give you a half day's holiday!"

A loud cheer broke out from the assembled school, and the clapping was quite deafening. The Headmaster held up his hand for silence and the clapping and cheers died away.

"I am sure," said the Headmaster, "that you would want me to thank the Mayor and Mayoress for visiting us today and for giving you a half day's holiday. We shall all give three cheers for the Mayor - Hip Hip Hooray!"

"Hooray!" yelled two hundred voices.

The only time Josie had actually seen an Indian she had been very scared and had run to hide behind her mother. The said Indian had been going from door to door with his suitcase full of small rugs and brilliantly coloured scarves. He was very tall and had a long bushy beard. His hair was covered by a turban. The clothes he wore looked to Josie like a dress with a wide belt. Everything he had worn had been of bright clashing colours. Josie had never seen such a colourful man. "Like a peacock," her mother had said, but nevertheless she had bought a scarf from him.

The Indian man could be seen in the neighbourhood for several days manfully carrying his heavy suitcase from door to door. Then, just as suddenly as he had appeared, so he disappeared again.

He was replaced a few weeks later by a band of gypsies selling sprigs of lucky white heather and clothes pegs which they had made from willow-twigs. One very elderly lady gypsy had ribbons, lengths of white lace and little lucky charms, made from some kind of white bone carved to look like elephants. The old lady also offered to "Read your palm, lady, you've got a lucky face dear, cross my palm with silver and I'll look into the future."

Josie's mother and many of the other women were more than a little afraid of the gypsies. It had been known in the past when one of them had refused to buy, the gipsy had put a curse on her. no one seemed to know whether the curse had had any dire effects on her, but it seemed that the threat was enough to make most of the superstitious mothers buy something or hide away and pretend not to be at home until the gypsies had made their way higher up the road.

Another less aggressive visitor to the road came each week on a Saturday afternoon when the children were enjoying the weekend with no school. He came in at the top end of the road, parked his barrel-organ near the kerb, turned the handle and produced the most delightful music. As soon as it started children appeared from nowhere. Some just stood, transfixed by the music, others did a jig to it.

On either side of the road windows would be thrown open. At the end of his recital the organ grinder would pass around the audience with his little wooden box with a slot in the top for coins. People in the houses who had been listening through open windows would throw a ha'penny or so out for him to pick up. When the collection was complete he wheeled the organ to the other end of the road, followed by the children, rather like the Pied Piper, where he would go through the whole performance again.

Jimmy had passed his eleventh birthday now and knew that the 'Eleven-plus' examination was looming over him. He and Pete and Willy had birthdays within a few months of each other and were all in the same class at school, all were due to take the exam this year. There was much discussion with class-mates as to their chances of passing and cramming from their teachers to enhance their chances. The exam was in two parts, the first part consisting of a list of short questions and puzzles of various sorts to unravel. Enquiring from older boys who had previously taken the exam, the general consensus of opinion seemed to be that the first part was easy. It did cross Jimmy's mind to wonder, if it was so easy, why so many of the boys had failed to pass. With so much emphasis on the importance of passing by the teachers, one got the impression that, without a grammar school education, one's life was more or less finished before it had begun.

After the first part of the exam was over, there was quite a wait before the results were announced. So it was some six weeks later when Jimmy found out that he had not passed. To his great relief neither had Pete nor Willy, which meant that after August they would all start at the local boys' Senior School. "I'm glad!" they confided in each other. "It's jolly hard work at Grammar School and it would have been rotten if we'd got separated." They began to quite look forward to going to their new school, mostly because it was a boys only school with a good reputation and an emphasis on sporting activities.

To cheer Jimmy up after his failure to win the scholarship, the children were told that on Sunday their parents were taking them on a trip to Yarmouth - not the usual one by train, this time they would go by boat from Brundall.

When the great day arrived they made their way to Brundall and boarded the steamer. It was the most exciting day of Josie's life, she had never been on a boat before. Her father glanced down at the people milling around the quay. One tiny little man stood out from she crowd.

"That's 'Billy Bluelight'," he said.

"What a funny name," giggled Josie.

"It's not his real name," said her father, "it's just a nickname, his real name's William Cullum."

"Why is he called 'Billy Bluelight' then?" asked Jimmy.

"No idea," said his father. "But if you watch him you'll find he starts walking when the boat pulls away, then he'll walk all the way to Yarmouth."

"Perhaps he can't afford a ticket," said Josie, feeling very sorry for the poor little man on the quay.

"I don't suppose he can," said her father. "But that's not the idea anyway, he doesn't want to go by boat, he wants to walk to see if he can get there before the boat."

"He couldn't do that, could he Dad?" asked Jimmy. "After all, the boat must be going quicker than anyone can walk."

"Maybe, but the river winds about a bit so it's probably longer than the road, anyway old Billy can get a move on when he likes!"

"Does he wait for the boat if he gets there first?" asked Josie.

"Of course he does," said her mother. "That's the whole idea, then everyone on the boat will make a collection for him."

"He does all right from these little jaunts," laughed Mr Brown as the boat began to pull away and Billy, waving to the passengers, shouted:

"See you in Yarmouth!"

Josie scarcely stopped chattering the whole way to Yarmouth, never had she enjoyed a journey so much. The boat glided through the water, strange plants and flowers grew along the bank, and every now and then she caught sight of a scurrying animal.

From time to time when turning a bend in the river they got a fleeting glimpse of the road. Josie stood up to see over the rail and strained her eyes in an effort to see 'Billy Bluelight'.

At last the first building in Yarmouth came into view, buildings which the children had never seen on their many previous visits to Yarmouth, because the river followed a course through an area seldom visited by holidaymakers.

As the quay came into view Josie spotted the small figure she had last seen walking away from Brundall. As he looked up at the boat and waved everybody clapped and cheered. The passengers began to file off the boat, putting coins into the hat of the little man who had once again beaten the boat to Yarmouth.

The months sped by and in no time at all the schools closed for the summer break. This year, instead of the usual week at Yarmouth, the grown-ups had decided to go to Hemsby. They were going to share a bungalow with their friends, who had two children about the same ages as Josie and Jimmy.

Kate was a couple of months older than Jimmy and Charlie was nearly a year older than Josie. Jimmy began moaning as soon as he heard the plan for the holiday.

"I can't stand that Kate, specially since she passed the scholarship, she's become a right stuck up little madam."

"Jimmy, I hope we're not going to have any quarrelling, I don't want you spoiling the holiday, I don't see any reason why we can't all get along together."

"We thought you'd be pleased, Jimmy, you're always grumbling about having to cart Josie about with you, now when you've got someone your own age you're still complaining."

"If it was anyone but that awful Kate, I probably would be."

"I'm pleased," Josie butted in. "I'll have Charlie to play with, so I won't have to worry if Jimmy goes off and leaves me on my own."

Jimmy's protests were ignored and on the Saturday before Bank Holiday Monday both families were assembled ready to start. The men-folk had devised an inexpensive way of getting the two families, plus a considerable amount of luggage, to Hemsby. They had prevailed upon a friend who owned an open backed lorry to transport them, for a small consideration, directly to the bungalow, thus eliminating the need for buses and trains.

The two women and baby John went in the cab with the driver, the men and the children sat in the back with the luggage. They had collected all the cushions they could lay hands on and a couple of blankets in case the children felt cold.

Thus settled for the journey, each with a bag of sweets to eat on the way, the children were highly delighted with this rather unusual mode of transport. With the exception, that is, of Kate who found the whole thing most undignified. First of all she objected to being man-handled on to the back of the lorry. It took both men a fair amount of pushing and shoving before they were able to heave her aboard. Kate was a plump, not very agile girl and her dignity was somewhat ruffled as she flung herself bad-temperedly down on a pile of cushions and tried to ignore the sniggers of Josie and Charlie.

"Why couldn't we have gone by train?"

Jimmy hopped easily on to the back of the lorry, followed by Charlie, then Josie, with a little help from her father. Jimmy piled up the cushions for the younger children and himself as far as possible away from Kate. Charlie settled himself with Jimmy and Josie.

"You're always grumbling about something," he told his sister. "Don't take any notice of her, she's not going to ruin our holiday is she?" he appealed to Josie and Jimmy. They were already beginning to warm to Charlie.

The two men settled themselves and lit a cigarette each and then they were away. It was surprising how much of the countryside was visible from their vantage point. Much better than trains or buses seemed to be the opinion of all, except of course, Kate, who sat in her corner looking disdainful.

When the assembled company broke into song as they sped along, Kate merely sighed loudly.

"S'pect they don't do that at the Blyth School," whispered Jimmy as Josie and Charlie broke into giggles.

By the time they were nearing Hemsby the children were all complaining of sore bottoms from the hard boards of the lorry, even the cushions could not prevent the jarring every time they went over a bump in the road.

Kate had more than her fair share of the cushions and had propped herself quite comfortably in the corner at the back next to the driving cab. Despite this she complained about the discomfort, she complained about the singing, she complained about going on holiday with a load of silly kids. This last complaint annoyed Jimmy who considered himself much more grown up than Kate, if her present behaviour was anything to go by.

At last the road sign said 'Hemsby one mile'. Jimmy, Josie and Charlie cheered. Kate merely remarked, "Thank heaven for that."

Finally, when the lorry could go no further, everyone disembarked and unloaded the luggage.

Thus heavily laden, they caught their first glimpse of the bungalow they were to occupy for the next week. It was new, having been erected at the end of the last summer season. Made of dark brown wood, it had a wide verandah running along the front, overlooking the sea. But, most marvellous of all, at the side were wooden stairs running up to the roof, which was flat with a balustrade running all round. There were coloured deck-chairs and tables all ready for use. On sighting the stairs the younger children made a dash to the top.

"Mum, Dad, it's lovely up here," yelled Josie.

The adults made their way up to admire the view once they had deposited the luggage inside.

"Oh! isn't the sea lovely, Jimmy," said Josie, peering through the balustrade. "We can get out of bed and run straight in the sea even before we have breakfast!"

"I'll come too," said Charlie enthusiastically.

Kate, who was following behind the grown-ups, sighed and sat down on one of the deck-chairs.

Having admired the view, the whole party made its way down-stairs again to inspect the bungalow. The only drawback, as far as Josie could see, was having to share a room with stuck-up Kate. For the sake of harmony she didn't complain. Kate, however, complained bitterly that, had she known she'd have to share a room with a child, she'd never have come!

Mrs Moore was extremely proud that her Kate had passed the scholarship to go to the Blyth School. Since the results had been announced, Kate had been able to do no wrong in her mother's eyes. Now, even her mother was getting a little tired of her continual moans. "And what would you have done while we were on holiday?"

"I don't know, but I wouldn't have come," insisted Kate.

"Stop finding fault with everything and everyone," said Mr Moore, also getting irritated by his daughter's attitude. "You're sharing with Josie and that's an end to it. You don't hear Jimmy complaining about sharing with Charlie."

"He's probably not got enough sense to complain," said Kate, spitefully.

"You'll apologise to Jimmy this instant," said her father.

"Oh, don't bother!" said Jimmy, shortly.

"I don't want to hear another complaint from you for the rest of the week." Mr Moore sounded very stern and Kate looked even more miserable.

Once they had unpacked the children ran noisily down to the sea to splash about until tea-time. Kate had stayed with the grown-ups on the roof, where she sat and sulked for the rest of the afternoon.

Tea over, the two families went for a stroll along the beach until it was time for the younger children to go to bed. Josie found that sharing a room with Kate was quite easy because she went to bed several hours before Kate and was asleep by the time she came to bed. In the mornings she was up and in the sea with the boys long before Kate began to stir.

The days took on a leisurely pattern, for the children an early morning bathe in the sea then back for breakfast. Josie and Charlie could play happily on the beach all day. Jimmy might long for the bright lights and noisy amusement arcades of Yarmouth, but to the younger children, the beach was heaven.

They wandered along the edge of the sand where the waves lapped gently on the bank of shingle. Shells and delicately coloured stones, and sometimes a lucky stone with a hole right through it, would be revealed as the tide receded. Best of all were the pieces of green glass worn smooth by the sea, these would shine among the shingle. As Josie gathered them her vivid imagination would weave stories of pirates, treasure and lost royal jewels from which the emeralds had come. Even Jimmy's disparaging remarks, "They're nothing but old bits of broken bottles," couldn't dampen Josie's enthusiasm.

Just before dinner-time the adults would go down the road for a drink at the nearby pub. Jimmy was left in charge of baby John, as neither Josie nor Charlie were anywhere to be seen and Kate was usually shut in her bedroom with a book. When they returned from the pub they prepared dinner, and usually had to go and look for Josie and Charlie who seemed to have no idea of time whatsoever.

After dinner was over the parents retired to the balcony on the roof for an afternoon of reading the papers and taking a nap. Jimmy, freed from looking after the baby, would accompany the two younger children to roam along the sand dunes and the cliff paths, usually walking for miles. Kate always turned her nose up at the very idea of indulging in such childish pursuits, but after a couple of days of getting thoroughly bored when the adults fell asleep in the sun, she reluctantly agreed to accompany them.

Getting together while they waited for her to change her shoes, they planned to go along the cliff path as far as they could and then make their way down the steep muddy cliff on to the beach.

"She'll be too windy to go down that way!" said Charlie, gleefully. "So we'll be able to leave her at the top - serve her right for being such a misery."

With a fair amount of bickering they made their way to the top of the cliff.

"We go down here," said Charlie, cheerfully.

"Oh no, I can't go down there," said Kate.

" 'Course you can, even little Josie can do it."

"No I can't, I can't," wailed Kate.

Jimmy, holding on to Josie, began to make his way, slipping

and sliding down the steep path. Although the children seemed unaware of it, this was quite a dangerous undertaking and had their parents known what they were doing they would have been horrified. Charlie, following behind, was also having difficulty keeping his feet.

They all eventually slithered to the bottom and jumped thankfully on to the sand, looking up they saw that Kate was still hovering at the top of the cliff.

"Come on then," said Jimmy. "It's not that difficult."

"I daren't," yelled Kate.

"Well then, go back the way you came," said Charlie.

"It's a long way back that way," said Kate.

"Then you'll have to come down the cliff, won't you?" Charlie reasoned.

"All right, I'll try," said Kate.

She moved a little way down and began to slide, screaming, she sat down on the mud and clutched at the grass to bring herself to a halt.

"You'll just have to slide down the rest of the way sitting down," said Jimmy, trying to be helpful.

Josie was beginning to get tearful.

"She'll fall Jimmy, she'll kill herself."

"Don't be silly Josie," said Jimmy sternly, trying to hide his growing alarm.

"Can you climb back up?" asked Jimmy.

"No," cried Kate. "It's worse getting up than it is down."

"Right then," said Jimmy, taking charge, "I'll try to get up and help you down."

He began the perilous ascent of the cliff. He would have found it quite simple to climb if it were not for the slimy slippery mud. Josie, on the verge of tears again, watched her brother climbing ever nearer to the terrified Kate.

They could see that Jimmy was talking to Kate and she seemed to have calmed down a bit. Jimmy started to descend slowly in front of Kate who, at last, started to move. He had told her not to worry about slipping because he would be able to stop her if she slipped too far. He was not really as confident in his ability to do this as he made out, after all she was bigger and heavier than he was.

Kate was carrying out his instructions and sliding foot by foot on her bottom along the muddy path. If she started moving too fast he had told her to grab the grass on either side to slow down her descent.

To the two scared children at the bottom their progress seemed painfully slow.

At long last they reached the bottom. Jimmy jumped on to the sand and held up his hands to assist Kate.

"Thank you Jimmy," said Kate, and burst into tears.

"Well, don't cry about it," said Jimmy as Josie also started to cry.

"You aren't half in a mess," said Charlie, eyeing his sister from the back. "You're absolutely covered in black mud."

Their enmity forgotten the children inspected each other. Josie and Charlie were both OK except for muddy shoes and socks. Their descent of the cliff had been made more or less upright so their clothes had escaped any damage. Jimmy had remained clean on his first descent but on going back for Kate he had crawled most of the way up on his hands and knees and had slid on his bottom coming down again. So both Jimmy and Kate were liberally coated with evil smelling black mud.

"What can we tell them when we go back?" asked Jimmy.

"Couldn't we wash your clothes in the sea?" suggested Charlie. "It's warm, they'd soon dry."

"We'd never get the mud off without soap," said Kate. "They'll kill us when they find out what we've been doing."

"They probably won't let us out on our own anymore. Let's think, what are the alternatives?" said Jimmy.

Luckily, this was a completely deserted part of the beach. They couldn't sit on the sand because they knew it would stick to the mud and make things even worse. So they stood in an unhappy little group discussing their plight, but at least they were now completely united in their efforts to avoid the wrath of their respective parents.

"They might be asleep on the roof when we get home," said Jimmy. "Supposing we can get in without being seen, then we could change and hide our muddy clothes, then when they go to the pub tonight maybe we can wash them."

They all agreed that this seemed a good plan - even Kate cheered up considerably.

"You two," said Jimmy, indicating Josie and Charlie, "will

have to go home first while we wait on the beach, then you can let us know if the coast is clear, but make sure you check properly."

Having decided on a plan they made their way quickly back to the beach in front of the bungalow. Jimmy and Kate hid in the sand dunes awaiting the report from Josie and Charlie.

Josie felt very important as she marched along with Charlie.

"I'll go up and check on the roof," said Charlie. "You keep out of sight till I come down again." With that Charlie began to creep up the stairs, carefully raising his head at the top, he surveyed the scene. The baby was sound asleep in his push-chair, his white floppy sun-hat pulled down over his eyes. Fast asleep in the deck-chairs were all four of the parents. Charlie crept down the stairs again.

"It's all clear Josie, they're all asleep, you run down and tell Jimmy and Kate. I'll stay here in case anyone wakes up," said Charlie.

Josie was off like a hare down the beach to where Jimmy and Kate were concealed. "It's OK," she told them, "Charlie's been up to the roof to check they're all sleeping."

"You're sure?" asked Jimmy.

"Yes quite sure, but hurry before they wake up."

"Don't make any noise Josie," said Jimmy. They ran silently toward the bungalow.

"You and Charlie keep watch," whispered Jimmy when they reached the veranda.

It was all very thrilling, thought Josie, crouching out of sight of the stairs, like playing 'cops and robbers'. She hoped they wouldn't be too long getting changed, the strain was beginning to tell.

Soon Kate and Jimmy emerged looking clean and tidy again.

"We'll wait until they go out tonight then we'll see if we can wash the clothes and hang them on the clothes line at the back. It's dark when they come home so chances are they won't see them. We'll both have to get up early in the morning before the grown-ups are awake so we can get them in again!" said Jimmy.

It's amazing, thought Josie, last Saturday Kate had been a stuck-up madam, beyond contempt. Now, it seemed, she was Jimmy's bosom friend. Well, she supposed Jimmy was something of a hero after this afternoon's rescue.

When they eventually returned to the bungalow for tea they did so in sets of two, Josie and Charlie arriving first.

"Where are Jimmy and Kate?" asked Mrs Moore.

"I don't know, they're around somewhere I suppose," stated Charlie.

"You mean they're together?" asked Josie's mother.

"Oh yes, they're definitely together," said Charlie.

"Well, fancy that," said Mrs Brown.

When tea was over Mr Brown said, "Right, let's make a move, Jimmy'll take care of the baby."

With that they all trooped off to pursue the evening's entertainment.

Kate and Jimmy retrieved their smelly clothes from their hiding places. Jimmy filled the kitchen sink with hot water, finding a bar of soap and a wash-board, he proceeded to scrub his shorts and shirt.

Josie had heard her mother telling her aunt how domesticated Jimmy had become since the birth of baby John. "I'll make sure I never become domesticated," thought Josie, eyeing the revolting mess in the sink.

Josie and Charlie were losing interest in the washing operation. They were forbidden to leave the bungalow whilst the parents were away so they settled on the veranda with a glass of lemonade and the 'snakes and ladders' board. When nine o'clock arrived they went to bed without a murmur, both being completely tired out.

After they had gone to bed Jimmy and Kate sat on the veranda.

"It's lovely here, isn't it Jimmy?"

"I thought you didn't want to come?"

"Well, I didn't to begin with and I didn't like the lorry ride," then she smiled, "I didn't like you very much either."

"I suppose it was a bit rough in the lorry," agreed Jimmy, remembering they had all been a bit unkind to Kate, laughing at her awkwardness, and really she wasn't so bad when you got to know her better. The moon came up casting a silver shadow on the sea. "Look, isn't it beautiful?" said Kate.

"Mm! I wouldn't mind living here all the time," said Jimmy.

Jimmy had never had such a long conversation with a girl before, girls had, up to now, been something he refused to bother with. At the beginning of the week he had pined for his friends

Pete and Willy and thought how marvellous the holiday would have been if they had been there. Now, he was not so sure, walking and talking with Kate had its compensations. He couldn't imagine either of his friends sitting here like this, watching the moon reflecting on the sea, no they'd want to be up and doing. Well, sometimes it was nice to just sit and talk, reflected Jimmy.

"What's come over them?" said Mrs Moore, when the adults returned from their evening out. "They seem to have been at each other's throats ever since they arrived."

"Let's be thankful Kate's stopped moaning, she seems to have been doing her best to spoil everyone's holiday up to now," said Mr Moore, who had no illusions about his daughter.

Jimmy went to bed very quietly so as not to wake Charlie. After he had turned out the light, he lay thinking about the holiday so far, up until today he had wished they'd gone to Yarmouth as they usually did. There was so much to do there, with the amusement arcades all along the front right down to the Pleasure Beach at one end and the Waterways at the other.

Yarmouth was more to Jimmy's taste. He wasn't like Josie, who was happy gathering wild flowers and making daisy chains, looking for crabs and shrimps in the pools left when the tide goes out. He liked the noise and bustle - but he liked it better here now that he was friendly with Kate. In the morning he was up and dressed by six-thirty.

Kate was waiting on the veranda wearing her swim-suit with a towelling wrap around her shoulders.

"I thought I'd come for a swim with you," she said.

They made a dash for the sea, splashing right in before the coldness of the water had time to register.

"Oh-h - it's cold!" shouted Kate.

"It is at this time of the morning," said Jimmy. "But you'll find it's all right after you've been in for a little while."

Kate was already out-pacing him, she was obviously a very good swimmer. They had walked out until the water was deep enough to make swimming comfortable then they swam parallel to the beach. Jimmy tired first and started to head for the beach, before he reached it Kate had overtaken him. She ran up the beach ahead of him and put her wrap around her shoulders. Jimmy, shivering a bit, put his towel around him and sat down on the sand. A watery sun was rising higher over the sea.

"It's the best time to go in, later on there are lots more swimmers. You're a jolly good swimmer, Kate."

"That's because I'm fat," said Kate.

"You're not fat," said Jimmy, gallantly.

"Well, my Mum says it's puppy fat and I'll lose it in a year or so."

"I don't know what you're worrying about," said Jimmy, "I think you're all right as you are."

"Thank you Jimmy," said Kate, sighing contentedly and pulling her wrap more tightly around her shoulders.

The second half of the week passed even more quickly than the first half had done. Josie and Charlie were seldom off the beach, they were either paddling in the rock pools or building sand castles, it was difficult to get them to come in for meals. Kate and Jimmy had taken to walking for miles along the sand dunes.

On Thursday Jimmy wheedled round his father for permission and the necessary cash to take a trip to Yarmouth. Kate had been equally successful with her father. Friday morning found them waiting for the 9 a.m. bus for Yarmouth, each with a packed lunch and a jacket in case the weather turned cooler. "Why can't I go?" wailed Charlie.

"Oh, who wants to go to Yarmouth, it's much better here. I thought we were shrimping today Charlie."

"That's right," said Charlie, all thoughts of the attractions of a visit to Yarmouth dismissed. Gathering their buckets and spades and shrimp-nets they headed for the beach.

On the journey home next day Kate sang as heartily as everyone else, never once complained and surreptitiously held Jimmy's hand when their respective fathers were occupied with other things so they didn't notice. Josie noticed and whispered to Charlie, who said, "Sloppy lot!" and then continued with his singing.

Following the holiday, there was a long period of friendship between Kate and Jimmy, each had settled well at their new schools. Jimmy made a practice of rushing out of school and pedalling as fast as he could to the Blyth School to meet Kate and walk home with her. Kate got a good deal of ribbing from her classmates about her faithful swain. But the two still stuck to each other.

6

Mr Moore on the Dole

Although the Moores were not aware of it, the storm clouds were gathering over their happy family life. One afternoon when Jimmy had made his usual frantic dash to meet Kate at her school gate, he found her already waiting for him. Almost before he had time to get off his bike, Kate grabbed his arm, obviously in great distress.

"Oh! Jimmy, something awful's happened, my Dad has lost his Job, half the workers at his factory have been sacked."

Jimmy was stunned, it was all so unexpected.

"That is awful Kate, what's he going to do?"

"I don't think he knows at the moment, there are very few jobs in the shoe trade in this area and that's all he knows, that's what he's done since he left school. Oh! Jimmy, whatever are we going to do?"

"Maybe he could find some other job not in the shoe trade."

"I doubt it, it's the slump, it's all over, not just the shoe trade, but I know he'd be prepared to take anything that's going. I've never seen my father so desperate."

They walked home in gloomy silence, their little world suddenly shattered by this turn of events. When Jimmy got home he informed his father of the situation.

"Poor old Sid," said Mr Brown, "Wish I could do something for him but I had to lay another couple of my chaps off last week, it's the same everywhere, don't know what things are coming to. Tell Kate to ask him to come round at the weekend, perhaps they could all come, how about asking them to tea on Sunday Em?" he consulted his wife.

"Yes, fine," said Mrs Brown.

Jimmy passed the message on to Kate when he met her the next day, she was still very upset.

"My mother and father were talking about it last night, they don't know how they are going to manage if Dad can't find another job," said Kate.

"You'll be able to get money from somewhere surely?" said Jimmy.

"My Mum said they do what's called a 'means-test', so what you get depends on whether you've got anything put by, or anything you can sell."

"Have they got anything put by do you think?" asked Jimmy.

"Well, a bit I think, but that's not going to last long if he's out of work for any length of time is it?" said Kate. "He'll get dole money to start with, of course. Poor old Dad, he's really cut up about it all."

Some weeks later Jimmy as usual rushed to meet Kate out of school only to find her looking more distressed than usual. Her father had been offered a job by his brother-in-law who owned a small restaurant in London and the family would be moving there in a couple of weeks time.

Kate and Jimmy were heartbroken. Charlie, although upset at the thought of moving and leaving behind all his friends, had to admit that the idea of living in London had a certain appeal.

The departure of Kate was an unhappy experience for Jimmy.

"He's such a misery," said Josie, unfeelingly.

"He's missing Kate," said her mother.

"I miss Charlie but I'm not making such a fuss," said Josie.

"But you didn't spend as much time with Charlie as Jimmy did with Kate."

"No, I'm not in love," said Josie with a smirk.

For the first two weeks after Kate had left, Jimmy retired to his room at some time during the evening to pen his long epistle to the 'love of his life'. Every morning he waited anxiously for the postman. Kate was just as regular with her replies.

During the third week Jimmy missed one letter because Pete and Willy persuaded him to go with them to join the Boys' Brigade. Jimmy, finding himself very much at a loose end, was glad of something to occupy his time. His one regret was that

d

Kate wouldn't be there to see him when he got his uniform. He had taken to knocking around again with his two mates. Pete and Willy had to admit that they were pleased to see the back of Kate so their twosome could revert to a trio again.

Jimmy was getting quite wrapped up in the Boys' Brigade. He was now a member of the band playing a drum on which he practised incessantly. Whenever possible he got Pete and Willy to join him in the garden shed for a practice session. Willy also had a drum and Pete had a bugle.

His letters to Kate were becoming less frequent.

"It's difficult to think of things to write about if I write every day," he confided to his mother.

"I'm sure it is," she said. "I don't think Kate would expect you to write every single day. It must be just as difficult for her to think of things to write about."

"I suppose so," Jimmy's conscience was salved by his mother's reasoned argument.

The letters became less and less frequent and eventually dried up altogether. Jimmy didn't seem to have time to wonder whether he was upset or not.

The holiday with Grandma took on a different pattern this year. For the first week Jimmy, Josie, John and Mrs Brown all stayed at Grandma's, with Mr Brown joining them at the weekend. By the end of the first week Jimmy was beginning to get bored and he was missing Pete and Willy. Couldn't he go back with his Dad, he pleaded? After some discussion between his parents and, with his Dad's agreement, Jimmy returned home with him on the second Sunday.

Josie heaved a sigh of relief as Jimmy departed remarking, "He's been a right misery all week."

"He'd rather be with his pals I expect," said her Grandma.

Josie settled for spending a happy week in the company of Mary from the farm. Mary was quite enchanted by baby John. He was now a sturdy little boy who liked nothing better than to follow his big sister around, much as she used to follow her big brother.

When Josie, her mother and the baby returned from holiday they were amazed to find that, whilst they had been away, the big house on the corner, which had been boarded up for more than a year, had suddenly been occupied.

The house was surrounded by a six foot high wall. Along the top of the wall were jagged pieces of glass set in cement. The last occupant of the house had been a reclusive old man whom the kids nicknamed 'the hermit'. Since he had died the house had remained empty and boarded up.

The boards had been removed from the upstairs windows which were the only ones visible from the road, and one or two curtains had appeared. The double gates at the back had been opened to allow the removal van access. Most of the neighbourhood's child population were interested spectators, Josie was itching to join them. There seemed to be several very dark, handsome young men helping to unload the furniture. Josie had not yet established whether they were employees of the removal firm or members of the family of the new residents.

"Can I go and have a look?" Josie pleaded.

"Oh all right, but come home at tea-time," said her mother.

As Josie worked her way to the front of the crowd she saw there was one very much younger dark boy of about her own age. He dashed about carrying small items into the house. It was several weeks and several rumours later that it was established that the new family were Italian. Eventually, the young boy ventured out into the road to investigate the evening game of cricket, attracted by the shouts as someone scored. The game stopped as the boys eyed the newcomer. Josie, who had been included in the game because they were one short, called "Hello!" The boy approached the group rather shyly.

"What's your name?" Jimmy asked him, wondering if he spoke English.

"Aldo," said the boy. "What's yours?"

"Jimmy, this is Pete and this is Willy. Oh, and my sister Josie," he added as an afterthought.

"Pleased to meet you," the boy had no trace of an accent.

"Want a game?" asked Jimmy.

"Yes please," said the boy, accepting the bat offered by Jimmy.

"Do you know how to play cricket?" asked Jimmy.

"Of course," said the boy.

"Right, you bowl Willy."

Willy bowled a fast one, Aldo cracked it up in the air and over his own high wall.

"Better go and look for it, come on," said Aldo opening the tall gate which had been padlocked for years.

All the children trooped into the garden.

"Might be a bit difficult to find," said Aldo, " 'cos the grass is so overgrown. I expect my brothers will cut it down as soon as we get properly moved in."

"Are they your brothers who were moving the furniture in?" asked Josie.

"Yes, Franco, Geno and Mario," said Aldo.

"What lovely names," said Josie. "Are you all Italian?"

"All my brothers and my sister Maria were born in Italy but I was born here in this country."

When school started again Aldo came to join Josie's class at school; as he knew no one other than Josie he tended to stick with her, especially as she seemed to be a force to be reckoned with when she got with the other kids. Because Josie had always had to stick up for herself when it came to dealing with her brother and his friends, she was viewed with some trepidation by those of her own age group. So a stranger in their midst would be treated with respect if he appeared to have Josie's backing.

Josie's protection of Aldo was to form the basis for a strong and lasting friendship between the two. The older boys, once the initial novelty of having a foreigner in their midst had worn off, dismissed Aldo with a scathing reference to 'That Iti Kid'.

Aldo often took Josie home with him after school, there she would sample the cakes his mother made. Aldo's mother seemed, to Josie, to never be out of the kitchen, she was always either baking or preparing meals for her large hungry family. All three of the elder boys and the father worked in the fish restaurant which they owned. They worked extremely long hours.

"This," said Aldo, "was to get the business established."

Josie was not exactly sure of the meaning of the word 'established' but she had no intention of betraying her ignorance, so she merely nodded wisely at Aldo's remarks.

Now that Josie was at Primary School the work was harder and they were often given work to do at home. In spite of this, Josie and Aldo managed to meet most evenings. Often they sat on the fish-shop doorstep at the side entrance which was never used.

"What do you do all evening when you're sitting on the doorstep talking 'non stop'?" asked Jimmy one evening.

"We have discussions," said Josie importantly.

"What about?"

"Oh everything, Aldo knows a lot about the world, he goes to Italy to see his Grandma and his aunts and uncles every year. They don't go in the summer 'cos that's their busy time. They go during the winter for a whole month so Aldo has to have a month off school."

"Lucky devil!" sighed Jimmy. "Well I don't mind what you do as long as you keep your gang out of my way."

Josie pondered over Jimmy's remark. Perhaps a gang might be fun, she would have to suggest it to the boys.

When they met after school the next day Josie put forward the proposal.

"Why don't we become a gang?" she asked the boys.

"What do we do if we're a gang?" asked Aldo.

"Well, er - we have meetings," said Josie, trying to think what else one did in a gang.

"Perhaps we could have an aim," said Ray.

"Like robbing the rich to feed the poor," put in Josie dramatically, having recently read *Robin Hood*.

"Perhaps we could take care of anyone who's down-trodden or put upon," ventured Duncan who, until recently, had been a bit down-trodden himself.

"That can be our aim," said Josie. "Now, what shall we call ourselves?"

"You should be the gang leader, Josie," said Aldo. "Don't you think so?" he asked the other two.

"Yes, Josie must be leader," chorused Ray and Duncan.

"Thanks, then," said Josie, very pleased to have been asked. "Now let's think what our gang can be called."

"The Disciples," suggested Ray.

"Mm, that's quite a good name, but think who was the leader of the disciples, I don't think I could live up to that!"

"What about Apostles then or Cavaliers?"

"Or Goodies, or Merry Men or the Foresters?"

"I know, what about the Samaritans?"

"Now that's good," said Josie. "After all, they helped people and that's what we want to do. I think we should be the Good Samaritans."

"That's settled then," said Ray, "I like it, 'The Good Samaritans'. Are we a secret gang then?"

"Yes, I think we should be a secret. Where could we meet where no one will know?"

"There's a disused stable in our garden," said Aldo. "No one's got around to doing anything with it yet, I don't suppose they'd even know we were there."

"Lovely," said Josie. "When shall we have our first meeting?"

"What about tomorrow?" said Aldo. "We could meet out here after tea and then I can show you where the stable is."

Josie was in a hurry to finish her tea the next day.

At their first meeting they decided that they would look for someone who needed help. Once they had selected the candidate for their good-work, they would meet to discuss the ways and means of accomplishing this. They would meet once a week, on Tuesday evenings. With the business completed, Aldo, who always had more money than anyone else, suggested Ray nip over to the fish shop and buy chips for everyone. Once Ray had departed clutching Aldo's four pennies the rest of them set about tidying up their headquarters.

They found an empty tea-chest which, when turned upside down, made an excellent table. There were enough beer crates to use for seating. It was quite dark and murky inside when the door was shut so a note was made for everyone to get hold of as many candles as they could. By the time they had completed the clean-up Ray had returned with four newspaper wrapped packages. Chips had never tasted so good they all decided, as they sat on their beer crates in a circle around the tea-chest table.

During the following week each Good Samaritan searched for someone who needed help. Josie studied her neighbours closely, then her class-mates - there must be someone somewhere who was needy or put upon. It was amazing how suddenly everyone seemed well adjusted and capable. Aldo, who didn't know many people anyway, was having an even more difficult task.

A fortunate, or unfortunate, occurrence, depending on which way you looked at it, was of great help to Ray. Two houses down from Ray's house lived elderly Mrs Parsons and her middle-aged bachelor son Alfred. Owing to the depression and the vast amount of unemployment Alfred had, for the past six months, been a member of the dole queue. He had been trying for the whole of this time to obtain employment locally. Finally, coming to the conclusion that he would have to look further afield, he had been offered a job in Northampton.

Due to leave the following week, Alfred's main worry was leaving his mother to fend for herself. Mrs Parsons was quite able to look after herself and cope around the house, but he didn't know how she would manage the shopping or the garden. Ray, thankful that his search seemed to be over, suggested to his mother that he should go and see Mr Parsons and offer his and his friends' services for shopping and gardening. Ray's mother was quite surprised at her young son's thoughtfulness and was happy to think that the other children were willing to rally round. Mr Parsons was considerably cheered after Ray's visit. Mrs Parsons was charmed by his enthusiastic offer to help with any tasks she had difficulty with.

The following Tuesday after tea The Good Samaritans assembled in the stable. Josie, Aldo and Duncan reported their lack of success in finding anyone in need of help. Ray, feeling very pleased with himself, stood up from his beer crate and told the other Samaritans about old Mrs Parsons.

"Good," said Josie when Ray came to the end of his summary, "we can all help her, so that will give us plenty of time to look around for other needy subjects."

They agreed to take it in turns to visit Mrs Parsons as soon as Alfred had left for Northampton.

With their involvement in 'Project Mrs Parsons' the gang found they had very little time for sorting out further candidates. They were, however, doing an excellent job of community care, although they didn't call it that. They merely thought of it as being neighbourly and following the example set for them by their parents, who always rallied round when anyone in the neighbourhood was in need of a helping hand.

Over the next six months the children kept up their visits to Mrs Parsons. After the initial enthusiastic everyday visits, Mrs Parsons herself sorted out the days of the week that she would require assistance so they were able to space out the visits to a more manageable level. Also, because of their devotion to their task, eventually both Ray and Josie's mothers got into the habit of visiting old Mrs Parsons. Once things had been sorted out with their first project they were on the lookout for another, preferably something which they could run in tandem with the first one.

Josie made a reappraisal of her class-mates; on closer inspection she had to admit that there was one particular boy who was certainly more poorly attired than the rest. While the rest of the boys wore shirts and striped school ties, Benny wore a jersey with a collar. Josie had never seen him wear anything else. To complete the ensemble he wore scruffy grey shorts, knee-length socks and lace-up boots with studs in the soles. Josie could just about tolerate the clothes but the boots were really the end. He must feel very unhappy about being different from the other lads, who wore black lace-up shoes in winter and sandals or black plimsolls in the summer, while a few sported white canvas tennis shoes. But winter or summer Benny wore his black lace-up boots.

Josie duly reported to the other members of the gang her concern for poor Benny. They agreed that he appeared to be a deserving case needing the attention of The Good Samaritans.

"What did you have in mind, Josie?" asked Aldo.

"Surely there must be some way in which we could at least get him some decent shoes."

"How?" enquired Duncan. "Shoes cost money."

"Yes, I know that, perhaps we could think of a way of earning some extra money."

Gloom descended on the four. Here, at last, was a worthwhile cause and they were stuck for the necessary cash to carry it to its fulfilment. The problem was eventually carried forward to the next meeting, with everyone charged with thinking up a solution.

Poor Josie now had a guilt complex every time she set eyes on Benny. She had previously had years of being in the same class with him and scarcely noticing him. Now, suddenly, she was acutely aware of him and found it difficult not to stare at his boots. She mulled over the problem for a whole week but was no nearer a solution by the time the evening for the next meeting arrived.

The 'terrible foursome', as Jimmy had nicknamed them, filed into the stable after tea on the following Tuesday. Aldo pulled the door shut, a late evening sun shone in through the dirty cracked window making the lighting of the candles unnecessary.

Josie, standing on an upturned beer crate, announced dramatically, "Has anyone thought of a solution to our present dilemma?" She was very pleased with the word 'dilemma', which she had heard in a film about an American lawyer.

The boys, already impressed, were even more so when she

used long words.

"It's all down to money really, Josie," said Duncan hesitantly.

"I've had a thought," said Aldo. "Are we concentrating on Benny's boots only?"

"Well, that would be a start anyway."

"Do you know what size shoes he takes?" asked Aldo.

"No, I've no idea, why do you ask?"

"It's just that I've got stacks of shoes I've grown out of, some of them are nearly new," said Aldo. "If we could find out his size perhaps we could find some to fit!"

"What a great idea," said Josie. "Would your mother mind, do you think?"

"I don't suppose she'd even know how many pairs are in my cupboard 'cos my brothers often buy shoes for me."

"Great!" said Ray. "All we need to know is his size then Aldo can check his shoe stock."

"Oh! Won't he be pleased," sighed Josie. "Thank you Aldo, you always seem to come up with the answer to our problems."

If Aldo had been a cat he would have purred or rubbed himself against Josie's legs, so pleased was he with her praise of his efforts.

"Who's going to find out the size?" asked Duncan.

"I can do that," said Josie.

"How exactly?" asked Ray.

"I'll just ask him."

"Won't he wonder why you want to know?"

"I'll think of something," said Josie. "Maybe I could say 'You've got awfully small feet Benny', then he's almost sure to say, 'Well, I take size whatever it is'."

"What if he hasn't got small feet?"

"Then I'll say 'You've got awfully big feet Benny', then I should get the same result," said Josie, confidently.

Everyone relaxed a bit now that the details of their second project seemed to be satisfactorily sorted out.

As winter was approaching again it was time for what Josie's mother called 'The winter outfitting trip'. Josie always enjoyed this outing as it meant she would be provided with a new winter coat and either a Sunday dress or skirt and jumper. The two boys were also kitted out for the coming winter. The boys' Sunday suits sometimes lasted for two years, it depended on how quickly they were growing. Their mother considered it was a false economy to keep a suit for best wear only to find it couldn't be taken in for every day wear because it didn't fit.

The same applied where Josie was concerned, after a year as a Sunday best, her attire was then relegated to school wear. Even older clothes, the year before last's Sunday best, while they were still wearable were retained for after-school activities. Occasionally when this scheme backfired, Josie might actually be supplied with something new for school. This was usually a black gym-slip and blouse, but it was considered beneath the pale to wear a gym-slip on a Sunday.

Underwear was also purchased on these visits to Frank Price's department store, where they stocked everything. Most items were priced to end in three farthings, for instance, six and eleven pence three farthings. The shop assistant referred to this as "Six and eleven three, madam!" Instead of the farthing change one was given a card of pins.

The thing which fascinated Josie was when the girl behind the counter, having written out the receipt and taken the customer's money, found that change was required. As there were no tills on the counter, she would place the cash and receipt into a little metal cylinder, clip it to an overhead cable, pull a lever and the cylinder whizzed away.

In some departments it was possible to see the cylinder reach its destination, which was the office in the centre of the store. Once there, the cashier would stamp the receipt and put it, with the required amount of change, back into the cylinder, pull the lever and it sped back from whence it came. As one walked from department to department it was to an accompaniment of clanging as the cylinders passed overhead.

Josie was quite excited as she was to have a new winter coat and dress, new underwear, navy knickers, white cotton vests and liberty bodices. Though these were Josie's pet hate, her mother insisted that they kept the body warm, which indeed she had to admit, they did. But they were the most unglamorous article of clothing imaginable, being shaped rather like a waistcoat without buttons, made of a kind of cotton stockingette with bands of cotton tape to help keep the shape.

At Price's many people, including Mrs Brown, shopped with what was called a 'draw'. These were obtained from a lady at the top of the road who ran the system. It meant that you paid a shilling in the pound for twenty-one weeks. You received for this a voucher for the full amount to spend in the shop as soon as you made the first payment.

Josie, dressed in what were at the moment her best clothes, soon to be relegated to everyday wear, accompanied her mother to Price's emporium. The underwear was soon dealt with, Josie was not really enthusiastic about underwear. While her mother sorted through a tray of vests, she wandered away to gaze longingly at the cabinets displaying elegant lacy slips, knickers sets and flimsy nighties. "Josie, will you please come and look at these vests."

Josie could not see what the fuss was about, it seemed to her that one white cotton vest was much like another and as for navy knickers, apart from some having a pocket, there seemed little difference between them. She was quite relieved when the underwear was safely in the bag and the cylinder had whizzed over her head on its way to the office.

"Is madam going to any other department?" asked the assistant.

"Yes, I'm going to the children's dress and coat department," said Mrs Brown.

"If madam would like to make her way over there, I will have the goods sent to that department, thank you for your custom madam."

As no cash was involved the goods would be moved from department to department until the amount of the draw was spent. It was almost impossible to spend the exact amount as it was usual to go slightly over and pay the difference in cash. By the time the customer got to the last department all the purchases were assembled ready for taking home.

Josie, anxious to get on with the interesting part of the shopping, was dashing ahead of her mother to the coat department.

"Can I help you, madam?" enquired the young assistant.

"I want a coat for my little girl."

"We have quite a selection in her size, madam."

The assistant began to take the coats off their hangers and pass them to Josie to try on. Josie gazed at her reflection in the large mirror, she was unimpressed by the first one or two. The assistant was holding a dark green coat with a fur-trimmed high-necked collar. The material of the coat was of softest wool.

"Oh, Mum, this one is lovely!"

In the mirror Josie noticed her mother checking the price tab on the back. "Josie, I can't afford this one, it's much too expensive."

"It looks lovely on her, it's just the right colour too," enthused the assistant.

"It's very nice but it's too expensive. Josie, take it off and try this nice blue tweed one."

Josie did as she was told with a heavy heart, the green coat was a dream and she really wasn't interested in anything else.

"This one is nice, it fits well too," said her mother as Josie put on the blue tweed.

"I don't like it," said Josie.

She fitted on a further half a dozen coats but none looked like the green one.

"We'll have the blue tweed," said her mother, deciding for her.

An unhappy Josie was shepherded by the assistant to the racks of dresses. Josie tried to look interested but she felt the whole trip was ruined, she wished she'd never seen the lovely green coat. Eventually, she settled for a blue checked dress, which matched nicely with the coat.

On the bus going home Josie's mother said she was sorry about the coat but as she had the boys to buy clothes for, it was just too expensive. Josie knew that she ought not to be so upset about it, she could appreciate her mother's difficulty, but she felt that she would never enjoy wearing the blue tweed.

Next week at school Josie made her overtures to Benny, seeking the information she required.

"Have you got extra big feet, Benny, or is it just 'cos you're wearing boots?"

"What's wrong with my boots?" said Benny, immediately on the defensive.

"Nothing," said Josie. "Nothing at all, don't you like shoes?"

"Never had any," muttered Benny.

"What, never? Not even when you were little?"

"Well, I suppose I might have when I was a baby maybe, but I can't remember that far back."

Josie felt she was getting nowhere with this line of questioning, it wasn't as easy as she had thought it would be. She tried another tack.

"I've got pretty big feet for a girl you know, I take size thirteen."

"That's nothing, I take size two," replied Benny.

Josie smiled to herself, Benny had fallen easily into the trap. At the gang's next meeting the boys were impressed with Josie's ability to come up with the information they required. Aldo, looking slightly perturbed, said, "That's the size I wear at the moment so that puts paid to using any shoes I've grown out of."

"Any other suggestions then?" asked Josie.

"Well, I've got two pairs I haven't ever worn, one of my aunts bought them for me when I was in Italy last year. There's a pair of brown lace-ups that pinch my feet a bit."

"But won't your mother wonder what happened to them?"

"I shouldn't think so, she knows they hurt my feet and I don't like the style much anyway."

"You mean you'd give them to Benny?" asked Duncan, amazed at Aldo's generosity.

"Yes, if it will help. What do you think, Josie?"

"I think it's very kind of you Aldo."

Aldo blushed and hung his head. "Think nothing of it," he muttered. "After all, I did say they hurt my feet."

"If you're sure it's not going to cause trouble with your mother, then the next thing we have to think about is how we're going to give them to Benny."

"We can't just say 'We've got some shoes for you so you won't have to wear those horrible old boots', can we?" said Ray.

"We don't want to offend him, he's quite a nice boy when you get to know him," said Josie.

"Do you think Benny is very poor?" asked Duncan.

"If the way he's dressed is anything to go by then I'd say he was very poor," said Josie.

"Yes, but is that anything to go by really? I mean sometimes millionaires look like tramps, don't they?"

"I don't know any millionaires," said Ray.

"Nor do I, unless Aldo's Dad is one. Maybe we'd better leave it for this meeting and we can all give it some thought ready for next Tuesday," said Chairman Josie.

"Good idea! Anyone got any money for chips?" said Duncan, looking hopefully at Aldo.

7

The New Park

Before the Good Samaritans were able to solve the problem of
Benny's shoes, something happened which temporarily put a stop
to the weekly meetings.

The children had for the past few months been watching the
construction of a new park. Josie had been gazing through the
railings on her way to school to check on the progress being
made.

It was all very exciting and, just prior to the official opening,
the local paper printed a plan of the whole park. It was, said the
paper, the most ambitious project at present being funded by the
local Council. On the evening of the opening day the gang went
to view the park to see if it came up to their expectations.

They found it beyond their wildest dreams, acres of grass, a
bandstand, a pavilion and flowers and shrubs blooming in
profusion. But, most impressive of all, was the children's playground - slides, rocking horses, swings and roundabouts, and in
the centre an enormous paddling pool surrounded by soft golden
sand.

By the time the park-keeper was ringing the bell to signal the
closing, the children had toured the entire park.

Tired and happy, the little group made their way home vowing
to visit the park again as soon as they came out of school the next
day.

"We could take John, he'll love the playground," said Josie.

It was some time before the novelty of the park began to wear
off. It had completely taken over the children, even Saturday

afternoon pictures had been shelved and Sunday evenings were spent listening to the band.

Now something happened which eclipsed even the attractions of the park. Mr Brown had purchased a wireless set. Even rich old Mr Vincenti didn't have a wireless. For a little while it was the sensation of the neighbourhood, even people with whom they had previously had little contact wanted to listen to the little dome-shaped box. Duncan's mother would ask Mrs Brown to turn it up louder so she could hear it from her garden. Soon there were aerials appearing in other gardens as interest in this new media took hold.

Radio Luxemburg was a great favourite with the children, who could sing along to the advertising Jingles, the favourite being 'We are the Ovalteneys little girls and boys'. BBC 'Children's Hour' with Uncle Mac and the Toy-Town adventures of Larry-the-Lamb and the Policeman were listened to with rapt attention.

Saturday nights used to be the one night of the week when Mr and Mrs Brown went out with their friends, leaving Jimmy in charge of the younger children. Since the advent of the wireless set, their friends, who hadn't yet acquired one, requested to stay in and listen, rather than visit the pub.

Jimmy seized the opportunity to make a practice of going out with his pals. When, at last, the wireless evenings began to pall and the adults wanted to resume their pub evenings, Jimmy was prepared to put up a fight for his freedom.

"Willy and Pete don't have to stay in on Saturday night," he protested.

"Neither of them have younger brothers and sisters," said his father.

"I know that, but I don't see why I should be penalised because I have, they're not my responsibility."

His father could see the point of the argument, he remembered Saturday nights with the lads had always been sort of special when he himself had been Jimmy's age.

"I'll speak to your mother," was as far as he would commit himself.

After a discussion with his wife it was decided that Josie was now old enough to keep an eye on John while they were out. At least they would give it a try and see how it worked out. Consequently, the next Saturday night Josie was left in charge of her little brother.

"Isn't it peaceful without Jimmy to boss us about?" said John, "I'd much rather be looked after by you, Josie."

Josie was too astute to be fooled by John's flattery, she knew when it was time for him to go to bed he would try to wheedle an extra half an hour.

"You're not getting round me to let you stay up," said Josie. "I'm in charge and I've got my instructions and if I don't carry them out we might be landed with Jimmy again!"

Although Josie had enjoyed the feeling of responsibility her parents had entrusted her with, she had felt bored with only John for company. She wondered how her parents would react if she suggested one of the boys could assist her with the baby-sitting. Having thought it over, she decided that she might stand a better chance of success if she approached her father with her request. When she inquired what he thought of the idea he said, "I'll talk it over with your mother."

"If she wants company, it would be much better if she had a girl with her," said Mrs Brown.

"I agree, but which girl? All her friends seem to be boys."

"I know that, but I don't think being on her own with a boy is a very good idea."

"I don't think Josie makes any distinction between boys and girls, she just looks on them as friends and they seem to consider her 'one of the boys'."

"I wouldn't be too sure about that," said Mrs Brown. "I think the only answer is for her to find a girlfriend or for Jimmy to have to stay at home on Saturday nights."

In the end a compromise was reached which suited everyone. Jessie, the girl who lived next door, was at Grammar School and was always burdened with homework, most of which she put off till the last minute. Therefore, most Saturday nights were spent catching up on a whole week's work. She had no objection to transferring her work to the Brown's dining-table, especially as she was making a bit of extra pocket-money into the bargain.

To soften the blow to Josie's self-esteem her mother agreed to one of the boys keeping her company, knowing that she now had Jessie to keep an eye on her. She issued strict instructions that the boys were to leave at nine o'clock which was Josie's bedtime. Aldo, who seemed to have no set bedtime, often stayed later, by using all his boyish charm to persuade Jessie to let Josie stay up a bit later. Sometimes Josie just had time to dash into bed as her parents opened the front-door. They were, however, unaware of this flouting of their instructions.

"She's such a good girl," said Mrs Brown, referring to Jessie. "It's lovely to be able to go out without having any qualms about the children and without having to deprive Jimmy of his Saturday night out."

Jimmy was now rapidly approaching his fourteenth birthday, he was due to leave school at Easter and would be joining his father as a learner at the shoe factory. Baby John, at four years old, would be starting at the infants school.

"One Brown out and one Brown in," said Mr Brown.

Jimmy was already making plans for what he would do when he was earning real money, not just the pittance he got for his paper-round. He planned to buy a racing bike and a pair of plus-fours, which were all the rage for serious cyclists.

At last the longed-for day arrived - Jimmy's last day as a schoolboy, from tomorrow he would be a fourteen-year-old adult. After Easter Monday he would be part of the working population, as would Willy, who was due to start working in the building trade, learning the ropes prior to signing for a five-year apprenticeship. His parents were willing to pay the premium for his indenture as an apprentice when he reached the age of sixteen, until then he would be a general dog's-body at the beck and call of the qualified tradesmen.

Both Jimmy and Willy were thankful to have found a job, although it seemed that the country was gradually coming out of the depression, there were nevertheless many of their class mates who would be leaving school without one.

Although Jimmy, Willy and Pete had taken a vow of eternal friendship as the 'three musketeers', Pete was wondering how this would work out now that two of them would be working and he would be left at school. He consoled himself with the knowledge that he only had one more term to complete then he, too, would be part of the wonderful world of work.

As they walked home Jimmy and Willy could talk of nothing but the prospect of going to their new job after the Easter break.

"They do say your school-days are the best days of your life," said Pete, in an effort to get a word in.

"Bosh!" said Jimmy.

"Utter bosh!" repeated Willy.

"It'll be rotten going back to school without you after Easter," said Pete sadly.

"Shame!" said Jimmy, completely without feeling.

Throughout the Easter weekend the boys stuck together. On Monday they visited the fair, but somehow to Pete some of the spontaneity seemed to have gone out of the relationship, he couldn't be part of their continual chatter about what would happen tomorrow when they started work. He was not to know that most of this was to cover the apprehension they were feeling about it. Jimmy was comforted by the fact that at least he would have his father for a foreman, but Willy had no such reassurance and he had heard frightening tales of the tricks played on new boys on building sites. A feeling of sadness and a conviction that nothing would ever be the same again seemed to haunt Pete as he said cheerio and wished good luck to his two friends at the end of the day.

"Shall we meet after tea tomorrow, then we can compare notes?" said Jimmy.

"Great," said Pete, considerably cheered that he seemed to have been included in the invitation.

The first few weeks at work were a struggle for both boys. Mr Brown was very careful not to show any favouritism to his son, consequently, he was actually harder on Jimmy than any of the other learner boys. At the end of the first month Jimmy was beginning to think he might have fared better with some other foreman. Willy, having weathered the first month's torment without giving way to tears, except in the privacy of his own bedroom, emerged a chastened but much stronger personality.

Their meetings with Pete were less frequent now, even the meetings between the two of them were often weeks apart. It was beginning to look as if the 'Three Musketeers' would finally break up. Funnily enough, it was Jimmy's new-found wealth which eventually ended it all. Having bought himself the racer bike it had long been his ambition to own, and having joined the local cycling club, he could be seen riding off resplendent in his first pair of plus-fours, fancy socks and cycling shoes every Sunday morning. Pete, watching him go, would sigh for the days that used to be.

Getting a bit bored with the park, the 'Good Samaritans' decided to resume their weekly meetings. The first item on the agenda was how to pass on the beautiful Italian shoes, which had been donated by the generous, well-meaning Aldo, to the shabbily-booted Benny. In the end, at a loss to know how best to achieve this, they had hit upon the idea of inviting Benny to one of their meetings. They would avoid mentioning that they were the 'Good Samaritans', since they still wished to operate under strict secrecy. It would have to be just a friendly invitation to join them for lemonade and chips in Aldo's shed, then they could present him with the shoes. Having checked that Aldo could afford the lemonade and chips and issued the invitation to Benny, Josie spent the rest of the week day-dreaming about how surprised and pleased Benny would be.

At last the great day arrived. After they had seated Benny at the make-shift table, provided him with chips and lemonade, Benny said politely.

"This is nice, thanks for asking me."

When they finished eating and drinking Josie announced, "We've got a present for you, Benny."

"What for?" asked Benny. "It's not my birthday or anything."

"We know that," said Josie.

"Just thought we'd like to give you something," said Ray, trying to look as if they were in the habit of giving presents to comparative strangers.

Benny looked amazed and not a little suspicious.

"What do I have to do in return?" he asked.

"Nothing," said Aldo. "Nothing at all."

Benny accepted the parcel, holding it a little gingerly as if he was afraid it might blow up in his face.

"All right then," he said. "If you're sure there's no sort of catch about it."

"None, none," said Aldo. "For Pete's sake, open it."

Benny's face was a picture when he saw the shoes, "Crikey!" he breathed, "I've never seen such beautiful shoes."

"They're Italian," said Aldo.

"But I can't take them," said Benny sadly.

"Why not?" said Aldo, looking hurt.

"My mother would kill me, she'd probably think I'd pinched them."

"We'd tell her we gave them to you," said Josie.

"She wouldn't like that," said Benny, still looking longingly at the shoes, "I wish I could keep them," he looked down at his ugly boots, "but I know it'd cause a right stink if I did and you'd all probably get into trouble. Where did you get them anyway?"

"They're mine, my auntie bought them for me when I was in Italy last year, but they pinch my feet a bit."

"We thought you might like them instead of those terrible old boots you always wear," said Ray tactlessly.

Benny turned bright red.

"What's wrong with my boots?" he asked.

"Shut up Ray," whispered Josie realising that Benny was getting embarrassed.

"It's very nice of you," said Benny in a frozen sort of voice. "But my boots are quite all right thank you. I think I'll go now if you don't mind, thanks for the chips."

With that, Benny made a dignified exit. The others listened to the sound of his boots clonking down the pathway. For a minute there was stunned silence, then Aldo burst out:

"You would say something like that Ray."

"What'd I do?"

"Well, it wasn't exactly tactful to mention his boots was it?" said Josie.

"But I thought the whole object of the exercise was to draw attention to his boots and give him some replacement shoes."

"Oh well, it didn't work that way did it?" said Aldo, putting the shoes back in their box.

"We'll never be able to face him again in class," sighed Josie.

"We never really had much to do with him in class anyway," said Ray.

"Nobody does," said Duncan. "Poor old Benny."

Josie felt really saddened, it seemed as if an opportunity for making a friend out of Benny had somehow been lost. They looked at each other, then they looked toward Josie expecting some sort of guidance.

"Let's not quarrel about whose fault it is," said Josie, resuming her role as leader. "Some things just don't work out the way you plan them and Benny's one of them."

"Who'd have thought it would be so difficult to do good?" protested Duncan.

"We've still got Mrs Parsons," said Aldo.

"Only until the end of the month," said Ray with a certain amount of pride that he was in possession of information not known to the others.

"What do you mean?" asked Josie.

"Alfred's coming back at the end of the month, my Mum told me," said Ray. "He's got a job at Holdenstein's shoe factory."

"You mean we won't even have Mrs Parsons after Alfred gets back?"

"Won't be any need, she'll manage just like she always did, and anyway my Mum and Josie's Mum both visit now."

"Shall we look for any more good deeds or shall we give up the idea of helping people?"

"Most of them don't seem to want to be helped anyway. Maybe it would be better if we just held meetings and didn't bother too much about finding someone to help for the time being. I expect something else will eventually turn up and we still have the park and Saturday pictures as well as our meetings."

After a while Josie became slightly less involved with the boys, having found a new girlfriend named Violet. Part of the attraction was Violet's older brother Jack, who Josie thought must be at least twenty and was as handsome as any of the film stars at the Saturday pictures. Josie admired him from afar and wove her dreams around the information she was able to glean from Violet. He worked in an office and always wore very smart suits. Josie took to hanging around outside Violet's when she knew Jack was due to come home from work. She never plucked up courage to speak to him, she would just gaze adoringly at him as he made his way through the back gate. In her day-dreams he rescued her from all sorts of dire situations. At home her mother would often ask the same question two or three times before it penetrated through the dazed expression in Josie's eyes.

"I don't know what's the matter with her these days, she seems not to be with us half the time," said her mother.

"Perhaps she's in love," grinned Jimmy.

"Well, if so, it's not Duncan or Ray or Aldo, she doesn't seem to spend so much time with them these days."

One evening as she hung around Violet's back gate, the object of her admiration appeared.

"Are you waiting for Violet?" he asked.

Josie blushed and hung her head.

"Yes," she muttered.

"Why don't you go to the back door and give her a shout?"

"Oh, thank you," said Josie as she dashed through the gate and down the pathway, not daring to look back. He had spoken to her, the wonderful Jack. By the time she reached Violet's back door she had almost forgotten why she was there. Was this what being in love was like?

Violet appeared in answer to her knock.

"You coming out?" asked Josie, still in a daze.

"OK! Let's go to the park," said Violet.

As they walked along Josie said hesitantly, "I saw Jack going out when I came for you."

"Oh! he's going courting," said Violet. "He's gone to meet his girl Doreen. My Mum doesn't like her much," she added.

Poor Josie, her little world was shattered. Jack courting, it didn't bear thinking about. Why couldn't he wait until she had grown up? The only thing which softened the blow was the fact that Violet's mother didn't like Doreen. Perhaps she'd stop him from marrying her! Josie had great faith in the power of parental persuasion.

As time went on Josie sometimes caught a glimpse of the glamorous Doreen. She had long, dark, wavy hair, she wore very smart clothes and very high heels. Oh, to be like her, thought Josie, looking at her sturdy little legs beneath her gym-slip. White socks and button-bar shoes seemed very unglamorous. If only she had got that lovely green coat with the fur collar! Josie was sure her life was ruined because of the dreadful blue tweed.

Violet, in one of her more informative moments, confided to Josie that she thought Jack wanted to get engaged to Doreen but she knew her mother was trying to put him off.

"She says Doreen is 'too common' for him."

Although Josie was not sure what 'being common' meant, she was glad Doreen was it; anything that Violet's mother could think up was all right with Josie, who was quite sure no girl was good enough for the lovely Jack.

While Josie still mooned around thinking all the time of Jack, actually seeing him would light up her whole day. For long periods she seldom saw her previously bosom pal gang members.

The boys muttered between themselves that they didn't know

what was wrong with Josie lately. It all seemed to be since she had acquired her new friend Violet.

"I can't understand it," sighed Duncan. "She always seems to be out. Whenever I ask her Mum she says she thinks she is probably at Violet's."

"Who is this Violet anyway?" asked Ray.

"She lives just down the road from me," said Aldo.

"She's not in our class is she?"

"No, she's in class four, I guess she's a year younger than us."

Saturday nights were now regularly taken up by helping Jessie to look after John. It was with some relief that Mrs Brown agreed to allowing Violet to keep Josie company.

"Far better than having boys, she's such a nice little girl," said Mrs Brown.

Christmas came once again. Because Jimmy was far too grown-up to share the excitement of the present-opening with Josie this year, she woke up baby John to tell him that Father Christmas had been! Although she no longer believed in him herself, she enjoyed keeping up the pretence because of John, just as Jimmy had done for her.

Josie had been rather disappointed with her array of presents, until she had found a note at the bottom of her pillow-case saying, 'I have left you something in the kitchen, love Father Christmas.' Dashing downstairs as quietly as possible with John hot on her heels she found her heart's desire, a bicycle, the model she had been admiring in the cycle shop window several months before when she had been pleading with her father to allow her to have a bicycle.

Violet had a bike and so did Ray and Aldo. Josie believed that untold vistas of enjoyment would be opened up for her if only she had a bike.

After Christmas her main activity became cycling, sometimes with Violet, sometimes with the boys and occasionally with both. As summer approached the rides got more ambitious and eventually, accompanied by Ray, Josie cycled all the way to her Grandma's at Tacolneston. Ray's enthusiasm had begun to wane before they had reached the halfway mark, but they received such a welcome from Grandma and Ray was so enchanted by the little thatched house and Grandma's home-made cakes that he was planning a return visit before they reached home again.

8

A Jubilee, an Abdication and a Coronation

At school, there was great excitement because of the coming Jubilee of King George V and Queen Mary. A great pageant was being rehearsed. Mothers were involved in producing costumes, lessons were geared to learning about the Empire and the achievements of the King's twenty-five-year reign.

Every school child received a commemorative mug and a medal. Josie especially liked the medal which had a red, white and blue ribbon and had an impression of the head of the King and Queen.

On the actual day of the Jubilee, which was a public holiday, several of the Brown's friends arrived to listen to the ceremony on the wireless. In the afternoon there was a street party organised by most of the mothers. The male population were delegated the task of putting up the decorations. Flags, balloons and streamers hung from the trees, many individual gardens were ablaze with colour and front windows had pictures of the King and Queen draped in red, white and blue bunting.

Jimmy divorced himself from the celebrations altogether, feeling that he didn't really fit in with his parents and their devotion to the monarchy anymore than he did with his little brother and sister and their street tea-party. Therefore, early in the morning, he went off with the other members of the cycling club, to take a trip to the sea-side.

Soon the Jubilee was just a memory and Josie, with her new bike, was cycling everywhere. After Empire Day they reached the period during the school year when all school children had a half day holiday on Thursday afternoon. Having a bike made quite a lot of difference to the choice of things to do. A favourite occupation was visiting Mousehold Heath, when the weather was fine.

Because of her preoccupation with the joys of cycling, John was no longer able to accompany his big sister on her various excursions. For a little while he pined and Mrs Brown began to wonder if a bike for Josie had been such a good idea, as she looked at John's miserable face every time Josie went off with her friends. Eventually, left to his own devices, John began to form his own friendships with children from his class at school.

Soon after the Jubilee, one of Ray's cousins started visiting him on Thursday afternoons. One particular afternoon the boys were sitting on their bikes at the corner of the road, idly chatting, when who should come past but Josie and Violet.

"Hello Josie!" shouted Ray. "Where are you going?"

"Oh, nowhere in particular," said Josie, alighting from her bicycle.

"This is my cousin Neville," said Ray, introducing a tall boy with a mop of black curly hair and bright laughing eyes. "This is my friend Josie and her friend Violet."

"Hello, friend Josie!" said Neville with a grin. "I've heard all about you from Ray."

Josie felt uncomfortable wondering what Ray had been saying. She quite liked the look of cousin Neville.

For the next few Thursday afternoons the foursome met beside the telephone box, sometimes they were joined by Aldo. Duncan felt very left out of things, but his mother still refused to allow him to have a bicycle fearing he would injure himself. For the first half an hour they would talk, argue and giggle, then having come to an agreement about where they were going, they would cycle off leaving poor Duncan watching enviously from his garden. One day he would have a bike and be able to join his friends again, thought Duncan as he turned disconsolately from his garden gate.

On the fourth Thursday the quartet went off to Ringland Hills. Riding high into the hills they found a likely spot to leave their bicycles so they could sit on the soft mossy grass. They chatted, sharing the bar of chocolate Neville had brought with him.

"I like it here," said Josie.

"Me, too," sighed Neville, spreading himself out on the grass

e

and shading his eyes from the sun.

"I s'pose you'll take the scholarship next year same as Ray?" he asked.

"Don't remind me," said Josie, "I guess you've already taken it?"

"Yes, I'm thirteen you know," said Neville.

"How'd you get on?" asked Josie.

"Passed the first bit, didn't do too well in the next part - it's much harder, the second part."

"Jimmy said that, although he didn't pass the first part.

"Neither did Len," said Ray, referring to his elder brother. "I'm trying not to think too much about it, I know my father is keen for me to pass. I'll feel awful if I don't. I bet Josie will though, she's always near the top of the class in exams."

"Clever girl," said Neville with a grin.

Josie blushed as she looked into Neville's laughing dark eyes.

On the way home Neville was careful to ride next to her, racing along they got a fair way ahead of the other two as Violet didn't ride very fast. As soon as they were out of earshot Neville said, "Josie, can you come out for a ride after tea?"

"On our own you mean?"

"Yes, I can tell my aunt I'm going home."

"I could tell Mum I'm going out with Violet I suppose."

"Good, I'll meet you at the top of Elm Tree Lane."

They slowed down to let the others catch up.

"You can certainly get a move on you two," said Ray. "Violet can't go that fast, can you?" he asked, turning to Violet.

"I try to keep up," said Violet puffing hard.

"It's OK, don't worry about it," said Neville - he had accomplished what he wanted by making a date with Josie.

"Do take your time Josie," said her mother. "If you bolt your tea like that you'll get indigestion."

"What's the hurry?" asked John. "Are you going out again after tea? I thought maybe I could go with you after tea."

"Well, you can't," said Josie shortly.

"You're always out," said John, a bit tearfully.

"Don't be such a baby, you've got your own friends."

"But we're not friends anymore, Josie."

"Yes we are, but sometimes I like to be with my friends and, anyway, you have to go to bed earlier than me don't you?"

"Are you going out on your bike, Josie?" her father asked.

"Yes, we're going for a ride," said Josie, trying to keep everything as vague as possible.

"All right, off you go," said her father, continuing with his tea. "But don't be later than half past eight."

Josie pedalled frantically up the hill, arriving five minutes late. Neville was already waiting, sitting on his bike trying to look nonchalant.

"Hello there!" he said. "Did you have any trouble getting out?"

"No, but I've got to be back by half past eight."

"Where shall we go?"

"I don't mind really," said Josie shyly.

"How about Ranworth Common? That's not too far, we could get back easily by eight thirty."

"OK!" said Josie.

As they cycled along, Neville asked, "Does your mother know you're out with me?"

"No, I didn't say who I was going with, so she probably assumes I'm either with Violet, Ray or Aldo."

"She wouldn't mind if you were with Ray or Aldo then?"

"No, 'cos I'm always with them."

"Would she mind if she knew you were with me?"

"She might do."

"Why?"

"Well, because you're older and she doesn't know you, does she?"

Neville was silent for a little while. At last he said, "Josie, do you think of either Ray or Aldo as your boyfriend?"

Josie laughed, "Of course not."

"Oh, good," said Neville. "Can I be your boyfriend then?"

"I'd like that, but don't let Ray know."

"Why not?" asked Neville.

"Well, he might tell his mother, then my mother will probably get to know, then I might not be able to go out with you."

"She'd stop you?"

"Well, I don't know but she might try."

"OK, then it'll be our secret," agreed Neville.

Lovely, thought Josie, how much more romantic to have a secret boyfriend. It would be their secret, her's and Neville's.

"Let's get a move on then if you've got to get back by half past eight," said Neville.

Josie had never been to Ranworth before and found it quite a hard ride. At last Neville slowed down.

"This is where the common starts," he said, indicating an area of trees, grass and shrub-land. Buttercups, cowslips and daisies grew everywhere in great profusion.

"Let's sit down for a little while," said Neville, "before we have to cycle back again. Have you ever had a boyfriend before?"

"Not really," Josie had never looked on Ray, Duncan or Aldo as actual boyfriends. She wondered if Jack counted, she supposed he didn't really as he had the glamorous but 'common' Doreen.

Neville shook his black curls and tried to look sad, but his eyes were still full of laughter.

"I had a girlfriend once," he said.

"What happened?" asked Josie.

"She ditched me for a chap with ginger hair. You won't do that will you Josie?" he said taking her hand in both his own and gazing into her eyes in mock alarm.

"I don't much care for ginger hair," said Josie primly, getting rather alarmed at the nearness of Neville.

He suddenly burst out laughing.

"Oh Josie," he said, "I think you're priceless, do you think I could kiss you?"

"I suppose so," said Josie, sounding rather doubtful about the whole procedure.

Neville kissed her quickly and a little awkwardly on the cheek.

"That wasn't too bad was it?" he asked.

"No, it was very nice thank you," said Josie.

They made their way slowly, still hand in hand, back to where they had left their bikes.

As they passed a large tree Neville took a penknife from his pocket and carved a heart with an arrow through it, with 'J' at one end and 'N' at the other. Josie watched, feeling very thrilled - no one had ever declared their love for her in this manner before.

"There we are Josie, now that will never grow out of this tree and when we're old we can come back and see if it's still here."

On the ride home, each time they were faced with a hill to climb Neville put a hand on Josie's shoulder and gave her a helpful push. It was really very nice having a sweetheart Josie decided, she wondered why in all the time she had known Ray, she had never before set eyes on his handsome cousin. When she broached the subject to Neville, he explained that there had been a long-standing family feud between his parents and Ray's parents, which had only recently been healed.

As they got nearer home Neville said, "Josie, do you mind if I leave you at the top of the hill?"

"So my Mum won't see, you mean?"

"Yes, your Mum and my aunt, 'cos she thinks I went home after I'd had my tea."

They stopped at the top of the hill and, waiting until there was no one in sight, Neville placed a hasty kiss on her cheek.

"See you Saturday little Josie."

Josie free-wheeled down the hill, I've been kissed, my first real kiss, thought Josie. You can't really count 'postman's knock', that's not really a proper kiss.

Josie now transferred all the love and admiration previously reserved for 'Lovely Jack' to Neville, still keeping him a secret from everyone including her parents. Her mother would have been horrified if she had known about her twice weekly rendezvous with Neville, but she was in blissful ignorance, thinking that she was, as usual, out with Violet and the boys.

In spite of his worldly-wise attitude, Neville was worried in case he didn't measure up to Josie's romantic idea of him. He now joined the Saturday afternoon trip to the pictures, always making sure he sat next to Josie but being very careful not to display his admiration in front of the others. Josie, for her part, became expert at almost ignoring Neville whilst in the company of the rest of the group. When they were on their own, they often laughed at their ability to deceive the others, believing that they had everybody fooled.

But both Ray and Aldo had their suspicions; there was something different about Josie they both agreed, they just couldn't quite fathom out what exactly it was.

"I think it must have something to do with your cousin you know," said Aldo, " 'cos it all seemed to happen after he started visiting you."

"Do you think so?" said Ray. "But they don't seem to take much notice of each other do they?"

"I wouldn't say that, I've noticed them smiling at each other."

"Have you? Well, I can't say I have, but I've noticed Neville always manages to sit next to Josie at the pictures."

After a carefully planned meeting on the next Saturday evening Josie and Neville had returned home at eight-thirty as instructed. They had spent a happy evening sitting and chatting among the heather on Ringland Hills, they had held hands a great deal and had exchanged a couple of chaste kisses.

Knowing that her parents were out, Neville had become very bold and had escorted Josie to her front gate, unfortunately just at the time when Jessie was looking out of the window. When Josie went indoors Jessie asked, "Who was that boy you were with? I haven't seen him before?"

"Oh, he's just a friend," said Josie airily. "He's Ray's cousin you know."

Josie was not as unconcerned as she sounded, she was secretly bemoaning the fact that Jessie had to be looking out of the window at that precise moment.

"He's a very nice looking boy," said Jessie. "Not a bit like Ray."

"No, I suppose not, old Ray's all right though."

Josie was trying hard to convince Jessie that Neville wasn't really anything special.

She wondered whether to ask Jessie not to mention anything to her mother, but on reflection, she decided this was a sure way to suggest to Jessie that her mother wouldn't want her to go out with Neville. The best policy was, obviously, to make light of the whole matter, so Josie changed the subject and enquired how her little brother had behaved.

By the time her parents returned Josie had long since gone to bed. Lying awake she heard them come home, she could hear muffled chatter, then the door closed as Jessie went home. There was no sound of them coming upstairs so she began to breathe a little easier. If Jessie had spilled the beans, she felt sure they would have immediately come upstairs to see if she was still awake.

Some time later, still laying awake in the darkness, the landing light had been switched on and her parents' footsteps echoed on the stairs, they passed her bedroom door making their way down the corridor to their own room. Josie heaved a sigh of relief, it only remained to see if anything was said at breakfast tomorrow, she didn't kid herself she was out of the woods yet. With that troubled thought, Josie drifted into uneasy sleep.

Next morning breakfast was uneventful, Josie and John did their usual visit to Grannie and Grandpa's, admiring the new hatchings in the canary cages and feeding the rabbits with cabbage leaves. Finally, each pocketing the pennies from Grandpa which made a useful addition to their pocket money, they made their way home.

Dinner was the usual Sunday roast of beef with vegetables and Yorkshire pudding. As they got to the sweet course, which was rice pudding, Mrs Brown suddenly said, "Jessie says a very pretty boy she hadn't seen before came home with you last night, Josie."

Josie felt her face going red, so she hung her head and concentrated on her plate.

"He's only Ray's cousin," she muttered.

"Oh, I see," said her mother. "Was he visiting at Ray's then? Why haven't we seen him before?"

"Their parents had fallen out, but now they're friends again."

"Why are you blushing?" asked Jimmy. "Look at her, I bet she's sweet on this cousin."

"Shut up Jimmy," said Josie hotly.

"Leave her alone Jimmy," said his Dad. "What's this lad's name Josie?" he enquired.

"Neville," said Josie.

"How old is he?" asked her mother.

"Thirteen," said Josie, who had decided there was no point in lying as they were sure to find out anyway.

"Cor, he's old for you," teased Jimmy.

"Jimmy, will you shut up," said his father.

John restored the situation by requesting some more pudding.

"Does he go around with the boys and you and Violet?" asked her mother.

"Yes, we all go to the pictures together and bike riding." Josie comforted herself with the fact that this was only partly untrue, as indeed sometimes they did all go bike riding together.

"Where does he live?" asked her mother.

"I don't really know," said Josie. "Over the other side of the city, Earlham Road way somewhere."

"You'd better hurry with that pudding John or you'll be late for Sunday School," said his mother.

"Come on John, hurry up or you'll make me late too," said

103

Josie.

As they made their way towards the Sunday School building Josie reflected that things had gone rather better than she had hoped. no one had forbidden her to see Neville again. Mind you, she thought, I don't think they realise we go out on our own, if they did it might put a different complexion on things. She'd got away without having to tell a downright lie, which she had to admit she had been quite prepared to do. If she was careful not to get involved in too much discussion about Neville and if Jimmy would keep his big mouth shut, perhaps all would be well.

When they got to Sunday School Josie took John to the front row of chairs and made her way to the back of the hall where her class sat. Josie's mind was still in turmoil, she had to work things out carefully, Perhaps next time they were all together she would find an excuse for them all to go round to her house then her parents would be able to see that they were all going out together. Maybe next Saturday when they were going to the pictures might be a good opportunity, she could say she'd forgotten her money and they could all come with her to collect it. She could alert Neville to the plan beforehand.

They were on the second hymn before Josie really returned to full consciousness again.

On Wednesday when Josie and Neville had their next clandestine meeting, Josie explained what she had in mind for Saturday.

"You think that once your mother has seen me I'll be accepted, do you Josie?"

"Well, I thought if she sees us all together she will accept you as one of the gang, so to speak. She did with Aldo when he first started going around with us."

"Sounds like a good idea then, as long as we don't let anyone know when we meet on our own, everything should be OK. You're a schemer Josie and no mistake, I'd never have thought of all that."

Josie was not quite sure if this was a compliment, she felt being a schemer smacked of being underhand.

Thus, by the time Saturday arrived the two were well rehearsed. As the group assembled at the telephone box Josie suddenly exploded, "Blow! I've left all my money at home."

"You'd better go and get it then," said Violet.

"Good job I noticed before we got to the pictures."

"No doubt Neville would have paid for you," said Violet spitefully.

"Why Neville?" said Aldo. "I'd pay for you Josie."

"I don't need anyone to pay for me," said Josie patiently.

"Let's all go back with her," suggested Neville.

"Can't see why we all need to go," said Ray but, as the others had already started to move off, Ray followed behind somewhat reluctantly.

When they reached the back door Josie went in while the others waited on the square of concrete outside the door.

"Mum," Josie called, "I forgot my money would you believe, good job I didn't get too far!"

"Are the others waiting for you?" asked her mother.

"Yes," said Josie as she went up to her bedroom to collect her picture money.

She would have laid odds on her mother's curiosity leading her to go and have a look at Neville so she delayed as long as she could in her bedroom. When she eventually came down, she found her mother surrounded by the gang on the doorstep chatting with Neville about where he lived.

"We'd better hurry," said Violet, "or you're going to make us miss the serial, Josie."

"Be home at tea-time Mum," said Josie as the gang made their way to the front gate.

When Josie and Neville discussed the whole matter when they secretly met after tea, they decided the whole thing had been an overwhelming success. Josie was certain that her mother had accepted Neville as just one of the gang.

When next the gang got together for their weekly cinema visit, they were joined by Duncan who informed them excitedly that his mother was, at last, going to allow him to join the rest of them when they visited the cinema. He was, as far as ever, off persuading her to let him have a bike, but at least she had relented on her ban on visits to the cinema. Duncan asked if he could join them on Saturday.

Josie thought she had never seen him so excited but when she remembered that he had never in his life been to a cinema, she supposed it was understandable that he would get excited. What to her had become a common occurrence, was to him a great new adventure.

Once they were seated in the cinema and the film had begun, Duncan's face was a picture. Buck Jones' daring stunts had Duncan enthralled. Thank goodness for Josie he thought, or more particularly, Josie's Mum who had put in a word for him to be allowed to visit the pictures. At the moment life held no greater joy for Duncan than Saturday afternoon at the pictures.

As they walked home after the film-show Duncan kept up a non-stop commentary on what he had seen. Reaching the telephone box which was their dispersal point, they hung about chatting until Duncan said he had better go home before his mother started to worry, whereupon Aldo came to the same decision and crossed the road to his home, leaving the two girls and two boys still deep in conversation.

"You going for a bike ride tonight?" asked Violet.

"S'pect so," Josie said vaguely.

"Are you going with her?" Ray asked Neville.

"What do you mean?" asked Neville playing for time.

"Come on, we know you go out together, Violet has seen you."

Neville looked at Josie to see if she gave any indication of what to do next.

"You might as well admit it 'cos we know anyway," said Ray.

"I can't think why you have to make such a secret of it." said Violet.

"We thought my Mum might object 'cos she didn't know Neville, but it seems to be all right now she's seen him."

"You're a couple of sly devils," said Ray.

There was an uncomfortable silence then Violet said, "Does this mean we can come out with you on Saturday nights then?"

"Well, sometimes I suppose, what do you say, Ray?" asked Neville.

"That's fair enough," said Ray. "A foursome."

"Then Violet can be my girl," he smiled shyly at Violet, who blushed and said:

"I'd like that Ray."

That evening and the future Saturdays all followed the same pattern of bike rides as a foursome, which they all seemed to enjoy. Josie had to admit that she felt considerably relieved that she was no longer having to deceive her parents. She could now say quite openly that she was going out with Violet, Ray and Neville and her parents made no objection to this.

As winter approached the bicycles were relegated to being used only for purely practical purposes. There was really very little enjoyment in just riding around as the weather became steadily colder and colder. Christmas came and went. Christmas parties followed. This year Neville was invited to Josie's and Ray's, much to Josie's delight.

Over the Christmas period listening to the wireless was very depressing as the King was ill and bulletins were broadcast every few hours. Finally, on January 20th, the King's death was announced. At the end of the broadcast the announcer said, "The King is dead, long live the King."

"Who will be King now?" John asked his father.

"The Prince of Wales will succeed his father."

"What will he be called?"

"He will be King Edward the Eighth."

"He's quite handsome," said Josie, "I've seen him on the newsreel at the pictures."

The King's funeral took place on January 29th and the Prince of Wales became King. Although he was not yet crowned, he continued his official functions and the duties of a monarch. The talk was of the future and a possible date for the Coronation.

By December there were newspaper reports and gossip about the King and a lady named Mrs Wallis Simpson. On the wireless Josie listened with her family to an address by the Bishop of Bradford who said, "We hope that King Edward the Eighth is aware of his need to commend himself to the grace of God. Some of us wish that he gave more positive signs of his awareness."

"What does all that mean?" Josie asked her parents.

"It's a bit hard to explain," said her father. "What it boils down to is that the King has this woman friend who is not considered a suitable partner for him."

"Do you mean he might want to marry her?"

"I think that's what is causing the problem."

"Would she be Queen then?" asked Josie.

"Well, the fact is she wouldn't be acceptable as Queen."

By December 8th there was talk of possible abdication. Josie, who was avidly following the saga of the King and Mrs Simpson and was still feeling sympathetic toward Mrs Simpson, felt her sympathy waning when she discovered the meaning of abdication.

On December 10th the King sent a statement to Parliament to say he was going to abdicate. On the following day at 10.00 p.m. the voice of Sir John Reith, Director General of the BBC, came over on the wireless. John had been allowed to stay up to listen to what was being called an historic broadcast. The voice said, "This is Windsor Castle" - there was a pause before he announced, "His Royal Highness Prince Edward."

Then, the man who had been King for the past 326 days, began to talk slowly and clearly and almost the first words he said were: "A few hours ago I discharged my last duty as King and Emperor and now I have been succeeded by my Brother the Duke of York. I have found it impossible to carry the heavy burden of my responsibility and to discharge my duties as King as I would wish to do without the help and support of the woman I love."

The Prince went on to thank his mother and his family and the Ministers of the Crown and, in particular, Mr Baldwin. The speech continued for several minutes more. As he neared the end the Prince said:

"I now quit altogether public affairs and I lay down my burden. It may be some time before I return to my native land but I shall always follow the fortunes of the British race and Empire with profound interest and if at any time in the future I can be found of service to His Majesty in a private station, I shall not fail. And now we all have a new King, I wish him and you, his people, happiness and prosperity with all my heart. God bless you all, God save the King." At the end of the speech all broadcasting ceased for the night.

"The Duke and Duchess of York will take over now," said Mrs Brown.

"Will she be all right for a Queen?" asked John.

"Most suitable I should think," said his mother. "We really couldn't have had Mrs Simpson could we?"

The beginning of the new school year brought with it problems. The time for taking the 'Eleven-plus' scholarship was rapidly approaching. Ray was beginning to go to pieces already. He felt such pressure because he knew his father was counting on him to pass, a feat which had not been achieved by either of his elder brothers. Ray was the youngest and last of the brothers left to accomplish his father's ambition to have a grammar school educated son.

Often now, Ray would have to stay home when the others were out enjoying themselves, always he seemed to have his head stuck in a book. But the thing that Josie and Neville found so distressing was Ray's complete lack of confidence in his own ability. He said quite often that he didn't think he had the remotest chance of passing. He was in despair as to how his father would react.

It was a waste of time for the others to reassure him that his father would soon get over it if he didn't pass, he had soon come round when the elder boys had failed.

"I know," wailed Ray, "that's what makes it worse, 'cos he could always console himself with the thought that there would be another chance with me. But if I fail, there's no one left for him to pin his hopes on."

With the weather being so cold and the bike-rides shelved until the warmer evenings, Josie's meetings with Neville were less frequent. However, they still had Saturday afternoon pictures to look forward to. Although these visits included the rest of the group, Josie and Neville usually managed a fair amount of private chatter.

It was no longer necessary for Jessie to baby-sit as Josie no longer wanted to go out on Saturday nights and could keep an eye on John. Josie quite liked the feeling of being in charge but she hoped her parents weren't expecting her to stay in every Saturday when the summer came again.

One particular evening when Violet had joined her for her baby-sitting stint they had played 'snakes and ladders' with John until it was time for him to go to bed. John had been unusually fractious and grizzly and the girls were quite relieved when he actually asked to go to bed, another most unusual occurrence for John.

After a while, Josie told Violet that she would just nip upstairs and make sure John was OK. When she came down again she was looking rather worried.

"He's so hot and flushed," she told Violet. "He says he's thirsty and I've given him some water."

Eventually Violet had to go home, so Josie was left to worry on her own about her little brother. She was very relieved when her parents arrived home.

"I don't think John's very well Mum, he's very hot and keeps asking for water."

"You're sure it's not an excuse to keep you running about after him?" asked her Dad.

"No, I think it's genuine, he really doesn't look at all well."

"I'll go and look at him," said her mother, making her way upstairs.

"Jack, come and look at him," she called downstairs to her husband.

John's father dashed upstairs in alarm, followed by Josie hot on his heels.

"I think it's measles," said Mrs Brown. "He's covered in a rash."

John sat in bed snivelling in his effort to get a bit of sympathy.

"It itches," he wailed, scratching himself.

"Don't scratch it," said his mother, giving him another glass of water. "I'll dab it with calamine lotion, that should take the sting out of it a bit."

John looked quite a picture when he finally dropped off to sleep with his red flushed face and blotches of calamine on his neck and behind his ears where the rash was worst. "You haven't had measles you know, Josie."

"Oh no! I don't want to be ill, not now when we're going through what to do in the exams."

"Perhaps you won't get it," consoled her mother.

But, sure enough, Josie did get it. She was pleased when she showed no signs of it on Sunday and, on her mother's advice, she stayed well clear of John.

On Monday she went off cheerfully to school convinced that all was well. It was not until she was undressing for bed that she discovered the first tell-tale signs, a red rash starting behind her ears. She called her mother to look and she confirmed that it looked suspiciously like measles. By morning there was no doubt at all what it was. Josie was covered with an angry-looking rash far worse than John's. She also felt decidedly under the weather.

"You're to stay in bed Josie," said her mother, "and I'll get the doctor to look at you."

Josie didn't need a second bidding to stay in bed, she was beginning to feel so dreadful she would have found it hard to get out of bed anyway.

"How are you Josie? Would you like any breakfast?" asked her mother after she had sorted John out.

"I'm hot and itchy and my head aches. In fact, I think all of me aches. My throat's sore as well," said Josie. "Could I have a cup of tea or a glass of milk?"

Mrs Brown settled for a glass of milk, reasoning that milk was as good as food.

Eventually, after morning surgery, the doctor arrived and confirmed that both John and Josie had measles. John's seemed to be a milder dose, poor Josie was by now in a sorry state.

"No school for you young lady for two weeks. Aren't we pleased about that!" joked the doctor.

"No, I'm not," said Josie with as much force as she could muster. "We're right in the middle of practising for the scholarship."

"Gracious, are you eleven Josie? Doesn't seem long since you were born. Well, I'm sorry but there's no way you can go back for the next two weeks because you'll be contagious, you wouldn't want to cause an epidemic would you?"

Josie thought an epidemic might be a good idea really, that would mean everyone would start even again after missing two weeks of school. But she lay back on her pillows and decided she was just too tired at the moment to plan how to start an epidemic.

For several days Josie had periods of not feeling too bad, followed by periods of feeling awful. During the awful bits she would drowse into a kind of nightmarish sleep during which she would be yelling at Neville who was chasing her up and down the hills at Ringland. Sometimes her mother, alarmed by the noise, would shake her awake.

"You were yelling," she told Josie. "What was Neville doing to you?"

But Josie had no recollection of what had happened.

Another time, the cat next door had got stuck in a tree and Josie, in her dream, had gone to rescue it. As she crawled along the branch, it had turned into a full-grown leopard and Josie awoke screaming. The doctor, who was visiting every day, told Mrs Brown that the hallucinations would go when Josie's temperature went back to normal. It was just that Josie had a far worse dose of measles than John. This was usually the case with older children.

After another couple of days Josie woke up in the late

afternoon, suddenly feeling better, much better and hungry.

"Mum," she called, finding her voice a bit croaky as she hadn't spoken very much for the past few days. "Mum," and, as her mother ran rapidly upstairs, "I'm hungry. What day is it?"

"Saturday."

"Is it, what happened to Thursday and Friday?"

"I expect you've been too ill to remember."

Josie ate a good tea, washed down with a couple of cups of tea, the first real meal she had eaten for days.

As Josie gradually began to feel better, she began to ask after her friends. Had they enquired how she was? Really she wanted to know if Neville had asked after her, but she disguised this by enquiring about all of them. Her mother informed her that Duncan, Violet, Ray and Aldo had all been round to ask if they could see her.

On Sunday morning they all trooped round again, Violet carrying a bunch of flowers gathered from her garden, Aldo with a large bar of her favourite chocolate. Josie sat up in bed to receive her guests, she had checked on the mirror and decided she didn't look too bad. She was looking forward to seeing her friends and wished that Neville was coming with them. But on reflection, maybe she didn't want to see him really, after all she was not exactly looking her best.

As they gathered round the bed and presented the flowers and chocolate Violet burst out.

"You've been very bad Josie, your Mum wouldn't let us come to see you when we came earlier this week."

"How are you feeling now?" asked Ray.

"Oh, tons better," said Josie, trying to think of a way to bring the conversation round to Neville without being too obvious.

"How's school?" she asked.

"Lousy," said Ray. "All we get is instructions on how to pass the scholarship."

"You still worrying about it Ray?" asked Josie.

"I'll be glad when the whole blessed thing is over," said Ray.

"Me too," said Aldo. "Though I doubt if I'll even get through the first bit."

"I'm glad I've got another year before I have to start worrying," said Violet.

"I'm going to be two weeks short on my revision," said Josie.

"Well, you can't help that, if you're ill," said Ray.

"I know, but they won't make allowances for that, will they?"

"No, I s'pose not, but you'll pass without any trouble Josie, with or without revision," said Aldo. Josie was touched by Aldo's faith in her.

"Did you go to the pictures yesterday?" she asked him.

"Ya, we all went," replied Aldo.

"All?" said Josie. "You mean Neville came too?"

"Oh no, not Neville," said Ray. "I haven't seen him for a couple of weeks, matter of fact my Mum was asking this morning why Neville hadn't been for tea. How long since you saw him Josie?"

"Well, not while I've had measles."

"I know that, but how long before that?" insisted Ray.

"I didn't see him the week before that," Josie admitted reluctantly.

Aldo grinned, "Do you like the chocolate Josie?" he asked, changing the subject.

"Thanks Aldo, it's my favourite chocolate."

Josie tried to smile. Privately she was thinking what could have happened to Neville. It wasn't just because she had measles either she thought. There was really no doubt that whatever had happened had nothing to do with her illness. After their last visit to the pictures Neville had not arranged things so that he could have his usual secret rendezvous with Josie.

Josie became aware that her friends were chatting to her and getting no answer as her mind was in turmoil. Neville, what had happened to her Neville? Had he found another girlfriend? Perhaps one who was thirteen like him. Girls of thirteen could be much more glamorous than eleven-year-olds.

"Josie, are you still with us?" said Aldo, waving a hand in front of her eyes.

"Sorry, er - sorry Aldo." Josie tried hard to pull herself out of her depression. They were her friends and they had taken the trouble to visit her while she had been ill and had waited until her mother allowed them to see her.

"It's good of you all to come," said Josie, "and thanks for the presents and everything."

A loud sigh escaped Josie's lips and she sank back on to her pillows.

"Sorry, but I think I feel one of my turns coming on."

Violet turned to the boys.

"Come on, remember her Mum said not to tire her. Cheerio Josie, we'll come again soon."

"Thanks," said Josie faintly from her sick bed.

Once they had left Josie gave way to the tears, turning her face into her pillow she had a real good cry. She didn't really know if she was crying over the possible loss of Neville or because she still felt unwell, or because she was overwhelmed by the kindness of her friends. How could she face them if she no longer had Neville? Now that Ray was fixed up with Violet this seemed to make things worse.

Josie cried some more then it crossed her mind that she still had Aldo, dear faithful Aldo who would do anything for her. And there was always Duncan waiting in the wings. She dried her tears and, sniffing a bit, consoled herself into believing that it wasn't the end of the world. She became so carried away with salvaging her injured pride that she completely forgot that she was only surmising this entire situation, as yet there was no proof that Neville had left her for another.

By the middle of the second week of isolation Josie was feeling nearly back to normal which made it even more frustrating not to be able to go back to school.

At the end of the long two weeks both children were declared fit to return to school. Josie, putting a brave face on things and hiding her broken heart, had decided to be very non-committal if anyone asked about Neville. She was surprised at how much seemed to have been happening in her absence.

Now that the date for the Coronation of King George and Queen Elizabeth had been set for May 12th, there was something other than the dreaded 'Eleven-plus' to command everyone's attention.

There were debates at the council meetings to decide what they could afford to give the local schoolchildren as souvenirs of the Coronation. Plans were already in hand for a street party; a group of mothers, including Mrs Brown, had been mulling over various suggestions for weeks.

Some people expressed regrets at the abdication of the previous King, they had mixed feelings about his brother who had taken over and was shortly to be crowned.

'He hasn't got the personality to make a good King.' 'He's not assertive enough and then there's that awful stutter.' 'How will he cope with making a speech?' These were sentiments often heard expressed.

There had been no further word from Neville. The thing that hurt most was that she had been abandoned in her hour of need, when she had been really ill, she couldn't forgive Neville for that. Aldo and Duncan, on the other hand, were quite delighted with this latest turn of events. Josie had returned to the fold, a quieter rather forlorn Josie the boys had to admit, but they were quite confident that they could soon jolly her out of her depression.

Amid the joyous arrangements for the Coronation the first part of the scholarship raised its ugly head. After sitting the exam the gang compared notes.

"Easy," said Josie confidently. "Some of the questions were downright silly."

"Not so bad," was Ray's rather non-committal assessment.

"Not half as bad as I thought it would be," confirmed Aldo.

"Same here," said Duncan. "Wonder if we'll pass though?"

"Wouldn't it be great if we all got through."

"Even if we do, I don't hold out much hope for the second bit," said the ever-gloomy Ray.

As the day for the Coronation drew nearer the wireless was on almost non-stop in the Brown's household. Of the gang of five the only ones not yet possessing a wireless were Ray and Duncan. Their parents were invited to the Brown's household to listen to the ceremony. Mrs Brown had been baking for several days in readiness for supplying refreshments to the assembled masses in her living-room on the Coronation morning and for the street party in the afternoon.

Everything went off remarkably well, all the children managed to get through the entire day without once falling foul of the slightly harassed adults. They had listened spell-bound to the crowning of the King and Queen.

The broadcast started with the commentator describing the crowds lining the streets along which the golden coach would pass. Then, at last, the announcement that the King and Queen were leaving the palace, the commentator waxed lyrical, 'A shaft of light falls on the golden coach and the eight grey horses as they enter the forecourt,' he gushed. There was a second's silence then a sudden burst of cheering as the Coronation coach swung into the view of the assembled crowds.

Of the hundreds of thousands who lined the route, many at the back could see very little. Looking down on the crowds the commentator at Piccadilly Circus said he could see a sea of periscopes held high as people struggled to get a glimpse of the coach.

By the time they returned from the ceremony and the coach reached the Palace a gentle rain had begun to fall. The policemen had donned their capes and those who had come prepared for all weathers had opened their umbrellas. As the coach passed out of sight through the Palace gate the crowds broke ranks and rushed to the Palace railings, shouting and cheering. An enormous cheer went up as the King and Queen appeared on the balcony some half an hour later, followed by the two Princesses and Queen Mary. The broadcast finished as the Royal family again appeared on the balcony.

There had been discussions among the mothers for most of the morning about the worsening weather conditions. With much forethought preparations had been made in case the weather proved unsuitable for an outside party. The Sunday School hall had been offered as an undercover alternative to the street. By the end of the broadcast, although no rain had yet fallen, the sky had become leaden and the temperature had dropped considerably. A quick consultation between the organisers had brought forth the unanimous decision to proceed with the arrangements in the hall.

The party was great fun, the boys made sure they looked after Josie. Aldo and Dunean were now competing for her affections. Josie, however, was still pining for her lost love Neville, so the boys' attentions went unnoticed. Although she joined in the festivities she seemed somehow detached from it all, as if she felt it was her duty to the Royal family to participate but really her heart wasn't in it.

Aldo was becoming increasingly worried about Josie's bout of depression which showed no signs of improving.

"I could kick your blessed cousin," he told Ray.

"Oh, she'll soon get over it," said Ray. "I know Josie, give her time. Anyway, I'm not taking the blame for Neville, I haven't seen him for months."

"That's no great loss is it?"

"No, I don't really care if I don't ever see him again," exploded Ray who, although he had no romantic attachment to Josie, was very fond of her and regarded her as his good pal. He secretly felt a bit responsible for the situation, after all he had introduced Josie and Neville.

9

The Eleven-Plus

Back at school the day started much like any other. Assembly in the hall, all classes standing in straight orderly lines, prayers and hymns, then announcements from one or two of the teachers, nothing concerning Josie's class. Then the unexpected appearance of the headmistress, who only attended when she had something of importance to announce.

"I shall be coming to Class 6A and 6B later in the morning as I have the results of the first part of the scholarship." An excited murmur from the classes mentioned. "Silence children," said the head, "I am pleased to tell you that our results are very encouraging."

Entering Josie's class later in the morning the headmistress said, "Be seated children, I'm very pleased with your results, you have more passes than the other top class, which is only right and proper as you are the A class. But, remember, although the school is pleased with your results, the important part of the scholarship is yet to come. If these results can be repeated then I shall be very pleased indeed. I will read the names of those who have passed in alphabetical order." Her voice droned on and everyone listened with rapt attention.

Grins from several with surnames beginning with A. Ray was wearing his usual worried frown until Miss Finch said, "Raymond Anderson," then passed on to those whose name began with B. "Josephine Brown." Josie sighed with relief and looked over to Ray who saluted and grinned. Josie crossed her fingers and held them up to Duncan and Aldo.

She had reached the S section. Duncan held his breath, he really wasn't expecting to pass he told himself so he wouldn't be too disappointed. "Duncan Scott," said Miss Finch. Josie waved and Duncan felt this was the happiest day of his life. He knew his mother would be overjoyed.

A few more S's and a couple of T's, there were no names beginning with U. "Aldo Vincenti," said Miss Finch. Aldo looked stunned but managed a wave. 'We've all passed,' thought Josie feeling happier than she had been for months. They were all through the first bit, they'd have to think of something to celebrate.

It was difficult to concentrate on Mrs Stubbs' history lesson as the children waited anxiously for the play-time break so they could get together. Once in the playground the hubbub could be heard for miles. Josie, Ray, Duncan and Aldo were joined by Violet who had been waiting for play-time to find out how her friends had fared.

"We've all passed," yelled Ray as Violet approached.

"Your dad'll be pleased," said Violet.

The little group huddled together oblivious of the activities of the rest of the children scattered about the playground.

"It's such a relief," said Aldo. "Whether we'd passed or not, just knowing is a relief."

"And the fact that we've all passed makes it even better," said Duncan, who still couldn't believe his luck.

"What shall we do to celebrate?" said the ever-practical Josie.

"Are we going to the pictures Saturday?" asked Aldo.

"Guess so," said Josie.

"Yes," said Ray and Violet together.

"Why do you ask?" asked Josie.

"Well, I was thinking," said Aldo, "I could ask my Dad if we could all go to the restaurant for a fish and chip tea when we come out."

"Cor! That'd be good," said Duncan enthusiastically, hoping his mother would allow him to go.

"Shall I ask him then?" said Aldo referring to Josie for consent.

"Be lovely if we could," said Josie patting Aldo on the shoulder in an effort to show her approval for his efforts.

The whistle blew. Mrs Stubbs was on playground duty. Everyone stood perfectly still. A second blast and everyone dashed into their lines to file back into school, class by class.

The following day they crowded around Aldo when he arrived at school to find out what his father had said about their proposed celebratory tea.

"He said it would be OK, he'd reserve a table for us for five-thirty, he said we'd all done so well we deserve it."

"Coo! I've never been to a real restaurant before," sighed Duncan. "I told my Mum you were going to ask your Dad and she said I could go if he said yes."

"Are you pleased Josie?" asked Aldo.

"Yes, of course I am," said Josie. "It'll be great all going out for tea."

"Even without Neville?" asked Aldo, trying not to sound vindictive.

"Who cares about Neville?" said Josie quickly but not very convincingly and she certainly didn't fool Aldo.

Josie had told her mother and father of Mr Vincenti's kind offer of tea at his restaurant.

"Hadn't you better put your best dress on?" said her mother after Josie had finished her dinner.

"Oh! can I please?" said Josie

"Well, this is rather special isn't it?"

Josie sped upstairs to her room to put on her Sunday clothes, a pink flowered creation and a pink cardigan which her mother had knitted for her.

Duncan was already waiting at the back door, as they walked down the path Aldo came to meet them.

"Ray and Violet are at the bottom of the road," he informed them, falling into step beside Josie.

Although the Buck Jones serial had reached an exciting pitch the children found it hard to concentrate on Buck's exploits as they were thinking of the fish and chip tea to come. It was not so much the fish and chips as the visit to a real restaurant that was the attraction. Other than 'Wooly's' tea-rooms and on rare occasions the station buffet, none of the children, with the exception of Aldo, had ever been to a restaurant before. The fact that they had no parental supervision for this first visit made it even more exciting.

Having been resigned to the loss of Neville, Josie was beginning to look on Aldo as a substitute boyfriend. She admitted

120

to herself that she didn't feel quite the same devotion to Aldo as she had to Neville but, she reasoned, that's because he was much more familiar to her. There wasn't the excitement of getting to know each other like there was with Neville. Perhaps there was a lot to be said for that anyway, probably if she'd known Neville a bit better, she wouldn't have been so surprised when he abandoned her without a word of explanation.

Josie suddenly became aware that the film was half over, she must stop this continual reminiscing about what went wrong with her romance with Neville. The rest of the film didn't make much sense and she was glad when it was over and they were able to make their way through the city and up to Aldo's restaurant.

Mr Vincenti had a great sense of occasion. He had set a table in a secluded corner. The table, covered in a snowy white cloth, had a centre-piece of flowers. The children filed silently in, with the exception of Aldo, all were rather overawed by their surroundings.

"Good afternoon my young friends!" said Mr Vincenti, appearing from the kitchen.

"Hello Papa!" said Aldo.

"Did you enjoy the pictures?"

"Yes," said the chorus, though Josie couldn't remember much about the main film, her attention had been otherwise engaged. Mr Vincenti drew out a chair for Josie and Geno did the same for Violet. When they were all seated Mario appeared carrying plates of steaming hot fish and chips, several other young waiters followed him until the table was finally laid with fish and chips and plates of bread and butter and glasses of lemonade.

Once the meal was in front of them and the waiters had disappeared, there was a sudden burst of chatter from the table in the corner. In their excitement they all spoke at once. There seemed to be overall agreement that if this was the grown up way of life then they couldn't wait to be grown up. Aldo winked at Josie through the foliage of the flowered centre piece and raised his glass of lemonade.

"Here's to us and good luck with the next bit."

"So say all of us," amended Josie.

Coming hard on the heels of the scholarship results and right in the middle of cramming for the second part came the much talked of wedding of the ex-King and Mrs Simpson, now to be

f

known as the Duke and Duchess of Windsor.

They had resided in France since the abdication. Josie had seen pictures on the Pathé News at the cinema of the magnificent chateau which they had made their home.

There were pictures in all the newspapers on the day following the wedding which was on June 13th. Pictures of the Duke in morning dress and his bride in a long gown.

It was the chief topic of conversation for about a week, both at home and at school, where it was discussed and debated in class with arguments for and much criticism against the Windsors. Finally, the interest died away and the Windsors were left to pursue the private life they had stated they wanted.

Sitting the second part of the scholarship became the vitally important issue. There were several sections to this part. Josie found English and History comparatively easy, Maths a bit harder and Geography harder still. After it was over the gang compared notes. Aldo and Duncan confessed that they had found most of it beyond them. Ray was his usual gloomy self, saying he wished he could honestly say that he had found one subject easy but he couldn't 'cos they were all blooming hard. He thought he might have done reasonably OK at Maths but then Maths was his best subject. They knew they wouldn't have too long to wait for the results as they would all need to know which school they would be attending after the summer break.

When the results were finally announced, again by Miss Finch in alphabetical order, Josie was somewhat dismayed when the headmistress passed from A straight to D and, by the time she had finished, which didn't take long, there were only five boys and four girls who had passed.

The quartet had not a single pass between them. Josie was the only one who was stunned and couldn't quite decide if she should quietly shed a few tears when play-time came or rejoice that she wouldn't be going to the Blyth School after all.

"I can't understand it Josie," said Aldo loyally, "I mean you're never out of the top half dozen when we have tests."

"My Dad'll kill me," said Ray.

"'Course he won't," said Josie. "You did your best didn't you?"

"Yes, I did but I don't think he'll look at it like that, he's so keen for me to get to Grammar School."

Ray looked near to tears, he felt he had let his parents down.

Aldo and Duncan hadn't had any great expectation of passing so they weren't feeling so bad about it. Josie had felt she had a good chance, judging by her form results and had felt she had had a stab at most of the questions on each subject. True, she had been nervous on the actual day of the exam so, perhaps, had not been capable of her best performance.

The group stood in a dejected little circle in one corner of the playground, awaiting the whistle to return to class for the remainder of the morning before they had to face the prospect of telling their parents of their failure.

Their progress home at dinner-time was unusually slow. Violet had joined them and tried to cheer them up without much success. Josie was silently praying that Ray wouldn't break down and cry but the more sympathetic Violet became the more likely this possibility looked. 'Don't do it Ray,' said Josie to herself, 'I'm sure I won't know what to do if you start crying and neither will Violet.'

"Oh, shut up, Violet!" said Josie suddenly. "You're only making things worse."

"Sorry, I'm sure," said Violet getting very prickly. "I'm only trying to help."

After the initial shock of failing to pass and the trauma of having to tell their parents, the four seemed to be welded into an even closer relationship, sometimes even Violet felt a bit excluded. She supposed this was because she hadn't shared their experiences, but she pointed out that her's was yet to come and she wasn't really expecting to fare any better than they had.

Ray's father had eventually got over his disappointment at Ray's results and had enrolled him at Brackendale Private School for Boys beginning next term. Ray didn't know whether to be pleased or not, he'd miss Aldo and Duncan but he supposed he'd make other friends. Josie was in a similar position, she would be losing all the boys and Violet wouldn't be eligible for senior school for another year.

Getting together on the last day of school they decided to put all these horrors behind them and enjoy the next six weeks of freedom.

It was surprising how quickly the summer holiday seemed to pass this year. The whole group, with the exception of Violet who was not changing schools, were dreading the end of the holiday and the prospect of starting at a new school.

On the last morning of the holiday at Yarmouth Josie and John decided to have one last session of kite-flying. This year they had a kite which was exceptionally good. Having got it soaring high in the sky, Josie in answer to John's pleading, had allowed him to hold the string. John's grasp had slipped and the kite went out of control, flying high over the promenade with the string dangling temptingly just out of reach. Out of breath with chasing it, Josie at last gave up.

"It's no good, it's gone," she said to John who came panting up behind her.

"Rotten luck," said a boy who had been watching the kite's progress. "Why don't you come with us?" he added as he joined a group of children who were all staring up at the sky where the runaway kite was still visible.

"We're looking for Lobby Ludd."

"Who's Lobby Ludd?" asked Josie.

"You have to have a newspaper," said an older boy in the group as they gathered around Josie and John. "We've got one," he said, producing one from under his arm. "There he is," he pointed to a shadowy indistinct photograph at the bottom of the paper. "You get ten-bob if you find him but you have to say, 'You are Lobby Ludd and I claim the reward,' then hand him the paper. We've challenged six men in trilby hats already this morning."

John stopped snivelling, this sounded like fun and it might take Josie's mind off the missing kite.

"Let's go with them Josie," he said.

The group consisted of four boys who were about Josie's age, one older boy who looked as if he might have left school and two small girls who looked about seven or eight. There were no formal introductions, Josie and John just tacked on to the rest of the group. As they walked along the older boy waited and fell into step beside Josie.

"Where are you from?" he asked.

"Norwich," replied Josie.

"So'm I," said the boy.

"We thought you all lived here."

"Well, all the others do but I'm staying for the week with my auntie, these are my cousins," he pointed to the two girls.

Suddenly, the boys in front came to an abrupt halt.

"Over there," whispered the leader, "that chap sitting on the seat, I bet that's him."

Josie and John listened as they discussed who should challenge him.

"You do it, I did it last time and Joe and Bryan have already done it, go on, it's your turn Reggie."

Reggie somewhat reluctantly approached the man and said his little piece, thrusting the newspaper toward him.

"Clear off!" said the man indignantly. "Go on, clear off the lot of you!" The man was beginning to get red in the face.

They all took to their heels and ran down the promenade, eventually coming to a stop at the entrance to the pier.

"He didn't say he wasn't Lobby Ludd," said the boy who had made the challenge. "Did you notice he didn't say he wasn't?"

"No, but he didn't say he was either," said Josie.

"No, but then he'd have to give me the ten shillings if he had. I bet they don't let kids win it. I bet he is Lobby Ludd, he's exactly like the picture."

"I think we might as well give up," said the older boy, who had told Josie that his name was Edwin.

"We'll have to go home now, it's nearly dinner-time," said Josie.

"What are you doing this afternoon?" Edwin enquired.

"Nothing much, we usually come back to the beach."

"See you down here then, opposite the pier," said Edwin, as they went their separate ways.

As they made their way back to the pier after they had finished dinner, they could see that Edwin and his cousins were already waiting.

"I want to see the Punch and Judy for one last time," said John as he jumped down on to the sand. The girls followed him as they claimed a place on the form in front of the booth.

"Josie and I will go for a cup of tea while you're watching," said Edwin as he and Josie walked towards the refreshment kiosk.

Edwin bought tea and shortcakes and came back to sit next to Josie. He chatted away as if they had known each other for years. Josie was rather more reticent, her confidence with the opposite sex had been considerably undermined by her experience with Neville. Within minutes Josie had discovered that Edwin was working at the Maypole store as an errand boy. His father was Manager of the store and Edwin hoped that he might one day equal his father's success.

"I'll soon be fifteen, how old are you Josie?"

"Twelve," said Josie, who actually had a month to go before she reached her twelfth birthday but twelve seemed so much more grown up than eleven, especially when you were speaking to someone who was nearly fifteen.

"I thought you were older than that," said Edwin.

Josie wished she had said she was thirteen.

"You going to senior school after the holidays then?"

"Yes," Josie outlined her apprehension about changing schools.

Edwin listened and was able to reassure her. "I felt exactly the same when I left primary school but you soon get settled, in the end I quite enjoyed my years at senior school."

By the time the Punch and Judy performance came to an end they had exchanged life stories, but Josie had carefully omitted any mention of Neville. John and the girls came to look for them. Edwin bought all of them an ice-cream. John was babbling away as he licked his ice-cream cone.

"Wasn't it good? I've seen it three times this week. Let's go and look at the sand picture," he said as he skipped along with Edwin's cousins.

Josie and Edwin walked behind at a more sedate pace, still deep in conversation. It seemed to Josie that Edwin was much more enthusiastic about his job than either Jimmy or Willy, who both seemed to regard it solely as a means of making money.

"My cousins seem to like your little brother," said Edwin. "Which is fortunate 'cos we can continue our chat. What a pity I didn't meet you earlier in the week, I've got a bit bored roaming around with my cousins and their friends," he grinned. "They're all a bit young for me, don't you think?"

"Don't you think I'm a bit young too?" asked Josie.

" 'Course not, you seem older somehow, I was surprised when you said you were only twelve, I reckon you must be a very sensible twelve," he laughed, "and my cousins are both young for their age, that's because they're completely spoilt by their mother."

"Are you going out tonight?" Edwin enquired.

"We're going to the Pleasure Beach with my Mum and Dad, we always do on the last night of the holiday," replied Josie.

"I'm going to see you again, aren't I?" Edwin pleaded.

Josie was quite taken aback, fancy a boy who was at work asking to see her again!

"I hope so," she said demurely, but she was already wondering how this would work out.

Except for Saturday nights she had to be home by eight-thirty. How would a boy who was working and could probably please himself what time he went home, react to this? It seemed to her that this friendship was doomed before it got started.

"Penny for your thoughts!" said Edwin with a laugh. "What's the problem?"

Josie looked at Edwin who gazed back at her, a frown puckering his brow. He brushed his floppy fair hair out of his eyes, eyes which were a surprisingly piercing blue.

"What's wrong, Josie?"

"Well, I was thinking," said Josie, who had decided that perhaps honesty was the best policy, "I'd like us to be friends, I'd like to see you again when we get home."

"Well then?" interrupted Edwin.

"How could we meet? That's the trouble, what time do you finish work?"

"I usually get home about six o'clock, sometimes a bit later on Saturdays, but Thursday I finish at half-past twelve."

"I have to be home by eight-thirty on school days, so it wouldn't work out very well."

"Why not?" asked Edwin, who seemed to be stubbornly refusing to admit to any problem.

"By the time you'd had your tea that wouldn't leave very long in the evenings would it?"

"I could meet you by half-past six, that'd give us a couple of hours, and what about Thursdays? Maybe I could meet you out of school?"

Josie brightened considerably, perhaps it wouldn't be such a problem. She'd realised that the reason she was being so cautious was because she was still nursing the hurt from Neville, she was reluctant to involve herself in anything which might cause her further heartache.

"Can I see you tomorrow night then after we get home, or will

127

that be too soon?"

"No doubt my Mum and Dad will be going out so I can probably be out until nine o'clock or half-past if I can wangle it with Jessie!"

Edwin grinned. "Good! That's settled then, where will I meet you?"

Josie thought for a moment - it mustn't be too near to home.

"At the park gates, do you know Waterloo Park?"

"Oh, sure," said Edwin, "I deliver around that way."

Josie told herself to stop anticipating trouble as she thought of her friends and, in particular, Aldo. She would have to be careful to keep Edwin a secret, at least to start with in case the whole thing fizzled out.

Finally, arriving home a little weary to a house which smelt stuffy from being shut up for a week, Mrs Brown flung open all the windows to 'let a little air in', as she put it.

"What's for dinner?" asked John about five minutes after arriving home.

"Josie, you'd better get fish and chips," said her mother, "I'm really not going to have time to cook anything today."

"I'll go with you," John volunteered.

Joining the queue at the fish shop there was a shout from the inside.

"Hi Josie, you back from holidays?"

Josie looked up to see Aldo waving from the front of the queue.

He wandered over to where Josie and John were waiting their turn.

"Coming out tonight Josie?" he enquired.

"No, I can't tonight, too busy after the holiday," lied Josie.

"Shame, will I see you tomorrow then?"

"S'pect we'll go over to see Granny in the morning," John chimed in.

"How about tomorrow afternoon?" Aldo persisted.

"OK," said Josie. "There's no Sunday School tomorrow."

"I'll come round after dinner then, I've got to go now, I'm having a quick dinner 'cos I'm going out with Mario this afternoon, he's got the day off. See you tomorrow Josie."

It was surprisingly easy for Josie to organise her evening out, her father's only comment was, "I expect you want to see your friends to tell them about your holiday. Jessie's coming in to keep an eye on John. Don't be later than nine."

Edwin, dressed in spotless white shirt, grey flannel trousers, looking even more grown up than he had in his seaside shorts, was waiting at the Park gate.

"Hello Josie, you made it all right then? No trouble with your Mum and Dad?"

"No trouble," said Josie. "Mind you they don't know I'm meeting you."

"You going to keep it a secret then?"

"For the time being while I think things out."

Edwin couldn't resist a smile, she seemed so serious and adult this girl he was making into a friend. She seemed, at times, more adult than he was.

"I told my Mum about meeting you," he said.

"Did you?" Josie looked slightly alarmed. "Did she mind?"

"Of course not, why should she?"

"Well, I don't know, did you tell her how old I am?"

"You're worrying too much about the difference in our ages Josie. I did tell my Mum, she said I was to treat you right and remember you are still a schoolgirl. She also said why don't I take you home for tea sometime?"

Josie looked startled, things were moving rather too quickly for her to cope with.

"Shall we walk in the park, or is there anything else you would rather do?" asked Edwin.

"A walk in the park would be nice," said Josie politely. "Have you been to the park before?"

"Only once," said Edwin. "Do you come in the park a lot Josie?"

"Quite often, there's a gang of us who play cricket and rounders."

Edwin laughed.

"Cricket," he said. "You're a bit of a tom-boy aren't you Josie?"

"I s'pose so," said Josie blushing. "That's probably 'cos I haven't got any sisters and most of my friends are boys."

"Are they? I'll have to keep an eye on them won't I? Are any of them your special boyfriend?"

" 'Course not," said Josie immediately, pushing to the back of her mind the fact that Aldo probably considered he was just that.

"Good," said Edwin as they walked up the steps toward the bandstand. "Let's sit for a little while," he said. "Can I come tomorrow and hear the band with you?"

Josie thought rapidly. Because there was no Sunday School she had agreed to meet Aldo in the afternoon. She knew she would prefer to meet Edwin, but she didn't want to hurt Aldo's feelings.

"I could come in the evening," she said.

"Right, that's a date then," said Edwin, "six-thirty at the park gates."

Before they parted for the evening Josie had learned that Edwin's father was the proud owner of an Austin Seven car in which he went to work each day, that Edwin was an only child and, reading between the lines, Josie had sussed out that he was the apple of his mother's eye. He had never had a serious girl-friend, in fact he didn't seem to have many friends at all.

For his part, Edwin had decided that Josie was a tom-boy with a generous streak, that she had many friends, was always looking for lame dogs to help, and had an elder brother Jimmy who didn't seem to like her very much. The other worry in her life seemed to be the prospects of changing schools after the holiday.

Edwin walked almost home with her when the park closed for the night. At Josie's request, he stopped short of the road in which she lived as he knew she was worrying about being seen by anyone she knew.

Sunday passed uneventfully, a visit to Grandma and Grandad in the morning, an afternoon spent in the park with Aldo and John, the evening spent with Edwin.

Listening to the band with Edwin, although very enjoyable, was tinged with anxiety in case any of her friends might have the same idea of spending the evening. She had actually lied to Aldo when he had suggested that they could meet again in the evening after spending the afternoon in the park. Josie had told him she couldn't come out in the evening as she had to look after John. She was able to justify her lie to herself by reasoning that she had, after all, given her full attention to Aldo for the whole of the afternoon and was only doing the same for Edwin for the evening. It was very reassuring being so much in demand and having to find ways of spreading oneself a bit.

Soon the summer holiday was over, the new school term was

due to start on Monday. As a last fling and in an effort to prevent Josie's brooding about starting at her new school, Edwin had suggested cycling to Sea Palling for the day on Sunday. Josie had agreed enthusiastically, a whole day at the seaside, just the two of them.

Her mother had taken it for granted that all her friends were going and Josie did not enlighten her for fear that permission to go would be cancelled. While packing a picnic meal with the help of her mother, Josie tried to avoid too much chatter, she was hoping that she could manage not to have to tell an outright lie, though she had steeled herself to do so if it became necessary.

However, Mrs Brown hadn't really given a second thought to the matter, the fact that Josie still roamed around with her gang all the time that Edwin was at work, had lulled her into the mistaken idea that this was her daughter's sole activity.

Meeting Edwin at a safe distance from home, they made their way to Wroxham Road to start their journey.

The ride was very enjoyable, the sun shone in a clear blue sky, the hedgerows and the fields were the slightly faded green of high summer. The corn was ripe, lots of it had already been cut and was standing in neat little pyramids made out of half a dozen sheaths stacked together.

"Josie, shall we stop for a little while, it's about another ten miles to Sea Palling, let's sit in this cornfield for a bit of a rest," said Edwin.

"OK," said Josie, "I could do with a cup of tea.

Edwin stretched out in the sun.

"Boy, it's hot!" he said. "Do you think you can manage another ten miles?" he asked.

" 'Course I can, I've biked to Yarmouth and that's further than Sea Palling."

"Have you? I've never biked as far as that. Who'd you go with?"

Josie wondered whether to tell him about Neville but decided against it. Edwin took the cup of tea she handed him.

"A boy I bet," he said.

"Well, yes," said Josie hesitantly, "but I don't have anything to do with him anymore."

Edwin sensed a reluctance to discuss this any further and, not wishing to upset Josie, he changed the subject.

131

"Have you been to Sea Palling?" he asked.

"No, have you?"

"I went in the car with my Mum and Dad. It's a nice sandy beach and there are some lovely quiet beaches further on at Horsey Mere."

"How much further on?" Josie enquired.

"Oh, only a few miles, do you want to look at them?"

"See how we feel when we get there."

"Let's sit here for a little while, there's no hurry is there? At least you seem to have stopped worrying about your new school tomorrow."

Josie's big brown eyes clouded over. Edwin could have kicked himself for reminding her about tomorrow.

"Sorry Josie," he said, taking her hand, "I'm sure it'll all be all right when you get there." He leaned over and kissed her cheek - their first kiss.

"Let's forget it," she said, rolling over on her stomach and gazing into Edwin's blue eyes.

Edwin tickled her nose with a piece of straw from the stack, he sighed.

"Josie," he said, "when you're back at school, when are we going to be able to meet? Let's sort it out. We'll still be OK for Saturday night and Sunday night and I could meet you out of school or after school on Thursday. Maybe we could go to the pictures if we went early so you were not too late getting home."

Josie was not going to admit that she had only ever been to the 'Cinema' in Magdalen Street and then only to a Saturday afternoon children's matinee.

"I could bring you some sandwiches. My Mum would do that for me, I know."

"What'd I tell my mother? Why I was not going home for tea I mean?"

"Couldn't you tell her you were going to the pictures?"

"Um!" - Josie thought about it, she supposed she could try, after all, the worst that could happen would be for her mother to say no. "I'll see what she says," said Josie, doing her usual trick of keeping everything as vague as possible.

"I'll be jolly glad when you feel you are able to tell her about me."

Josie daringly patted his cheek.

132

"Let me decide when it's the right moment then maybe I will."

"Good," said Edwin. Then reluctantly, "I suppose we'd better get started again."

After another hot and tiring ten miles the signpost read 'Sea Palling - one mile'.

"Nearly there," said Edwin with some relief.

Eventually, the beach and the sea were in sight.

"It's a lovely beach," said Josie. "Such clean sand and look at the dunes."

"Yes, it's almost silver coloured isn't it?"

They walked along at the edge of the sea, hand in hand, the sea was so calm it seemed to have to make an effort to even make a slight ripple as it reached the shore.

The further they walked the thinner was the sprinkling of people enjoying the sun on the beach or in the sea.

"This looks nice," said Josie. "It's sheltered and quiet."

"Good," said Edwin, "let's have dinner."

He took a towel from his bag and spread it out for Josie to sit on.

"I didn't think of bringing a towel, thanks Edwin," said Josie sitting down.

They sorted out and swopped some of their sandwiches and cakes, then finished off with cups of tea.

Having packed their flasks, cups and empty wrappings back in their bags, Edwin flopped on his back in the sand, placing an arm around Josie.

"Relax Josie," he said as he felt her stiffen at his touch. "You still worrying about tomorrow?"

"No," said Josie, "I'm not even going to think about it."

"What's wrong then?" Edwin was puzzled. "You're not afraid of me are you Josie?"

" 'Course not," said Josie without conviction.

"Josie," Edwin ran his hand down her back as she still sat tensely on her towel, "you know about - er - things, don't you, men and women I mean?"

"Yes," said Josie very quietly, she was not really sure her scant knowledge was correct or not, never having got around to asking for further details from her mother, who had given her basic information when she had started her periods. Most of her information had been gleaned from Violet, and Josie had her doubts about the reliability of information from Violet who was given to exaggeration.

"Josie, I wouldn't do anything to hurt you. I know you're younger than me," he grinned. "I can wait until you grow up. My mother would kill me if I led any girl astray."

Josie felt reassured, Edwin seemed so straightforward and honest.

By the time they returned to their bikes for the ride home, Josie felt that their relationship had entered a new phase. She no longer felt on edge every time Edwin came near her, they had after all discussed things that she had previously thought it impossible to discuss with anyone, especially a boy.

Josie awoke next morning with very little enthusiasm for the day ahead. On arriving at St. Augustines School she stayed close to the girls who had been her classmates for the previous years at Angel Road Primary.

Usually, on the first day of term, Josie would meet up with the boys and Violet at the school gate; now, of course, there were no boys and Violet had another year before she transferred to a senior school. Things are so different, thought Josie as she filed with the others into the Assembly Hall.

After a few weeks Josie had established a close friendship with the twins Milly and Maggie and another ex-classmate who was called Penelope.

The girls had taken to drawing and cookery lessons like ducks to water. Though they had always enjoyed art at their Primary school, this was their first experience of cookery. In the art lesson they could run riot over the very elderly mistress and in the cookery lesson they all developed a crush on the young and pretty Irish cookery teacher.

By the time Christmas came Josie, Penelope, Milly and Maggie were all settled into a routine. The old gang had split up, the boys had made other friends at their all boys' senior school.

Ray, who was now attending his Private school, had also made a new friend who attended the same school.

Violet, left at Primary school, found the boys and Josie always otherwise engaged and Ray no longer keen on the idea of having a girlfriend. She felt obliged to make other friends for herself.

The only thing from her old way of life that remained constant for Josie was Edwin. At Christmas Edwin had been so insistent about wanting Josie to come to tea that she had finally plucked up courage to tell her mother.

Mr and Mrs Brown had been a bit alarmed at the news that their daughter had a fifteen-year-old admirer who wanted to take her home to tea. But, having talked it over, they suggested that perhaps she would like to ask Edwin to come to tea with them on the following Sunday.

When Josie conveyed the message to Edwin when they next met, he expressed his pleasure that she had, at last, brought their friendship out into the open.

On the following Sunday afternoon, wearing his best suit, it was with some trepidation that Edwin knocked at the Brown's front door - he was thankful it was Josie who opened it. Her mother had lit a fire in the front room in Edwin's honour.

"This is Edwin," said Josie introducing him.

Edwin nervously brushed his hair out of his eyes.

"Pleased to meet you," he shook hands with both parents.

"Well, sit down lad," said Mr Brown.

"I know Edwin," John piped up, "and his cousins. How are your cousins? Do you think I'll ever see them again?"

Mrs Brown laughed.

"Don't say you've got a crush on Edwin's cousin?"

"Cousins," said John, "there's two of them, I don't know which one I like best."

John had broken the ice and soon they were all chatting.

Tea was a very jolly meal. Edwin was, by now, feeling quite at home, even the arrival of Jimmy shortly before tea had left him quite unperturbed. The family banter between the brothers and their sister was something he had never before experienced. By the time he took his leave of the Brown family he felt that he had been accepted by them all.

On the following Sunday the procedure was reversed. Edwin called to collect Josie to take her to his home for tea. His parents were enchanted by this shy little girl with her big soulful brown eyes. Josie, for her part, thought his mother was both smart and pretty and his father, who teased her quite a lot, was great fun. Thus, with everything turning out much better than either had dared hope, they no longer had to avoid meeting anyone they knew when they were out together.

For Christmas this year Mr Brown had purchased an electric

record player. Once again, because none of their friends possessed one, they all delighted in coming round to listen to the Brown's record collection. When he had selected the dozen or so records to start the collection, Mr Brown had consulted all the family members for their choice of record.

Josie's choice was a song from a film she had recently seen entitled 'Hawaii Calls' starring a young boy named Bobby Breen who had a beautiful voice. After seeing the film, Josie's romantic daydreams were centred around Bobby Breen, with whom she lived on a South Sea Island, but thoughts of Edwin kept intruding on her daydreams, partly because Edwin was the one who had taken her to see the film and had held her hand during the sad bits.

By the end of the Christmas holiday Mr and Mrs Brown were heartily sick of the sound of Bobby Breen's high notes; although Josie protested that she was just as sick of Jimmy's choice of George Formby singing 'Leaning on a Lamppost', and she was even less enamoured with her father's favourite 'Marta' sung by Arthur Tracy the 'Street Singer'. There were times when the new record player was almost red hot, as were the arguments between the young Browns about what to play next.

After Edwin had returned to work Josie spent quite a lot of time with Penelope, who was now her best friend. She accepted that Josie would spend her time with Edwin whenever he was not working, however, she knew that Josie was very glad of her company when he was. This arrangement seemed to work quite satisfactorily for all concerned.

A couple of weeks after Christmas Josie was, as usual, hurrying through her tea, anxious not to be late for her date with Edwin.

"We've had a German trade delegation at the factory for the past week," said Mr Brown, "I seem to have befriended one of the younger members, a young chap named Otto."

"I've seen him," said Jimmy. "Chap with dark curly hair."

"I thought all Germans were blond," said Josie.

"He's a German Jew," said her father. "Things are not too good for Jews in Germany at the moment, so he was telling me."

"Could I have another cup of tea?" said Josie, who had decided to linger a bit longer to hear about Otto.

"How about asking him round for a meal?" said Mrs Brown.

"Or do they have to stay in their hotel?"

"I was about to suggest that," said Mr Brown. "I'm sure he'd love to come, he's asked about the family. He's not married himself, he lives with his mother and young sister in Berlin."

"Sunday for tea then," said Mrs Brown.

"Edwin's coming for tea on Sunday," Josie reminded her mother.

"Well, that won't matter, will it? He can meet Otto too."

On the following Sunday, promptly at four o'clock, Otto presented himself for tea with the Brown household. He was not very tall and of sturdy build, he had an undistinguished sort of face, the most striking feature being his bright intelligent eyes. His hair was black and curly. He reminded Josie vaguely of Neville.

After all round introductions, Otto was soon swamped with questions about Germany from Josie, Edwin and John. As he told of the plight of the Jews, his eyes clouded over. He, himself, was at present all right. His father had been a well-established industrialist who had left a thriving shoe-factory, when he died, to Otto and his two elder brothers who were, at present, running things with Otto as junior partner.

For the next two weeks Otto became a regular visitor to the Brown's house. He had confided in Mrs Brown that he hated being in the hotel. Most of the other German representatives were older than him and none of the others were Jewish, they tended to ridicule him at every opportunity.

The Browns invited him to treat their home as his own during his stay and he had taken them at their word, visiting every evening. Josie felt sure her mother would have taken him in altogether were it not for the shortage of beds.

By the time Otto reluctantly returned to Germany, he left behind a deeply anxious Brown family. He promised to write and keep them informed of the situation, which he had described as getting desperate. His fear of the Nazi party and its leader Adolf Hitler was very apparent. And if he was to be believed, terrible things were already happening to the Jewish population.

Josie knew her father had discussed with him the possibility of his coming to live in England but Otto was worried about the rest of his family. His widowed mother and his young sister were his chief concern, he felt responsible for them, as both his elder brothers were married with families of their own.

Soon after his return to Germany a large parcel was delivered to the Browns. It contained a variety of delicious biscuits and chocolates and a letter expressing his gratitude for the hospitality he had received and a promise to keep in touch.

At school Josie had informed all her friends of Otto's visit, explaining and, as usual, exaggerating a bit about the plight of the Jews and the dreadful dictator named Adolf Hitler. In the middle of a somewhat graphic description, with her friends clustered around listening with rapt attention murmuring "Oh, no!" and "That's awful!" occasionally, they were pounced on by the history teacher.

Understandably annoyed at this interruption to her lesson she really let fly at Josie.

"You're talking a lot of rubbish Josie Brown, corrupting the minds of your classmates. Adolf Hitler is doing wonderful things for Germany, it's a pity we haven't got someone like him in this country. If I ever hear you mentioning anything like this again, I'll report you to the head."

"But Miss, my Uncle Otto . . ." began Josie.

"I don't want to hear about your Uncle Otto, he's a liar," she said furiously.

Josie, who was by now bright red with embarrassment and trying hard not to shed any tears, which she knew would give the teacher great satisfaction, slumped in her chair and remained silent for the rest of the session, only giving way to her tears of frustration when she reached home at lunch-time.

"He wasn't lying was he Mum?"

"I see no reason why he should want to lie about anything to us," said her mother.

"Perhaps someone should start taking notice of what's happening in Germany. I hate that blessed Miss Greenaway," said Josie with some heat. "She seems to know all about it and actually approves of this Adolf Hitler."

In February a new cinema opened situated in Botolph Street. It was called the Odeon, a name no one in Norwich was familiar with. It was the very latest thing in cinemas, far grander than any of the older ones. Painted in striking colours and beautifully carpeted throughout, the seats were plush covered and extremely comfortable. It was, perhaps, less ornate than some of the old style cinemas, but Josie quite liked its uncluttered style of decor. The price of the seats was a little higher than some of the others charged but, as Edwin always paid for Josie, she didn't have to worry about this unduly, although she did enquire whether he could afford the extra expense.

Josie and Edwin went quite often to the Odeon, partly because it was much nearer to Josie's home, so they didn't have to worry about her being late home. Edwin was very conscientious about always getting her back at the correct time under strict instructions from both his own mother and also from Josie's parents.

The world situation, with regard to Nazi Germany, took a turn for the worse in March, when they closed the frontier between Germany and Austria. The wireless reported that German troops were massing on the border.

It became clear that neither Britain nor France were prepared to go to the defence of Austria. By March 13th German troops had entered and taken over Austria. Hitler appointed himself Chancellor of Greater Germany which now included Austria.

There were discussions at school about whether Britain should have gone to the aid of Austria. Those who were against any form of action pointed out that this would be a sure way to start another war with Germany. Those who thought some assistance should have been offered were of the opinion that Germany was hell bent on war anyway and if Britain and France stood idly by Hitler would simply over-run the rest of Europe and then turn his attention to Britain.

Every day there seemed to be news of atrocities being carried out by Germany. Josie thought often of 'Uncle Otto' and wondered what had become of him and his family. It was months since they had had any news of him. After a particularly depressing news bulletin Josie said sadly:

"It all seems so awful there now, the Germans seem to be behaving like maniacs toward the Jews. Perhaps that rotten Miss Greenaway will believe it now."

In August a letter arrived with a French postmark and stamp. "It looks like Otto's writing," said Mr Brown, quickly tearing open the letter as the family gathered round.

"It is from Otto," he said.

"What's it say Dad?" asked Josie and John, almost in unison.

"Just a minute and I'll read it. He's escaped to France. One of his brothers and his entire family have been arrested by the Nazis. Otto and his mother and sister, his other brother and his family are all in France seeking asylum.

Reading further he stopped suddenly.

"Oh no!" exclaimed Mr Brown.

"What is it?" asked his wife.

"He says he and his brother intend to return to Germany to try to rescue the others, once they have got permission to stay in France."

"Cool like the 'Scarlet Pimpernel' sighed Josie, who's romantic fancy was already creating a film-like scenario, with Uncle Otto, heavily disguised, rescuing his brother and family.

At school on Monday Josie had another furious exchange with the hated Miss Greenaway.

"My Uncle Otto's brother and his entire family have been arrested by the Nazis. In spite of what you say, Hitler is killing as many Jews as he can." Josie paused only to draw breath, so great was her feeling of frustration. "It's time we did something about it," she finished.

Her friends began to rally behind her, there were murmurs of agreement.

For a moment Josie felt like Joan of Arc leading her troops into battle.

"I'm very sorry to hear that, Josie," said Miss Greenaway. "What do you think should be done about this situation with Germany?" she asked the class.

There were shouts of "We should go to war," but the less aggressive pupils were all for continued negotiations in the hope that war could be avoided.

At play-time Josie became the centre of attraction.

"You told her Josie," said one of her classmates admiringly.

"I wonder what will happen in the end. Do you think Hitler might start invading other countries?" asked one of the girls.

"I wonder what England will do if he does," said another.

"Declare war I should think," said Penny.

"Do you think there'll be a war, Josie?" asked another of her classmates, who was greatly impressed by what she considered was Josie's inside information.

10

War Clouds Gather

Anxiety about the possibility of war was once more occupying the wireless and newsreel headlines.

There was trouble in Czechoslovakia where there had been pro German demonstrations by other German communities living in the west of the country. The Czechoslovak authorities had recently declared martial law.

In the crisis that followed three men were ranged against Hitler: Neville Chamberlain the British Prime Minister, Edward Daldier the French Prime Minister and the Czech President Edvard Benes.

Benes did not want to risk the whole of Czechoslovakia for the non-Czech part. The British and French Prime Ministers had some sympathy with the Sudeten, Germany's desire for what they termed 'National Self Determination!'

It was becoming obvious that their main object was to preserve peace in an effort to re-arm their own armies. Further alarm for the British population was an announcement on the wireless and notices in the local paper giving details of the issue of gas-masks to the entire population.

The Brown family duly collected theirs from the distribution point.

Despite the apparent normality of everyday life, everyone was well aware that in many countries things were far from normal. The family listened to Mr Chamberlain's speech on September 27th: "How horrible it is that we should be digging trenches and trying on gas-masks because of a quarrel in a far off country between people of whom we know nothing," he said.

Two days later he flew to Munich to confer with Hitler, Daldier and the Italian dictator Mussolini. The next day it was announced in a news bulletin that just after midnight an agreement had been signed giving Hitler 11,500 square miles of Czechoslovakian territory. Mr Chamberlain had a further meeting with Hitler the next day in which the two leaders agreed 'to continue our efforts to remove all possible sources of difference' and thus to contribute to assure the peace of Europe.

On his return home Mr Chamberlain had reassuring words for the British people. The following morning the national newspapers were emblazoned with uplifting headlines:

'Chamberlain says I believe it is peace for our time.'

'Peace with honour' said another.

Everyone heaved a sigh of relief, perhaps they wouldn't need the gas-masks or the Anderson air-raid shelters which were now being issued. In the House of Commons, however, conflicting reports were emerging via the newspaper and wireless reports. Winston Churchill was stated to have said: "England has been offered the choice between war and shame. She has chosen shame - and will get war."

The news that other areas of Czechoslovakia were to be given to Poland and Hungary, costing Czechoslovakia a third of its population and large parts of its industry, still brought no help from either Britain or France.

Josie and many of her school friends were of the opinion that Britain should have put up a fight on behalf of the Czechs. Josie's mother, on the other hand, was all for protecting the peace at any price and for Britain not to involve herself in other people's affairs. For most people of the age of Josie's parents the horrors of the 'Great War' were still uppermost in their minds.

Mr Chamberlain sincerely but naively believed that the agreement he had signed with Adolf Hitler would bring lasting peace and indeed many people were lulled into a false sense of security.

October saw German troops marching into Czechoslovakia, to take the largely German speaking area of Sudetenland.

At Jimmy's factory the boss was offering a five pound bonus to any of his employees who joined the Territorial Army. Jimmy, figuring that if war came, his age group would be the first to be conscripted, reasoned that he might as well take advantage of this offer, which also guaranteed time off with pay, needed for training. Because of his experience of first aid in the Boys' Brigade, Jimmy was duly drafted into the Medical Corps. After some weeks he arrived home from an evening training session resplendent in uniform of khaki and shiny black boots.

An important event was to take place in October, namely the opening of the new City Hall, which momentarily diverted the attention of the citizens of Norwich from the possibility of world conflict.

The opening would be at the culmination of Civic Week, for this short period all thoughts of war were banished. At last the great day arrived. The opening ceremony was to be performed by King George VI accompanied by Queen Elizabeth. As the opening day, October 29th, was a Saturday and the ceremony was at midday, this enabled even the working population to join the crowds who thronged the streets and market place to see the King and Queen.

The fact that both the King and Queen were making this visit was indeed a great honour and the citizens of Norwich were fully aware that this was the first time since the visit of Charles II and his consort in 1671 that a reigning King and Queen had made a joint visit to the city.

Josie, John and their mother got to the market place early to get a place at the front of the crowd. John had a Union Jack to wave. Josie, although fiercely patriotic, felt she was too old to wave a flag.

It seemed ages getting to midday although the banter from the crowds made the waiting less of a bore. By eleven-thirty all the officials and their ladies were seated in the enclosure outside the City Hall.

Suddenly the band of the Royal Norfolks began to play the National Anthem and the school children burst into song. The crowds pressed forward all hoping to catch a glimpse of the King and Queen. After a speech of welcome from the Lord Mayor, the King declared the new building officially open.

Jimmy and his father had not bothered to attend the opening ceremony as they knew that the King would be attending the football match at Carrow Road between Millwall and Norwich City. Being avid supporters of their local club, they concentrated on getting there as early as possible to obtain a good view of both the match and the King. Sadly Norwich lost the match by two-nil but fortunately the King had already left before either goal was scored.

At school there seemed to be a determined effort on the part of the entire staff to make sure the general gloomy atmosphere reigning, because of the world situation, did not permeate the school's preparations for Christmas.

The art class, in particular, had been enjoyable for the past month. Christmas cards, calendars, paper chains and lanterns had all been produced with great enthusiasm by the pupils. By the beginning of December the school itself was looking quite festive. The decorations produced in the art class were in place and the assembly hall boasted a large colourful Christmas tree.

The days grew shorter and the weather colder as Christmas approached. To Josie it seemed to lack the usual feeling of excitement. In the same way that Guy Fawkes night had seemed to lack something this year. She tried to analyse the reason for this lack of enthusiasm. Could it be that she was getting too grown-up to get the same enjoyment from these celebrations? The world was in such a state that it seemed almost sinful to be thinking in terms of enjoying oneself. Perhaps, thought Josie, that could account for the way she was feeling.

Her parents, on the other hand, were reacting in a totally different way. If war was as inevitable as it was beginning to look, then having a really splendid Christmas while the family was still intact assumed overwhelming importance to Mr and Mrs Brown. The preparations were more elaborate than ever before.

On Christmas Day there was a rather forced air of jollity. Everyone tried hard to put their worries behind them, at least for the day.

For Edwin it must have been quite an ordeal to meet all the relatives assembled at Josie's house but he showed no sign of his anxiety and carried the whole thing off with great aplomb. After tea they settled down in the front room, John and his friend Albert busy with their Meccanno set. Jimmy sprawled in an armchair, only stirring himself occasionally to tell the boys which bit went where.

Gazing into the flickering fire Jimmy said, "Wonder what we'll all be doing next Christmas!"

144

"Depends if there's a war I suppose," said Edwin.

"It looks as if there probably will be."

"Hope it lasts till I can join up," said John.

"Let's not talk about it," pleaded Josie.

"OK, but not talking about it won't make it go away you know," said Jimmy.

They lapsed into a gloomy silence.

On Old Year's Night there was, once again, a supreme effort to pretend everything was normal. Mr Brown did his usual 'first footing' at twelve o'clock. The family group was enlarged by Edwin and Jimmy's new girlfriend. It seemed a sad irony to wish each other a happy New Year.

Though Mrs Brown still clung to her belief in Mr Chamberlain's power of negotiating, most people were becoming disillusioned with him. They felt he was weak and his excuse that Britain had no treaty with Czechoslovakia was wearing very thin.

By March German troops had occupied the whole of Czechoslovakia. With the whole of Austria and Czechoslovakia now in his hands, Hitler turned his attention to Poland.

All over England householders were being issued with Anderson shelters to be used in case of aerial bombardment should war become a reality. The shelters made of galvanised iron, were delivered in sections which had to be bolted together. Then a hole had to be dug in the garden large enough to take the assembled shelter. Mr Brown and Jimmy, with occasional help from Edwin, had soon dug their hole and got the shelter in place, covering it with the soil from the hole. The shelter was partly above ground level to allow for entry. The floor which started as trampled down soil was eventually covered with an old piece of carpet. A curtain made from black-out material covered the entrance to make sure no chink of light could be seen by enemy planes, should they come. No other comforts were added at this stage because there was still hope in every heart that the shelter would never be needed, that the threat of war would somehow miraculously recede.

Having made a satisfactory job of their own shelter the Brown's labour force moved next door and, with Duncan's enthusiastic efforts to help, managed to erect another shelter for the use of Duncan and his mother. In spite of the gloomy news bulletins and the crop of air-raid shelters springing up in every back

145

g

garden, life on the whole went on much as usual.

Hitler, in the meantime, was still pursuing his policy of threats and conquests. He now had his eye on a corridor of land that gave Poland its only access to the sea at Danzig. On March 21st he stepped up his demands that Danzig be restored to Germany and that Germany be allowed to build road and rail links to East Prussia across Polish territory. Poland, of course, refused to allow this.

Two days later Hitler scored a notable success on the other side of East Prussia. He had been threatening the use of force against Lithuania in answer to his demands for the return of the Memet district which Germany had been compelled to cede after World War I. Fearing that Germany would now threaten force to seize Danzig the Polish government warned Hitler that any such threat would mean war.

On March 31st Britain promised Poland immediate military aid if Germany made any move against them. France also made a similar agreement with the Poles. This positive stance seemed to deter Hitler from making any further moves against Poland at least for the time being.

Everyone in Britain rested a bit easier in their beds. Perhaps the whole thing would now fizzle out. On April 7th, which was Good Friday, they were forced to reassess the situation. Far from fizzling out, it now seemed to be escalating.

Mussolini, taking a leaf out of Hitler's book, had ambitions to expand into the Balkans and the news broadcast of the day announced that Italian troops had entered Albania and annexed it. With Romania and Greece now clearly under threat from Italy, Britain and France gave them the same guarantees that they had given Poland. A hint of how serious the European situation had become was emphasised by an announcement in May of limited conscription of males into the army.

On May 22nd Hitler and Mussolini signed a pact, guaranteeing to support each other in any future way.

At school, Penny, who was very good at art, had decided to have a shot at passing the entrance exam for the Junior Art School. The twins, interested in a clerical career, were attempting the exam for Commercial School.

"Why don't you try for the art school?" Penny pleaded.

"I don't think I'd pass, I'm nowhere near as good as you."

"Oh, come on Josie, you're pretty good you know, I'm sure you could pass."

Horrified at the possibility of losing not only Penny but the twins as well and being left to struggle on alone against Miss Greenaway, Josie decided it was at least worth a try.

Having persuaded her father that she was serious in her endeavour to at least have a shot at the exam, Josie waited anxiously for the day of the exam to arrive. When it did the girls found it was much less of an ordeal than they were expecting. The atmosphere at the school seemed very relaxed. The collection of nervous pupils waiting instructions to commence the first drawing, of a vase of flowers, included boys as well as girls. This pleased Josie whose memories of co-education were much happier than the all-girl Senior School. The fact that the all-boy Technical School was housed in the same building seemed like an added bonus.

The exam took the whole day to complete.

"How did you get on?" Josie's mother asked anxiously as soon as she got home.

"Oh fine, it was all quite easy," said Josie airily. "Mum, you should see the school, it's lovely, some of the rooms look out on to the river. All the teachers were terribly polite, one of them called us young ladies. It didn't seem like being at school at all."

In a short time, to the girls' relief, the exam results were announced. All four had passed and when play-time arrived, they were busy congratulating each other when the dreaded Miss Greenaway approached.

"Well done girls, I hear you've all got through."

"Yes Miss," they chorused politely to Miss Greenaway as she paused to talk to them.

"I hope you'll enjoy your new school," she said.

"Well, beggar me," said Josie as soon as she was out of ear-shot, "that's the first kind word she's ever said to me."

Penny grinned.

"Probably because you'll be leaving and she's glad to see the back of you."

For the rest of term Josie surprised even herself by establishing a reasonable relationship with her arch-enemy. Miss Greenaway even enquired after her uncle and expressed sorrow when Josie told her what had happened.

147

"It's a terrible world to be living in," said Miss Greenaway.

Josie and Penelope, for once, were quite looking forward to the end of the summer holiday so they could start their new school.

Edwin teased Josie by saying, "Do you remember when you were due to start at St. Augustines and we went to Sea Palling and you were miserable all day thinking about it?"

"I was not," said Josie indignantly.

"Yes you were, you were scared stiff."

"I was a bit apprehensive," said Josie standing on her dignity.

"Apprehensive's a good word for it," laughed Edwin. "You don't seem bothered about changing schools this time."

"I'm not, I'm really quite looking forward to it."

"I'm not sure I am," said Edwin.

"Why not?"

"You'll be in a mixed class again. I'll have to keep an eye on you with the boys!"

"Don't be silly Edwin, they'll all be so young, even the second year's will only be a year older than me."

"You prefer 'em mature do you Josie?"

Josie had woken up to the fact that this was all just a tease, when Edwin put an arm around her.

"I'm pleased for you really," he laughed. "If this is what you really want to do."

During the holidays Josie had been invited to join Edwin's parents and Edwin for several runs out into the country in their Austin Seven. Looking like a little square box on wheels outside, it was surprising how comfortable it was inside. When Josie sat in the back with Edwin they seemed to be in a little world of their own. They were able to picnic in lots of places which were accessible only by car. It was a lovely summer break marred only by worry about the whereabouts of Uncle Otto and the increasingly tense situation in Germany.

On the home front there was much activity. Most houses now had an air-raid shelter at the bottom of the garden. Many of these were quite comfortably fitted out with bunks or mattresses in case it became necessary to spend the night there. The Browns had installed a primus stove and tea-making facilities. No matter what the crisis, a nice cup of tea was seen as a first priority.

During this period of comparative calm the Western Allies were tentatively discussing pacts with Soviet Russia. But on

August 23rd a stunned world heard that Molotov and Ribbentrop had signed a non-aggression pact in Moscow between Germany and Russia.

Britain began to speed up its preparations for a possible war. Reservists were called back to the Forces. On August 24th an organisation, recently formed, known as the ARP (standing for Air Raid Precautions) were put on full alert.

Each day, it had to be admitted, war seemed ever more likely. The Nazi-Soviet pact removed any fear that Hitler might have about waging war on two fronts, he seemed to be in a state of euphoria about having stolen a march on the Western Allies. On August 26th Hitler gave his generals orders to attack Poland, but at last Britain caused him to delay.

Pressure was brought to bear, not only from Britain, but also from the USA, France and even the Pope, for Germany to settle its differences with Poland by negotiation. Britain converted the guarantee, given to Poland in March, into a formal alliance. Though Hitler did not believe that the Western Allies would go to war for Poland's independence, he made the gesture of asking the Poles to send an emissary to Berlin to settle the Danzig question. This was a very uneasy truce and the world held its breath waiting for the outcome.

During the warm but troubled days of summer, Josie and Edwin were happy to escape the war-talk, by taking bike-rides to the seaside to visit Edwin's aunt and to the country to see Grandma. At Grandma's little cottage after a good dinner, they would walk hand in hand down to Tacolneston's leafy lanes, forgetting for a little while the problems of the world, content in each other's company. If the day was excessively hot they usually made their way back to the orchard to lie full length under the shady apple-trees. Peering through the faintly rustling foliage at the cloudless blue sky they wondered how much longer the fragile peace could last.

Usually lulled into a state of blissful contentment and almost on the point of dozing off, Grandma would summon them for tea. She always kept a careful eye on the young lovers. Though convinced of Edwin's honourable intentions toward her grand-daughter, she knew that the present highly volatile situation could put an uncomfortable burden on young people. Added to this she was not sure that Josie was either old enough or experienced enough to deal with her more mature boyfriend. But she needn't have worried, in matters of the heart Edwin was much less experienced than Josie, to him a kiss and a cuddle was being very daring.

One of their other favourite pastimes whilst in the orchard was to pick dandelion 'clocks' (which for some obscure reason were called 'Billy Busters'). As they blew the seeds away they chanted, instead of the usual 'she loves me, she loves me not', 'there will be a war, there won't be a war', carefully making sure that the last few seeds confirmed that there wouldn't be a war.

Finally it was time to resume schooling.

Josie and Penny met at the telephone box at eight-fifteen as arranged, thus allowing plenty of time to get there, find the bicycle sheds and assemble in the playground as instructed. It was the first time each had seen the other in school uniform. "Hello Penny, don't we look 'posh'?" grinned Josie.

Reaching the school, they dismounted and pushed their bikes past the impressive front entrance, through the opening between the school and St. Andrews Hall, arriving at the playground at the back. In front of the high stone wall which divided Art School and Technical School pupils were the cycle sheds. There were plenty of empty spaces, there was still twenty minutes to go before school commenced.

Soon there were fifteen or so new girls and almost as many boys patiently waiting for the appearance of a teacher or a bell, or whatever it was that would summon them to class.

They had not long to wait, through the gate in the wall it was possible to see the lines of Technical School boys beginning to move off toward the school building. Threading his way through the lines of boys was a tall, dark-haired man. He came through the gate.

"Right," he called. "Let's have two lines please. Second years here, first years this side."

Josie and Penny joined the line, there was a great hubbub of chatter.

"Less noise please," said the teacher. "Second years shut up please, how are the new people going to hear what I'm saying? Right, lead off Colin if you please," he patted the shoulder of the boy at the head of the line of second years.

Up two flights of not very wide stairs went the procession.

Finally, reaching a corridor running the whole length of the building, the walls on either side were covered with pictures and designs obviously produced by the pupils. Finally they entered what could only be described as a large classroom. Most of the children coming from ordinary senior schools were used to enormous assembly halls which also served as gyms for P.T.

There were lines of chairs facing a raised wooden platform, upon which a small man was seated, surrounded by three other men and one woman, all wearing black scholastic gowns. They were joined by the teacher who had been on playground duty also now attired in a black gown.

Josie was most impressed, she had never seen teachers dressed like this, except in films. She would dearly have liked to make some remark to Penny, but all the assembled pupils were now absolutely silent, so Josie curbed her enthusiasm.

The small man stood up - he wasn't much taller standing up than he was sitting down. He had a round cheerful little face and receding grey hair.

"I want to welcome all the new students," he said. "I hope you will be happy with us for the next two years. You will find that you are working in a more relaxed atmosphere than you experienced at the schools you have attended previously. Because you will now be specialising in Art subjects, there is less need for rigid timetables. You will find your tutors will treat you as young adults, not children, and in return they will expect you to behave in a suitably responsible manner. First year students, your form tutor is Mr Moore, who you will have encountered this morning on playground duty."

All eyes turned toward the tall dark-haired man standing at the far end of the platform. Josie nudged Penelope and grinned, each remembering the cheerful un-teacher-like voice saying 'Shut up second years and get moving'. Things were looking up thought Josie, 'I'm very willing to exchange stuffy old Miss Greenaway for him.'

One thing Josie had noticed was that they were no longer called pupils and teachers as they had been all her school life so far. She would have to get used to thinking in terms of students and tutors. Sounded very grown-up thought Josie.

The headmaster was nearing the end of his speech.

"Thank you for your attention. One final thing, I hope that this year's second year students will be as helpful as possible to the new young people we have in our midst. I would ask you to remember how you were feeling this time last year when you were the new intake. Perhaps you will take over Mr Moore."

"Thank you headmaster," said Mr Moore, rising from his chair. "Right, second years, off you go now, you know where your classroom is for this year."

The room gradually cleared leaving the thirty or so new students awaiting their instructions.

"We're in the first room on the right-hand side of the corridor, follow me please."

He led the way into a classroom which overlooked the river. The newly-named 'students' crowded to look out of the window.

"Kindly find seats for yourselves, you will have plenty of time in the future to admire the view."

Josie and Penny managed to find desks next to each other.

Before the girls had completed their first week at their new school, on September 1st the thing which all the world had been dreading happened at dawn - Hitler gave his generals orders to invade Poland.

Britain continued making preparations for what now seemed almost inevitable war, evacuation of children from London and other large cities began. At night a black-out was imposed. All street lighting was extinguished and all public entertainment was closed. Gas masks now had to be carried at all times. Mrs Brown had purchased a roll of black material and had made black-out curtains for all the windows, these were now in place.

On Sunday morning, September 3rd, Josie and John, despite the precarious state of the country, made their usual visit to their grandparents. When they arrived, they found an air of gloom, Grandpa couldn't even work up any enthusiasm for his beloved Canaries.

A statement by the Prime Minister was expected at 11.00 a.m. Josie, John and their grandparents clustered around the little wireless set awaiting an announcement. Neville Chamberlain's voice was heard at last. In a voice charged with emotion he said: "This morning the British Ambassador in Berlin handed the German government a final note, stating that unless the British Government heard from them by 11.00 o'clock that they were prepared at once to withdraw their troops from Poland, a state of war would exist between us."

There was a slight quiver in the Prime Minister's voice as he continued:

"I have to tell you that no such undertaking has been received and that consequently this country is at war with Germany."

"Coo! war at last," said John with some enthusiasm.

The Prime Minister continued:

"It is evil things that we shall be fighting against - brute force, bad faith, injustice, suppression and persecution; and against them I am certain that right will prevail."

As the calm, quiet voice finished, Grandad said. "I wonder how many of our young men will be lost this time. Your father survived last time, this time it'll be your brother who has to go."

Grannie looked near to tears.

"I think you should go straight home to your mother now."

Josie and John had never covered the distance between Grandma's home in such a short space of time. John was quite convinced that German planes would be overhead any minute, so he raced along, keeping an anxious eye on the sky.

Although common sense told Josie that an immediate attack of this kind was not within the realms of possibility, nevertheless she felt her heart beating fast as they hurried home over the Dolphin bridge. One heard such terrible tales of the power of the Nazis that really no one knew what to expect.

Edwin, who had been due to call for Josie after dinner, was waiting when they arrived home.

"Oh, Josie," he said sadly, giving her arm a comforting squeeze, wanting to kiss her but afraid to do so in front of her parents.

Jimmy had been instructed that, if war was declared, he should report immediately to his unit. He appeared on the stairs carrying his packed kit-bag, his respirator and tin hat slung over his shoulder, looking every inch a soldier. His mother burst into tears.

"Come on Mum," said Jimmy embarrassed by this show of emotion. "It'll all be over before you know I've gone."

"I hope so," sighed his mother.

"Look after yourself boy," said his father gruffly.

"Cheerio Josie, Edwin, John," he ruffled his brother's blond curls affectionately. "Probably be able to get home at the weekends till we get posted," he added quite cheerfully. He straightened his forage cap, heaved his kit-bag on his shoulder and marched off down the road to wait for the bus.

Edwin stayed for dinner, which was a very gloomy meal, with Mrs Brown trying very hard not to let her emotions get the better of her. The only cheerful one seemed to be John, who had quickly recovered from the initial shock and was making plans to capitalise on the novelty of having a soldier brother, before it all became common-place.

In the evening at 6 o'clock the King broadcast a message to the Empire.

"For the sake of all that we ourselves hold dear," said the King, "and of the World's order and peace, it is unthinkable that we should refuse to meet the challenge." There was a slight pause "To this high purpose, I now call my people at home and my peoples across the seas, I ask them to stand firm and united in this time of trial."

As the weeks went by, apart from reports of war from other countries and the inconveniences at home, life went on much as usual. Large silver-coloured barrage balloons floated majestically over the city. With these and the artillery emplacements springing up on the outskirts of the city, the population slowly began to feel more secure.

The autumn seemed more beautiful than usual, the days balmier, the colours more vibrant; perhaps this heightened awareness was because of the state of the world and the feeling that one lived for today as tomorrow was very uncertain.

Jimmy, still stationed locally, managed to get home most weekends, either on Saturday or Sunday for tea. On several occasions he brought one of his new-found friends home with him. Edwin began to have misgivings about Josie's ability to remain true to him in the face of this undoubtedly attractive soldiery parading at the Brown's house most weekends.

The weather got colder as the year drew to a close. Christmas looked like being better than had been anticipated as Jimmy had still not been posted away from his home town.

Since September there had been very little in the war news to shout about. The RAF seemed to spend most of their time dropping leaflets on the German population, with as far as one could see, very little result. The Navy, organising a convoy system, set about hunting down U-Boats. In September they had their first success by sinking a U-Boat, but this had been followed by two disasters when the Aircraft Carrier HMS *Courageous* was sunk, and even more dramatic was the loss of the Battleship *Royal Oak* in Scappa Flow.

The army, meanwhile, was on the move. Now known as the British Expeditionary Force, they had crossed the Channel to France during the second half of September.

As the first war-time Christmas approached the first big story of success was thrilling the tired and somewhat despondent nation. On December 14th the wireless news bulletin stated that the German pocket battleship *Admiral Graf Spee* had been intercepted by the British crusaders *Achilles*, *Ajax* and *Exeter*. Although the armament of the *Graf Spee* was superior to all three British ships put together, the *Graf Spee* had broken off the encounter and raced for the sanctuary of Montevideo harbour, but not before it had crippled the *Exeter*. Seventy-two hours later the wireless reported that the *Graf Spee* had been turned out of the neutral harbour. Afraid to face British ships waiting for him her Commander had scuttled his ship in the estuary of the River Plate and had then committed suicide.

The run up to Christmas had been very different from last year. At their previous schools there had been class parties, nativity plays, paper chains and Chinese lanterns to be made.

At Art School, however, things were rather more sedate. A large Christmas tree, very artistically trimmed, had been placed in the foyer. On the Art School landing the students had arranged a nativity scene with scenery and figures they had made themselves.

Mr Hobbis, in his end of term speech, thanked everyone for their efforts in making the building delightfully festive. He wished everyone a happy Christmas and asked them to remember the brave boys in the Forces in their prayers. He hoped they would return refreshed and eager to work at the end of their Christmas holiday.

When Josie finally got home later that afternoon her spirits were considerably improved.

In the run up to Christmas the most popular request played on the wireless was for Gracie Fields singing a song that began with the words, 'I'm sending a letter to Santa Claus to send my Daddy back to me'. No matter how many times Josie heard it sung, it still brought a lump to her throat.

In spite of the state the world seemed to be in, everyone made a special effort for Christmas. Various items of food were beginning to get a bit short, ration-books had been issued but were not yet being used. Josie put up the Christmas tree and carefully trimmed it, plugging in the set of lights they had purchased last year.

Going for a walk on Christmas Eve with Edwin, Josie was suddenly struck by the difference between this year and last Christmas. When they had walked after dark last year they had played a joyous game of looking in the uncurtained windows of the houses to see which ones had illuminated Christmas trees. This year there was nothing but blackness, every window was closed and shuttered because of the black-out. Josie thought this was one of the saddest sights of the whole Christmas season.

Soon after Christmas, Jimmy failed to turn up for tea, as was his practice on Sunday afternoon. The family were only slightly perturbed as this had happened several times before when Jimmy was on unexpected duty or confined to barracks for some misdemeanour. They fully expected he would turn up the following Sunday. However, on Thursday a letter was received from Jimmy to say he had been posted and was now stationed at a place they had never heard of called Hetton-Le-Hole.

On January 8th the ration books, already issued to every adult and child in Britain, came into use. The first items to be rationed were butter or marg. 4 ozs, sugar 12 ozs, bacon or ham 4 ozs.

At the beginning of April the lull in the German's activities came to an abrupt end as they invaded Norway and Denmark. In Denmark it was an almost bloodless victory for the Germans. The slight resistance put up by the Danes soon came to an end when King Christian broadcast to his people to say that resistance would be hopeless and that the German occupation had been accepted by the Danish Government under protest.

It was, however, a different story in Norway when on April 9th, aided by traitors led by Major Quisling, the Nazis seized Oslo. Called on to surrender, King Haakon refused to have any dealings with the Nazis.

Josie saw all the action in dramatic fashion in the newsreel at the Haymarket. Edwin, feeling rather flush with his week's wages and money received in tips from his customers, had taken Josie for a special tea and then had splashed out for a double seat on the back row at the Haymarket. It was the first time he had dared to suggest a double seat to Josie. Apart from feeling slightly embarrassed at the ticket office when Edwin had requested a double seat, once they were seated in the darkened theatre Josie felt this was quite a cosy arrangement. She had no objection to Edwin's arm placed around her, especially as everyone occupying the double seats seemed to be likewise engaged.

After the Pathé newsreel the theatre lights came up and, to a great crescendo of noise, the theatre organ rose out of the floor with the organist working frantically at the pedals. There were the usual raucous remarks from a few members of the audience, which were completely ignored by the organist, who worked his way steadily through his repertoire and with a stirring finale disappeared into the floor again.

In May the Prime Minister made a speech to the House of Commons explaining the Allied failure in Norway, at the end of which a Division was taken, as a result of which Mr Chamberlain resigned. By evening the whole of Britain was aware of the situation by wireless broadcasts. In his farewell address to the nation Neville Chamberlain sounded tired and dispirited. He announced the name of the man who would take his place: 'Winston Churchill'.

The news on the evening of May 10th informed the nation that German panzers were pouring through the Low Countries. French and British Divisions were moving up to Belgium. For Mr Brown this brought back memories of the 1914 war, he felt thankful that his own son was not among the British Divisions.

The German drive pushed on toward Northern France, as Mr Churchill sorted out his new coalition Government. When he had completed this task, he made the first of the many memorable speeches he would make during the course of the war.

Josie carefully noted in her diary word for word the stirring speech from the new Prime Minister:

"I have nothing to offer but blood, toil, sweat.and tears. We have before us an ordeal of a most grievous kind, we have before us many many long months of struggle and suffering. You ask what is our policy? I will say it is to wage war, by land, sea and air with all our might and all the strength that God can give us and to wage war against a monstrous tyranny never surpassed in the

157

dark lamentable catalogue of human crime. That is our policy!"

This speech, made by an orator with the power to send shivers down your spine, was a totally different 'kettle of fish' from the weak, tired tones of his predecessor. No matter how grave the situation, there was at the helm a man with the power to inspire the nation to even greater effort.

The BBC, which had set up the Home Service station just prior to the outbreak of war, had broadcast Mr Churchill's speech in full. They now had a new format for the news bulletins. The newscasters, whose voices had become familiar to listeners since the outbreak of war, were now allowed to give their names when reading the news. Thus, for the rest of the war, they said, "This is the BBC Home Service. Here is the news and this is . . . reading it." The names of Bruce Belfrage, John Snagge, Alva Lidell and Freddie Grisewood became as familiar as any film-star and almost as glamorous.

The wireless, the newspapers and the cinema newsreels kept everyone up to date with the war news. For those who were regular cinema-goers, each week's newsreel reports were not only concerned with world news but included information about things at home, the work of the Auxiliary Fire Service and the Air-raid Wardens. Attention was also given to information about how to eke out the week's food ration. In newspapers and magazines the suggestions for pea-pod soup, soya-bean loaf, potato and chocolate pudding and carrot jam, sometimes proved to be more palatable than they sounded.

The wireless provided another source of comfort with programmes like 'Workers Playtime', meant principally for those working in munitions factories, but also listened to by most housewives. Songs were composed or altered to suit the occasion. Vera Lynn, who had become very popular and was now known as the 'Forces Sweetheart', sang heart-warming songs like *There'll Always be an England* and *There'll Be Blue-birds Over the White Cliffs of Dover*. Arthur Askey had changed the words of *Run, Rabbit Run* to 'Run, Adolf Run'. Everyone now knew the words to *We'll Hang Out the Washing on the Siegfried Line!*

Comedy shows on the wireless and variety shows at the theatres which had re-opened had performers like Robb Wilton, with his deeply depressed voice he always opened his act with the words, "The day war broke out, my missus said to me . . ." What his missus said varied from show to show, but in the end he had only to start with "The day war broke out", to be drowned in peals of laughter.

The British had always had a great capacity to laugh in the face of disaster and they got plenty of practice as the war progressed. In addition to the 'Home' service on the wireless, there was now a 'Forces' station, this specialised in record requests from personnel in the three Services.

Belgium and Holland clung desperately to their neutrality until May 10th when the news flashed around the world that Germany had commenced an attack on these two countries. At the request of Belgium's King Leopold for help, French and British troops hurriedly moved into Belgium. The Pathé newsreel had pictures of British troops receiving a tumultuous welcome from the Belgians. The next week there were reports of heavy fighting at the River Meuse and in the Ardennes. The might of the German air-force, the Luftwaffe, was unleashed against unprotected Belgian cities, including Brussels. There were reports and harrowing pictures of German planes machine-gunning helpless refugees. A few days later there was a statement from King Leopold announcing that Belgian resistance had ended, followed by a report that the Belgian Government had escaped to Paris.

If anything, Holland was faring even worse than Belgium. Their attack had also begun on May 10th with dive-bombers, tanks and mechanised columns invading neutral Holland. There was news of merciless bombing of civilians and the encirclement of the small, ill-equipped Dutch army who, though hopelessly outnumbered, were putting up a fight. To add to their defence, they opened the dykes and allowed the water to sweep over the land.

German paratroopers showered from the skies to terrify and confuse the population. It was becoming increasingly obvious that Germany had long been planning this invasion, they had Nazis planted everywhere. Thousands of disguised troops had been in hiding on Dutch barges and Fifth Columnists were assisting the paratroopers when they landed.

Soon the enemy were in control of all the strategic sites. Their attempt to capture Queen Wilhelmina was foiled by the British Navy who sent a destroyer to bring the Royal party to England. Once again, the Navy had provided a little light in an otherwise dark period.

On the evening of May 14th the Dutch nation gave up the hopeless struggle in an effort to avoid the further massacre of the refugees.

Realising the war was taking a turn for the worse, the defence of Britain was assuming greater importance. Anthony Eden broadcast on May 14th an appeal for men to join the Local Defence Volunteers. Police stations all over Britain were besieged with men anxious to join this new force, who would be trained and armed to face a possible German invasion. In every town and village groups of men, either too old or too young to join the Army, could be seen drilling, armed with a motley collection of firearms, knives and homemade coshes. On August 24th, Mr Churchill's name for this civilian army was officially adopted. Henceforth, they would be called the 'Home Guard'.

All the news lately had been very confusing partly because much of it was withheld from the general public on the grounds of security. It was, however, becoming obvious that things were not going well in France and the news which was managing to trickle through was all very depressing. By the 19th the reports said that British troops fighting with their backs to the sea were withdrawing to a coastal town named Dunkirk.

There had been an air of high drama at school when a rumour was rife that one of the Technical School tutors was missing. It was well known that he was the proud owner of a Broad's cruiser and the rumour persisted that he had left in his boat in the early hours of the morning for a special assignment. Groups of excited schoolboys discussed the situation at break-time and their missing tutor was rapidly assuming the mantle of hero in their eyes.

Soon it became obvious just what 'special assignment' he had been drafted to help with, as the news broke to the world that 335,000 soldiers had been rescued from the Dunkirk beaches and brought safely back to England by, as the report put it, 'anything which would float'. Most of the small privately owned boats were manned by their owners. Mercifully, the sea was calm, thus most of the ships setting out from England arrived safely at Dunkirk. The smaller ships ferried the exhausted troops out to the larger ships which couldn't get near the beach because of shallow water.

The wireless was turned on from morning until bedtime in

most houses. What might have been considered a terrible defeat was rapidly assuming the status of a glorious victory.

Although the wireless reports were realistic, it was not until the following week at the Haymarket, watching the newsreel, that Josie and Edwin were able to witness the full horror of the evacuation from Dunkirk.

On his first day back at School, the Technical School's own hero teacher, Mr Johnston, was overwhelmed by the welcome he received from his students.

At the cinema the newsreels showed the scenes as the troops landed at unnamed ports in England. The whole population had turned out to welcome them home. The Salvation Army and WVS had piles of food and gallons of hot tea for their arrival. There were gifts of chocolates and cigarettes for the weary men as they filed down the gangplanks. Crowds cheered and flags waved, homemade banners proclaimed, 'Bravo' and 'Welcome Home'. Amazingly, the exhausted men managed to smile and wave to the assembled crowds.

Mr Churchill, in his usual blunt way, did not attempt to dress up Dunkirk as anything other than a defeat. It had brought home to everyone that the war for survival had truly begun. The Home Front looked like becoming the War Front at any moment as the threat of invasion loomed. Signposts and place names were removed or painted out in order to confuse the potential invader.

With France beaten, Hitler believed that Britain couldn't stand alone and would soon come to terms.

Britain now stood alone on the only bridge-head of Western Europe not under Nazi domination. On June 30th the German army invaded and captured the Channel Islands, bringing them even nearer to the British mainland. Hitler believed that Britain couldn't stand alone and would soon surrender.

The enemy broadcasting station poured forth threats against the British. One particular broadcaster was actually British by birth, one William Joyce. His derisive nickname coined by the British press was 'Lord Haw-Haw', this was arrived at because of his most peculiar accent. His clarion call, "Germany calling, Germany calling," sounded like 'Jermany calling, Jermany calling." Needless to say British impressionists had a field-day and did much to ridicule the propaganda issuing from his lips. The Brown family, in common with a large part of the population, listened to these broadcasts, mainly to scoff and wonder what other fantastic lies would be forthcoming.

There was dramatic news of a more personal kind for Josie. Returning from school, she had been confronted by her old friend Aldo.

"Hello Aldo, seems ages since I saw you. How's school?" Josie greeted him cheerfully.

On closer inspection, she realised that Aldo was very close to tears.

"What's up?" inquired Josie, instinctively putting a hand on his shoulder.

A tear trickled down Aldo's cheek.

"We're being interned for the duration of the war," he said.

"Why?" demanded Josie hotly. "Why should they intern you? you're British, you were born here."

"I know," explained Aldo sadly. "But the rest of my family aren't, they're Italian, which makes them enemy aliens."

"Rubbish," said Josie. "Everyone knows they wouldn't do anything against Britain."

"The authorities don't."

"Can't you do anything about it?" asked Josie.

"Well, I don't have to go, but all the others do, so my mother wants me to go with them. Anyway, I couldn't stay here on my own could I? I don't have any relatives in England."

"This rotten war," sighed Josie. "I don't suppose your relatives in Italy want to fight us, do they?"

"I shouldn't think so, but we haven't heard from them for nearly a year."

"Is there anything I can do?" asked Josie.

"Don't s'pose so, I just wanted you to know, Josie." Aldo self-consciously wiped his eyes.

"When do you have to go?"

"We've been told to pack and be ready to close up the house."

Josie hesitated, not quite knowing what to say or do. Suddenly, Aldo seemed like her very best friend again. Her little world seemed to be rapidly disintegrating around her ears.

By next day the whole family had disappeared. It was not until some time later that a letter was delivered to the Browns. There was no indication of where it had come from, it was mainly to assure them that all the family were well, including Aldo, who sent his love to Josie. It concluded with the hope that when this dreadful war was over, they might all meet again.

Workmen appeared at the house and boarded up the windows, the grass in the garden grew knee-high again. Josie worried a lot about what had happened to Aldo and his family, it all seemed so unfair. She wondered if the internment was proving to be too awful: even if the conditions were reasonable, being locked up must be dreadful.

Things were beginning to get tough nearer home, when on July 9th Norwich was bombed, twenty-six people were killed and many more injured. The sirens were now an everyday and every night occurrence and an uninterrupted night's sleep had become a thing of the past. The lists of casualties were displayed in the public library and added to almost every week.

One day when Josie and Penny were cycling home for dinner, they had to throw themselves into a hedge at the side of the road as a German plane with machine guns blazing flew low overhead. When, still shaking, they picked themselves up and retrieved their bikes, Josie swore she had seen an evil smile on the pilot's face as he pulled the trigger. Penny was inclined to think that Josie had done exactly the same as she had, which was to cover her head with her arms and lie face down in the hedgerow. Their lucky escape provided a talking point at school for the next few days.

Shortly after this, Jimmy arrived on the doorstep late one afternoon on seven-day embarkation leave. At the end of seven days he departed for no one knew where.

The weeks passed when a letter from Jimmy finally arrived. Although the letter had been censored and whole sentences deleted, they were able to decipher enough to know that their Jimmy was in an area of warfare which had been much mentioned of late, both on the wireless and in the newspapers.

There had been reports from Libya about the Italians advancing and taking Sollum and Sidi Barrani, where seemingly they were carrying all before them. Suddenly there was a change in their fortunes and General Wavell and his numerically inferior forces broke through and surrounded the Italians. As Jimmy's letter said, 'We're very busy at the moment, at times all hell breaks loose.'

11

The Battle of Britain

Having a few days holiday from school, Josie had spent her morning helping her father in the garden. These days the garden had assumed great importance, almost every inch was taken up with growing vegetables and fruit to augment the somewhat meagre rations.

They had been encouraged to put in an even greater effort by the wireless programme that morning entitled 'The Kitchen Front', introduced by Freddie Grisewood. There had been many useful recipes aimed mostly at using un-rationed fruit and vegetables. Adverts supporting this campaign featured 'Potato Pete' and 'Doctor Carrot'. It was this advert which encouraged people to believe that eating carrots helped you to see in the dark. Pilots who flew night sorties were reported to practically live on a diet of carrots.

Going into the house for dinner in answer to a shout from Mrs Brown, they found the news bulletin on the wireless about to start. The announcer's voice was quiet and controlled, "This morning Britain was attacked by a massed formation of bombers, they were escorted by large fighter formations. No details were given of where exactly they had attacked." The announcer continued, "The enemy formations were attacked by spitfires and Hurricane fighters."

By evening the information was updated with the heartening news that 60 enemy aircraft had been destroyed.

Three days later an even larger formation of aircraft attacked Portland, Weymouth and convoys in the Thames Estuary. Next day came attacks on Dover, Portsmouth and the Isle of Wight. RAF Spitfires and Hurricanes continued to take a heavy toll of the enemy aircraft.

The next attacks concentrated on fighter aerodromes in an effort to destroy fighters on the ground before they had a chance to get airborne.

This period of high activity by the RAF was later to be called the 'Battle of Britain' and Mr Churchill, referring in one of his most famous speeches to those taking part, said, "Never in the field of human conflict was so much owed by so many to so few."

After the war when many an inspiring speech would be forgotten, this one quotation would be quoted word for word by anyone who had lived through this period. It so perfectly summed up the feeling of the nation at that time.

As the last vestiges of summer began to disappear, it was becoming apparent that the RAF had gained the upper hand against the Luftwaffe.

Amid the general feeling of satisfaction at the outcome of the air battles of the past months came the horrifying news of the sinking of the passenger liner *City of Benaves*, whilst engaged in evacuating children to Canada. The announcement said that of the ninety children and nine escorts, it was feared that eighty-three of the children and seven of the escorts had been lost. Later in the day further broadcasts spoke of the horror and indignation that a German submarine captain could torpedo a ship which was over six hundred miles from land, in a tempestuous sea, in which passengers had very little chance of survival.

In October, the Luftwaffe switched its attention to night raids. Many famous buildings, including Buckingham Palace, were bombed. The loss of life among the civilian population from these night raids was roughly seven times greater than the casualties from the daylight raids. By this time, the reports stated that two thousand, three hundred and seventy-five German planes had been shot down and the RAF had established complete superiority over the Luftwaffe.

Despite the hardships being borne by the civilian population, no one lost track of what was happening to the allied forces during this period. Early in October the Italians began a press campaign against Greece, accusing her of encouraging disorder in Albania, and by the end of October an ultimatum from

Mussolini was rejected by the Greek Prime Minister. Half an hour before its expiration Italian forces operating from Albania entered Greek territory. Winston Churchill lost no time in assuring the Greek Government, "We will give you all the help in our power. We fight a common foe and will share a united victory."

On a visit to the pictures with Edwin, Josie was beginning to notice how preoccupied he had been all evening. Several times she made remarks about the film they had been watching, only to receive monosyllabic replies. It was not until the organ burst into life and the lights went up that she was able to ask if something was wrong.

"Not wrong exactly, it's just that I've signed on for the Navy," said Edwin, in a breathless rush.

"You didn't have to go for another six months."

"I might not have got in the Navy if I'd waited to be called up," Edwin explained.

"When do you have to go?" she asked.

"First of January, report to Portsmouth," he sounded quite cheerful, even excited. "You don't mind, do you Josie?"

"I'll miss you," said Josie sadly. "But I can see the point, you're very keen on the Navy aren't you?"

Edwin put an arm around her, a thing he had never done when the lights were up.

"We've got another ten days and I'll get leave sometime Josie," he whispered comfortingly. "And we can write, can't we?"

"Oh, every day," vowed Josie, rather rashly.

She had long ago accepted the inevitability of Edwin's joining the Navy as soon as he reached the magic age of seventeen and a half. This didn't prevent the actual announcement coming as something of a shock.

Several letters had arrived together, just before Christmas, from Jimmy. Although they had obviously been written at different times and all had been heavily censored, reading between the lines the family were able to establish that Jimmy was now one of Wavell's men.

The news from this theatre of war was very encouraging and just before Christmas the newsreels were proudly showing the twenty thousand sad, dejected-looking Italian prisoners streaming back to the hastily erected prison camps.

166

By February the strange sounding names of Benghazi, Cyrenaica and Tobruk had almost become household names in England. The British troops were now nicknamed the 'desert rats'. There were pictures in the newspapers and the news reels of victorious 'desert rats' carrying all before them. "On to Tripoli!" was the call. Josie always scanned the news reels with great care, hoping to catch a glimpse of Jimmy. It seemed that Hitler, faced with imminent collapse of his Italian ally, decided he had better do something about the situation. Germany now had superiority and crack Nazi panzer troops rolled along the highway to Cyrenaica entering Benghazi on April 3rd.

Although British troops were now forced to abandon most of their hard won territory, they continued to hold on to Tobruk. The next letter from Jimmy confirmed that he was now part of this heroic garrison.

Edwin's letters had dwindled to a trickle after what had, at first, been a flood. Whilst he was completing his basic training, he had had plenty of time for letter-writing; as the training progressed and was interspersed with several sea- trips, there was less time for correspondence. Until the joyous day when Josie received a letter to say, 'Home on seven days leave at week-end.' She was beside herself with excitement.

Josie thought she would remember for ever the sight of Edwin striding down the road to meet her when he arrived home. He seemed to have grown a couple of inches. With his cap worn at a jaunty angle and his bell-bottoms flapping in the breeze, he was, to Josie, the stuff heroes were made of.

In spite of being apart for months, their first shy kisses were not exchanged until after dark, when the moon came out and the world was covered with a soft silver sheen.

"I've missed you so much Josie," sighed Edwin, encircling her with his blue-serge arms and pressing her head to his chest.

"Coo, that uniform's tickly," giggled Josie, thrilled but at the same time a little scared of this new very grown-up Edwin.

For the next week, Edwin, being a considerate boyfriend and a conscientious son, did his best to give equal attention to Josie and his parents. Josie, for her part, was always delighted to be invited to spend time with Edwin's parents.

Eventually, swearing eternal love, they had to part and Edwin returned to his ship. Josie spent a miserable week after Edwin had left, for some reason she seemed to miss him more than when he had first joined up.

Listening to the news later in the week, the usual breakfast-time pandemonium in the Brown household was suddenly silenced by the announcer's voice.

"A statement has been issued from Number Ten Downing Street this morning - Rudolph Hess, Deputy Fuehrer of Germany and party leader of the National Socialist Party has landed in Scotland, he has crashed in a Messerschmitt 100 near Glasgow. The very well-dressed German officer who was taken from the plane was found to have a broken ankle and has been taken to Glasgow hospital."

A later announcement stated that a Whitehall expert had confirmed that the man was indeed Rudolph Hess - medical opinion seemed to agree that Hess appeared to be quite sane.

For quite some time after this event there were many theories about the real motive of this flight. Hess, himself, insisted that he was hoping to induce Britain to 'bury the hatchet' with Germany and join with Hitler against Russia.

The war news was very depressing, everywhere the Allies seemed to be in retreat. In the midst of the general gloom, there was further bad news with the sinking of HMS *Hood* by the German battleship *Bismarck*. The nation mourned the loss of the great ship and, even more, the loss of her entire crew, except for three survivors.

Josie spent every waking hour, when she was not at school, listening to the wireless reports with a sort of morbid fascination for any mention of Edwin's ship, the *Intrepid*. Knowing that Edwin was now in the heart of the battle was worrying, to say the least. Every time the reports actually named ships Josie would tingle with fear and her heart would race. She wondered what state Edwin's parents were in by this time.

On the 26th the bulletin took on a decidedly more cheerful note, even the announcer's voice seemed to have a new bright-ness in it.

"The mighty *Bismarck*, the pride of the German navy, has been sunk," he announced. Later bulletins gave more details of the sea battle with a full report on the vessels involved, including the *Intrepid*, and the difficulties they had to face before they had finally cornered their prey.

In June, Russia entered the war, somewhat reluctantly on the side of the Allies. They had little choice in the matter as Germany launched 'Operation Barbarosa' and invaded Russia. Totally unprepared for war, Russia needed vast supplies of arms, which had to be shipped to them, and Edwin's ship became part of the escort for the merchant ships plying the dangerous northern route to Murmansk. Now that Hitler had to turn his attention to the Soviet Union, it seemed that the worst of the blitz on London might be over.

Edwin's letters had become very infrequent and Josie worried about where he was and how he was coping. Letters from Jimmy, on the other hand, although vague about where he was and what was happening, were at least being received regularly.

By the middle of the year, things were getting tighter on the home-front. As the supply situation deteriorated, rations were curtailed. The weekly allowances per person were now 8 ozs of meat, 1 oz cheese, 4 ozs bacon or ham, 8 ozs fat, including not more than 2 ozs butter, 2 ozs jam or marmalade: Many other foods were now only obtained on a 'points system'. Shopping became not only boring because of the scarcity of the choice of food, but also time-consuming because of the time spent by the shopkeeper cutting out the various coupons needed for almost every purchase. Queues became an accepted way of life.

Clothes rationing began on June 1st with the issue of yet another book of coupons. The allowance was sixty coupons per year, which to begin with didn't seem too bad as most people had a fair stock of clothes, but as time went on, it became increasingly harder to juggle the allowance.

There was further depressing news getting through from the Russian front. German troops had poured across the frontier and German aircraft were attacking Sebastopol and Kiev. As the war in Russia continued it was becoming obvious that the Russian army was in retreat and suffering grievous losses in both men and material. Mr Churchill made a speech rallying help for the Russians.

"We shall give whatever help we can to Russia and the Russian people. We shall appeal to our friends and allies in every part of the world to take the same course and pursue it as we shall, faithfully and steadfastly to the end!" thundered Mr Churchill.

Josie, listening intently to his speech, felt inspired once again

h

by Mr Churchill's oratory.

The newspapers and newsreels now contained more information about action on the Russian front than any other war zone. The Russian soldiers in their astrakhan hats with the red star on the front became as familiar as the uniforms of the Allied troops.

12

Josie Leaves School

As the time approached for Josie to leave school, the frantic search for suitable employment began. Josie was luckier than most of her fellow students. By having a father already employed in a local shoe factory, Mr Brown was able to put in a word for his daughter, who had ambitions to become a shoe designer. After an interview with the factory owner it was agreed that she should start in the pattern-room as a trainee pattern-maker/designer.

As her days as a student drew to a close, Josie realised that after the initial excitement of actually obtaining a job which had some relevance to the past two years of study, the fact remained that this was the parting of the way. After July her life would be completely changed. All her old friends would be scattered to the four corners of the city, some even leaving the city altogether. Others still without jobs wondered what the future held for them.

It was with some trepidation that Josie presented herself at the end of the August Bank Holiday to begin her career as a designer.

Nothing could have prepared Josie for the noise in the factory.

Although the pattern-room was the haven of comparative peace, she found that she spent much of her time checking on the progress of various sample shoes as they made their journey from department to department.

As winter began to bite the news from the Russian front improved. It appeared that Hitler, in his over-confident way, had expected his troops to have overwhelmed the Russians before the onslaught of the bitter Russian winter. There was now evidence that the Nazi troops were ill-equipped to deal with the extreme cold of the Russian winter and many were literally freezing to death. The Russian army, warmly clad, were dug in to hold Moscow at all cost.

On December 8th the wireless reports were full of the bombing, by Japanese planes, of Pearl Harbour the day before. After a few hours everyone in Britain was aware of the location of Pearl Harbour and what had happened to it. It was reported that President Roosevelt had made a speech to the American people denouncing, "This act of treachery on the part of Japan, made worse by the fact that even after the attack had begun, Japan's representatives were with the American Secretary of State discussing the future peaceful relationship between Japan and America." He then announced that a state of war now existed between the United States and the Japanese Empire.

In Britain Mr Churchill announced that Japanese forces had begun to land on British territory in Northern Malaya so Britain was now at war with Japan as well as with Germany.

Though everyone had made a supreme effort to stay cheerful on Christmas Day, on Boxing Day the news broadcasts informed a very subdued population that Japanese troops had accepted the surrender of Hong Kong on Christmas Day.

In spite of all the bad news, Mr Churchill made one of his stirring speeches to the United States Congress. He began by saying that, "The forces ranged against us are enormous," and ending with the statement that, "In the days to come the British and American people will walk together, in majesty, in justice and in peace." When the recording was broadcast to the British people, they applauded the sentiments expressed by their Prime Minister, licked their wounds and carried on.

The Christmas holiday had passed in a frantic whirl, it was over so quickly, Josie found there was a vast difference between two days off and the sort of holidays she had enjoyed when at school.

The Japanese continued to sweep away all Allied opposition. In a matter of a couple of months they had overrun Singapore and the final surrender was signed on February 15th.

By April, the war on the home-front had taken a turn for the worse. Almost every night the sirens' mournful sound filled the air, it was not unusual to get three or four 'alerts' each night. Sleep became almost impossible; although many nights were now spent in the safety of the shelter, the noise of the bombs and gunfire made it impossible to doze off for long.

Toward the end of April, there was one terrifying night when the 'alert' sounded while the Brown family were still in the house. As they started to make a run for the shelter, there was an ominous drone of planes and then the sound of bombs dropping alarmingly close.

"Under the stairs, all of you!" shouted Mr Brown who, on reaching the door, could actually see bombs exploding.

They huddled under the stairs. The next bomb seemed closer and with the next one it seemed as if the house had fallen in on top of them with an almighty bang.

After several more explosions, mercifully seeming to be a little further away, there was a slight lull when only the sound of artillery fire could be heard.

Eventually, the all-clear sounded. Picking their way through a carpet of glass and debris, the family emerged to inspect the damage. Both front and back doors had been blown out and were reposing, still intact, in the garden. Some of the windows, both upstairs and downstairs, had been shattered.

There was no longer any drone of planes or artillery fire but the sky was as bright as day with incendiary bombs burning.

Very much later, although feeling tired and extremely grubby, Josie and John sallied forth to take stock of the neighbourhood. There was a crater as big as a bus only half a dozen houses away. When they tried investigating in the other direction, they found another one almost as big. There were dozens of houses damaged by fire. Their own shattered house appeared to have got off lightly in comparison with a number of others.

The nightly bombings continued. The citizens of Norwich, bleary-eyed with fatigue and lack of sleep, carried on and the shops left standing opened for business as usual. Factory employees, when not clearing debris from the previous night's onslaught, got on with their jobs. Air-raid wardens and fire watchers still managed to turn up for duty. The list of casualties in the library grew longer. Neighbours helped each other, offering beds to those made homeless, water to those whose water supply had ceased owing to burst pipes, even the use of a bathroom to those without water who wanted to remove the grime of several days.

By the end of the next week, Mr Brown had decided enough was enough and he banished his wife and son to the country. Josie refused to go, opting to stay with her father.

For the next week or so Josie and her father cycled to Tacolneston, not only at the weekends but quite often during the week, to stay the night and return in the morning. On one such occasion as they approached Norwich, they were appalled to see the sky was still a brilliant red over the city.

Once in the city they found it impossible to get along many of the streets where fires were still burning fiercely. Finally arriving at the factory, they found it practically roofless, with hardly a window left intact. The employees who had managed to get to work set about clearing up the mess and inspecting the damage.

The factory struggled back into full production with a depleted staff as more and more young men were called up. Quite often, jobs previously done by men were now undertaken by women. But, somehow, despite the bombing, most of the employees managed to put in a full day's work.

Josie, rushing for the cycle sheds at dinner-time a couple of weeks later was surprised to see Edwin waiting for her.

"Hello Josie," he said, kissing her as the boys from the clicking-room cheered, "I've got seven days' leave."

"Why didn't you let me know?" asked Josie, blushing slightly at this open show of affection.

"I didn't have time to let anyone know, I didn't know myself until late yesterday afternoon. Boy! how I've missed you Josie."

"I've missed you, too," said Josie, feeling strangely shy. Edwin seemed to have grown even taller and filled out as well, he was no longer the skinny little boy who had joined up.

"How have you been getting on? Why didn't you write more often?" he said, in a rush. "I've been worried about you."

"It's been pretty rough lately you know, bombs almost every night. I've been going to Grandma's after work most nights, I've tried to write as often as I could."

"It's OK," said Edwin, tightening his grip on her shoulder, "I know it's been tough, my mother's been telling me, she said your area seemed to have been pretty badly hit."

Josie found it hard to concentrate on her work during the afternoon, she knew Edwin would be waiting for her as soon as work was over.

Edwin was standing at the gate, as he placed an arm around her shoulders, he grinned.

"I was going to put my civvies on to go out tonight but I found nothing fits me anymore."

"You've grown taller."

"Not only taller, I seem to have put on a couple of inches all round."

"I'm glad you didn't wear civvies," said Josie as they made their way towards the city centre, " 'cos you look lovely in your uniform."

Edwin blushed and muttered something about it being comfortable once you got used to it.

The next few days passed all too quickly, Josie and Edwin's visits to the pictures and the theatre were interspersed with long walks into the country.

Edwin's father had been hoarding his small amount of petrol coupons with the idea of visiting his sister in Yarmouth on Whit Monday. Permission had to be obtained to visit the coast. Now, with the formalities completed, he would be able to take his son and Josie with him.

The trip to the coast was something of a disappointment. It was not possible to get anywhere near the beach as it was covered with barbed-wire barricades and signs saying 'Danger mines'.

Soon it was time to return home. Josie and Edwin, sitting in the back of the Austin Seven, held hands and gazed into each other's eyes, afraid to express their feelings in the presence of Edwin's parents.

The seven days leave seemed to speed past and soon Josie was waving goodbye at Thorpe Station to Edwin, who had gathered her into his arms as the train puffed noisy funnels of steam into the air.

"Don't forget me, Josie and stay away from the boys!" he joked, trying to ease the pangs of parting as he banged the carriage door shut. As the train disappeared into the distance, Josie walked sadly toward the barrier, vowing to be forever true.

After tea that evening, as Josie sat thinking of Edwin and feeling miserable, her father said, "Why don't you give Violet or Penny a look, at least it'll take your mind off your troubles, you can't become a hermit until Edwin gets his next leave."

"I suppose not," said Josie as, somewhat reluctantly, she made her way to Violet's. As she knocked at the door, it was opened by Jack attired in a khaki uniform bearing two stripes.

"Vi, your friend's here," he shouted.

Josie gazed at Jack and waited for the usual thrill at the sight of him, but nothing happened.

"Get a move on Joan," he called and an attractive blonde girl appeared in the hallway. "If we don't soon get started we'll miss the start of the film."

The girl grabbed Jack's arm and tottered down the path, her high heels clicking on the concrete.

Violet appeared at the door and watched them go.

"Fine old mess he's got himself into," she said doing a creditable impersonation of Oliver Hardy.

"What do you mean?" asked Josie.

"Didn't you notice she was a bit fat around the middle?"

"Oh dear, I see what you mean."

"Come in Josie, seems ages since I saw you, everyone's out so we can have a cup of tea and a good old natter. My mother is absolutely furious," said Violet. "She wants to live here until the baby's born."

"Who is she? I don't think I've ever seen her before."

"Comes from Aldershot, that is where Jack's stationed."

"What happened to Doreen?"

"Oh, they fell out soon after Jack joined up."

"I expect your mother was pleased about that, she never liked her much did she?"

"No, but she likes this one even less, but she's insisting Jack must marry her."

"Why's that, if she dislikes her so much?"

"She can't stand the idea of a grandchild being born out of wedlock I suppose."

"Does he want to marry her?"

"I can't really make out whether he does or not but she certainly wants to marry him."

"Is he on leave at the moment then?"

"Yes, he's due back next Thursday, he's leaving Joan here, can't say I'm looking forward to that very much."

"Why can't she go home?"

"Because her father threw her out when he found out about the baby."

"Golly, poor girl, maybe you could make a friend of her when you get to know her better."

"I doubt that, I don't think she's my type somehow. Let's not talk about Jack and his problems, he'll have to sort them out himself. How's life treating you then?"

"Well, Edwin's been home on seven days' leave, he went back today."

"I've been going to the dances at the 'Samson' lately," said Violet, "with some of the girls from work. Why don't you come?"

"I can't dance," said Josie.

"Neither can I, well not properly anyway, there's always loads of servicemen there and most of them can't dance properly either, so it really doesn't matter much."

"Mm! I'm not sure Violet, I think I'd prefer the pictures."

"Oh! come on Josie, it's quite fun really."

Josie felt considerably cheered by the time she left Violet's.

The following evening the girls made their way to the 'Samson & Hercules' ballroom.

During the interval Violet asked, "Have you met anyone nice, Josie?"

"An airman who seems quite nice, his name is Gerry."

"Oh yes, I've seen him here before, I think he comes every week, he must be stationed near here."

"St. Faiths," said Josie. "He wants to walk home with me but I don't know about that."

"Why not?"

"Well, what about Edwin?" said Josie

"I s'pose you could tell him about Edwin, if you think it's strictly necessary that is."

"I think it's only fair."

"Let's go back now, we've had a breather. I'll see if I can get someone to walk home with me then we can all go together."

"Oh good, that would be better, but if you can't I'll tell him I have to go home with you, after all I came with you didn't I? And I can't leave you to go home alone."

When they returned to the dance floor the band was playing a waltz.

Gerry approached, accompanied by a good-looking dark haired young man in air-force uniform.

"Hello girls!" said Gerry. "This is my mate Robert, this is

Josie," he said introducing her to Robert. "And her friend, sorry, I don't know your name?"

"Violet. How do you do?" said Violet, shaking hands with Robert.

"Care to dance?" asked Robert.

"Love to," said Violet.

After the dance finished the four of them walked home together until they reached the point where Josie's and Violet's paths separated. Violet and Robert said a cheerful goodbye. The two boys arranged to meet in a quarter of an hour, so they could return to the pick-up point for the transport back to their base. Walking the short distance to Josie's house still chatting, they reached the front gate. "Can I see you again, Josie?" asked Gerry. Josie hesitated.

"Er, I think I ought to tell you, I've got a steady boyfriend who's in the Navy."

"You engaged or anything?"

"Well, no, but we've been going together for ages."

"We can still be friends surely, after all he's at sea isn't he and I'm sure he wouldn't expect you to sit at home until he returns."

"Put like that, no, I don't suppose he would, but as long as you know the situation, yes, I'd like to be friends."

"Life's too short to sit and mope, isn't it Josie, how about meeting at the 'Samson' same time next week?"

"OK, do you think Robert will be coming too?"

"Should be, provided he's managed to make a date with Violet," Gerry laughed. "I confess we'd agreed to try to make a date with the two of you while we were waiting for you to get your coats."

Next day, after yet another night with very little sleep, Josie met Violet to compare notes about the young airmen.

"Robert seems nice," said Violet. "How did you get on with Gerry?"

"Fine," said Josie. "I told him about Edwin."

"What did he say?"

"We can still be friends and he was glad I had told him."

"Good, 'cos I said we'd meet them outside the 'Samson' next week."

"Gerry asked me the same question and I said we would, I think they'd got things planned, don't you?"

"Well, we had a good time, didn't we? I'm quite looking forward to meeting them again."

"Me too," said Josie, rather hesitantly.

Much to everyone's amazement, there was a lull of several nights in the bombing. Not even an alert. It felt strange to be able to sleep in the house and not have to get up at all during the night.

13

War-time Entertainment

In the Brown household, the wireless was turned on almost from waking to sleeping.

Although the news bulletins were probably the most important of all BBC transmissions, Josie, who was an avid listener, also enjoyed many of the comedy programmes. One of the most outstanding of these was ITMA - initials for 'It's that man again'. The man in question being Tommy Handley, as the mayor of 'Foaming at the Mouth', Jack Train played Colonel Chinstrap. The charlady, Mrs Mopp, was played by Dorothy Summers who was responsible for the catch-phrase 'Can I do you now Sir?' which swept the nation. Other catch-phrases attributed to ITMA were 'I don't mind if I do' and 'After you Claude, no after you Cecil'. It certainly made the life of anyone named Claude or Cecil a bit of a nightmare for a time.

The Saturday night show entitled 'Band Wagon' starring Arthur Askey and Dickie ('Stinker') Murdock provided comical entertainment for a population which was settling into staying at home more often than had been the practice before the war. Again the catch-phrase which quickly caught on was Arthur's opening gambit 'Hello Playmates!' Arthur and Dickie were supposed to be living in a flat on the roof of Broadcasting House. Many people came to believe they really lived there and mail would be addressed to Arthur and Dickie, The Flat, Broadcasting House.

Another firm favourite was 'Garrison Theatre', this was broadcast from Clifton Parish Hall in Bristol where the BBC's Variety Department had been evacuated. The show was supposed

180

to be performed by men from the Services in front of an audience of troops. Jack Warner played the cheeky cockney soldier who performed monologues and sang comic songs, like 'I'm a bunger up of rat holes'. He also read letters which he was supposed to have received from his 'Bruvver Sid'. These letters, written from a variety of war-zones, were subject to army censorship. Jack would fill in the missing bits with the words 'Blue Pencil'. The show always began with Jack making a somewhat unusual entrance by riding his bike down the centre aisle yelling 'Mind my bike'.

Bebe Daniels and Ben Lyon, an American husband and wife team, had a very popular show entitled 'Hi Gang'. Ben and Bebe, who refused to return to America when war broke out, preferring to stay to entertain the British, among whom they had lived for a number of years, were held in great esteem. As was their stooge Vic Oliver, who, although an accomplished musician, could be relied upon to make a terrible racket playing his violin. Vic was of Austrian descent and had been a Cavalry Officer during the First World War. Now, as a naturalised Briton, he was helping to boost the morale of his adopted country.

All through the last winter the reports from Moscow were of continued advances by the German forces. Russian troops eventually pulled back to the outskirts of Moscow. Marshal Stalin refused to leave the Kremlin although government officials and diplomats had been evacuated.

When it seemed that nothing could stop the German advance, nature stepped in to lend a hand. Suddenly the Russian winter with its freezing temperatures, mud and slush, halted the Germans in their tracks. Thousands of tanks and armoured vehicles were bogged down in the mud. The German troops were not clothed to stand the intense cold. It was reported that they were still wearing tight nail-studded jack boots and many were suffering from frost bite.

Now that Josie was becoming interested in dancing she had become a fan of the 'Big Bands'. To the tunes of Geraldo, Joe Loss, Jack Payne, Harry Roy and Mantovani, she would secretly practise her steps, but the best band by far for dancing was Victor Sylvester, whose strict tempo dance band almost suggested the steps for you. Victor himself usually gave instructions on dance steps sometime during the programmes.

All the band-leaders had their own style of introduction, but perhaps the most distinct was the cool rather hesitant voice of Henry Hall, the leader of the BBC Dance Orchestra who always concluded his programmes with the words "And so we end tonight's programme by the BBC Dance Orchestra, directed by Henry Hall. Goodbye everybody and here's to the next time," and the orchestra would play itself out with their signature tune entitled *Here's to the Next Time*.

For the next few weeks the girls had regular dates with Robert and Gerry visiting the dance hall, the Theatre Royal and the Hippodrome. Gerry had, so far, stuck to his promise to just be friends, which meant Josie stayed happy with this arrangement.

When they were on their own the girls discussed their feelings for the airmen. Josie had a feeling that Violet was really smitten with Robert.

"Don't get too involved Violet," said Josie. "You're only young and the chances are the boys may get moved to another station, then you'll be terribly upset."

Meeting the boys about a week later they had decided on a visit to the 'Samson'. As they walked up the stone steps between the statues of Samson and Hercules, Robert said, "Gerry's got something to tell you Josie."

Josie, blushing slightly, said, "Really, what have you got to tell me Gerry?"

"Wait till we get inside," said Gerry mysteriously.

After leaving their coats in the cloakroom they joined the boys at the bar.

"Let's dance," said Robert quickly to Violet.

As they glided away Josie faced Gerry, "What've you got to tell me?" Josie asked.

"I've been posted for training as a navigator."

Josie, slightly startled, asked, "Is that what you want then?"

"I've always wanted to get into flying. I'd really like to be a pilot but I'm considered more suited to navigating, which is fair enough, I'll get to fly, that's if I pass out, of course."

"I'm sure you'll pass," said Josie.

"Well, there's a crying need for air-crew at the moment, so perhaps I might."

"What about Robert?"

"He doesn't want to fly, anyway he's not been selected."

"He won't be posted then?"

"Not at the moment."

"That's good, I think Violet would be heartbroken if he were."

"I know he's quite taken with her, so you think she feels the same way about him do you?"

"Oh, I'm sure she does. It's getting difficult to have any other sort of conversation with her, we always seem to end up talking about Robert," said Josie.

"Good, I'll tell him," said Gerry. "I'll be sorry to leave you, it's been fun the past couple of months, even though you've got your sailor. Will you write to me, Josie?"

"Of course I will," said Josie cheerfully, taking on more correspondence. "Let me have your address."

The rest of the evening passed quite happily, even the air-raid siren was silent for once. Josie told Violet about Gerry's posting.

"I'm so glad it's not Robert," said Violet. "Josie, will you mind if I continue to go out with him?"

"Of course I won't, you don't think I'm likely to play gooseberry do you?"

Violet's eyes had taken on a soft dreamy look as she talked about Robert.

'She's got it bad,' thought Josie.

At a loose end on Saturday, Violet being out with Robert, Josie decided to bike to Tacolneston to visit her mother and brother.

There had been a lull in the bombing for more than a couple of weeks. Josie was anxious to convey this information to her mother to prevent her worrying about how they were coping. She was surprised, when arriving at Grandma's, she was almost pounced upon by her mother who announced that she and John wanted to come home and would she and her father come to fetch them next weekend.

"Are you sure you're doing the right thing?" Josie questioned. "You're much safer here and John seems to be settled at school, it's doubtful how much schooling he'll get if you come back to Norwich."

Her mother remained adamant so Josie had no choice but to pass this surprising information on to her father.

Her weekend of relaxation had got off to a bad start, but in the peace and tranquillity of the countryside, Josie quickly recovered her good humour - it was difficult to remain anxious when the countryside seemed so strangely undisturbed by all the hardships that the war had brought. The corn was ripening in the fields, looking almost ready for reaping, the beautiful golden colour interlaced with the blood red of the poppies, which might be the bane of the farmer's life, but undoubtedly added to the beauty of the scene.

In the evening when the air cooled after another hot stifling day, this was the time to enjoy the orchard. The bees were still buzzing in and out of the daisies and buttercups which covered the ground. Birds twittered in the fruit trees and every now and then a rabbit, unconcerned about Josie, who was lying peacefully still in the shade of the trees, ventured out to nibble the grass.

Josie's thoughts drifted to her childhood, the happy holidays with Jimmy and her friend Mary from the farm. Things hardly seemed to have changed, except for Jimmy, who was now thousands of miles away on foreign soil, fighting for the very survival of everything they held so dear. She thought of Edwin and Gerry, if only this war would end so they could all go back to leading a normal life again.

When she returned home, much refreshed, on Sunday evening, her father was somewhat perturbed by the message from his wife.

When the next weekend arrived, Josie and her father prepared to collect the other members of the family. Mr Brown was still extremely doubtful about the wisdom of this move but he knew if his wife had made up her mind then that was the end of it. It was decided that they would stay overnight and make their way home on Sunday morning.

The first news bulletin of the day on Sunday reported heavy raids in East Anglia. More often than not East Anglia meant Norwich, but Mrs Brown refused to be persuaded to stay in the country where she would be safe.

It was with some trepidation that the family returned to Norwich, not knowing if they would have any home to go to, or if indeed the raid had been on some other town in East Anglia. When they eventually reached home they found they had been lucky because their house was still intact, although the one next door was extensively damaged.

Mrs Brown made a tour of the house, throwing open all the windows, "Lovely to be home," she said.

Although the British population were trying to live up to their reputation for keeping a stiff upper lip, in areas suffering the worst of the bombing, sometimes this took a lot of effort! Most of the young people were determined to do so, they tried hard to bring some semblance of normality into their shattered lives by continuing to visit picture houses, theatres and dance halls. The pubs tended to be populated by older members of the population. Groping about in the dark with the aid of carefully shaded torches had become a way of life, which no one really questioned. In the same way, no one really seriously thought that the Allies could lose the war, no matter how many set-backs they suffered.

The next news report bolstered the flagging spirits. "The Eighth Army has forced Rommel to make a withdrawal and the Germans are now digging in." General Alexander had become Commander-in-Chief with General Montgomery at the head of the Eighth Army. Soon he became known to all his troops simply as 'Monty'.

By the end of August Rommel ordered the German troops and tanks to advance on Cairo. The British public, acquainted with bad news, listened gleefully to bulletins which reported Rommel's tanks bogged down in quicksands and British mine-fields. The RAF was reported to be pounding German lorry concentrations. After a few days of this, the Germans retreated again. The second assault on Egypt had failed, with heavy losses in the armoured strength of the Africa Corps.

Listening to 'Lord Haw Haw' to hear the German interpreta-tion of the battle, the family were amused to hear the defeat explained away: "The Germans," said Lord Haw Haw, "Had merely mounted a reconnaissance force which, having completed its task, had successfully withdrawn again."

The reports now were of Allied advances, taking thousands of German and Italian prisoners. By the beginning of November the German retreat had become a rout. Monty, rallying his troops into further action, said, "I call on all troops to keep up the pressure and not to relax for one moment. We have the chance of putting the whole panzer army in the bag."

The number of dejected-looking prisoners grew with each newsreel sent from the front.

"There were now estimated," said the war correspondent covering the battle, "to be at least thirty-thousand prisoners, including nine generals."

Christmas became the joyous affair it used to be before the war. Despite the austerity there seemed at last to be something to celebrate. True, there were important members of the family missing, but letters had been received from both Edwin and Jimmy, confirming their safety and the safe arrival of their Christmas parcels despatched several months previously.

Soon after Christmas there was good news from Russia. Ever since September messages from Russia told of the heroic stand by the Red Army and the citizens of Leningrad to prevent the city falling into German hands. The city was reported to be under siege, its citizens starving.

In November a report spoke of a powerful offensive by the Red Army from the north-west of the city. Going behind the German lines, the Red Army had succeeded in cutting the railway lines bringing supplies to the German forces surrounding Leningrad.

By Christmas it was reported that the ill-equipped German troops were running short of food and ammunition and were still no nearer to breaking the will of the defenders of Leningrad.

By the end of January the relief of Leningrad meant that food and ammunition could pass into the Baltic port. It was very moving when newsreel pictures were finally released showing the starving citizens taking the first deliveries of food. It was only later that the numbers who had died of starvation could be calculated.

Toward the end of January there was excellent news from the Middle East. General Montgomery had entered the important town of Tripoli. The Eighth Army had advanced 1350 miles in 80 days. The Italian African Empire had ceased to exist.

Although the wireless reports were fairly up to date it was not until the following week that cinema newsreels were again showing the thousands of prisoners, guns and tanks captured. The date was May 13th, almost exactly three years after the evacuation from Dunkirk. It seemed that the wheel had indeed turned full circle.

14

Enter the Yanks

In a mood to celebrate this improvement in the war situation, Josie contacted Violet, Penny and the twins to arrange an evening when they were all available to go to the 'Samson' for an evening out.

Several weeks later, attired in their very best clothes, which in most cases had entirely exhausted their supply of clothing coupons, they entered the dance hall. They had decided not to invite any boys to join the party; in any case, with the exception of Robert, most of their boyfriends were abroad fighting for their country.

Anyway, there was never any shortage of males at the dance. All the military personnel based locally congregated here on their nights off. Not only were there the usual air force, army and sometimes the odd sailor or two, they had now been joined by a sprinkling of American Army Air-Force boys from the local air-base.

When the American forces had first arrived, they had almost seemed to come from another planet. They had beautifully tailored uniforms, totally unlike the rough serge of the British uniforms. They chewed gum and many spoke with the slow drawl, previously only associated with the cowboys on films. Large trucks with white stars painted on the cabs were becoming a familiar sight as they ferried the GIs from their base into the city.

The evening went with a swing, the band was good. The girls got together to compare notes after each dance.

Having danced almost every dance, they were sitting together at the bar when they were approached by a group of American GIs who offered to buy them a drink. Accepting the offer they stayed at the bar, chatting with interest to the GIs hearing where they came from and what their homes and families were like.

Eventually, at the end of an enjoyable evening, they parted at the entrance, the boys making their way to their pickup point, the girls to make their way home.

"See you next week girls," shouted the GI named Buck as he sped down the step and disappeared from sight.

"Oh, I did like them," said Penny. "They're . . . well . . . so different aren't they?"

"I thought they were a bit loud and brash," said Josie.

"Mm, I did too," said Violet. "I much prefer my Robert."

"They seem to have plenty of money, not like our soldiers."

"Money isn't everything," said Violet rather primly.

"They never stopped chewing gum," added Josie. "I found that a bit disconcerting."

"We've really had a great night out," said Penny. "They want us to go again next week."

"We're working," said the twins.

"Shame," said Penny. "Anyway, I think I'll go, anyone else coming?"

"I might," said Josie. "But I'll have to think about it."

"Depends whether Robert is on duty," said Violet.

"Oh, you and Robert!" said Penny despairingly. "It's like Josie and Edwin, you can't spend the rest of the war never going anywhere. After all, they're only asking to be friends."

Josie knew that when she had time to think about it she'd probably decline the invitation when she got her usual feelings of disloyalty to Edwin.

Surprisingly enough, under great pressure from Penny and much soul-searching, Josie finally agreed to accompany Penny a couple of weeks later.

"They might have found someone else as we didn't turn up last week," Penny sounded rather anxious. Her doubts were soon dispelled as they entered the hall, Buck bounded up.

"Hi girls!" he waved his hand. "We missed you last week. How about a dance?" he said, taking Penny's hand and leading her onto the floor. "I'll teach you to jitter-bug," he said.

Josie watched in amazement as Penny was propelled all over the floor in this very energetic dance. Other couples scattered leaving the floor clear for Buck and Penny.

At the end of another very pleasant evening Buck and a dark haired boy with bright blue eyes insisted on accompanying the girls part of the way home.

"I guess we'd better make our way back now or we'll miss our transport. See you next week Penny," said Buck, planting a hasty kiss on her cheek.

"Don't get any ideas," said Josie to her escort as Buck continued to hug Penny.

"You've already warned me off by telling me about your sailor."

The visits to the dance-hall became weekly events, sometimes with all five girls, sometimes with only Penny and Josie when the twins were working and Violet was meeting Robert. Josie had to admit she quite looked forward to Friday nights, not just for the dancing and the GIs, but the renewal of her friendship with both Violet and Penny. There had been long periods when, owing to circumstances, they had seen very little of each other.

Violet appeared to be getting more and more involved with Robert, whenever she mentioned him she had the typically dazed look of the love-sick.

"No good'll come of it, you mark my words," Violet's mother had said to Josie when she had called to visit Violet.

"I don't think she really likes him much," said Violet when they were alone.

"Why not? He seems quite nice to me."

"He's lovely," said Violet, going into a trance again.

By putting all thoughts of Edwin out of her mind, Josie had begun to enjoy the company of the bright eyed American boy who laughed a lot and teased her unmercifully.

Just when life had begun to settle into a pleasant pattern, Josie was suddenly unpleasantly reminded that there was a war on when she received a letter from Edwin, no longer at sea, but confined to a base hospital with shrapnel injuries. His letter gave very little indication of the seriousness of his wounds.

"Does he say where he's wounded?" asked her mother.

"No, just that it was a sea battle and he got hit with shrapnel and I'm not to worry as he's OK."

"Well, you mustn't worry then if he's told you not to and if he's written the letter himself then I shouldn't think he's badly injured."

Josie, slightly comforted, tried to eat her tea. Her father, returning home, reiterated what had been said by her mother. By the time she went to bed Josie was feeling a little better. Once in bed she was unable to sleep with thoughts churning around in her head of Edwin lying injured in hospital. She was overcome with guilty feelings that while all this had been going on she had been enjoying herself with the GIs.

Morning seemed a long time coming. Josie thought this was one night when she would have actually welcomed the sound of the sirens, if only to have contact with other people to take her thoughts away from this awful feeling of guilt. In her troubled mind she almost convinced herself that it was all her fault.

In a matter of three weeks Edwin was home, his arm still in a sling, looking every inch the wounded warrior.

It had been three weeks of self-doubt and self-denial for Josie, doubting whether she really cared for Edwin as much as she had always supposed. In her confused state she had refused for three weeks to go to the dance-hall for fear of getting more involved with Mick the American boy.

The instant she saw Edwin again the doubts vanished. Meeting her from work he had been surrounded by young lads from the factory wanting to know how he had got wounded. Edwin turned slightly pink, looked rather embarrassed and muttered something about not being able to discuss it as it was confidential information.

However, he was a bit more forthcoming to Josie and told her that his ship had been on escort duty with the merchant convoys, taking supplies to Russia. They had been attacked by a German cruiser and he had been hit in the shoulder by shrapnel. His ship had been damaged but not sunk, the German ship had fared worse and had broken off the engagement.

The next ten days seemed to pass in a flash. Every evening Edwin was either waiting outside the factory or waiting for her when she got home. They visited all their favourite cinemas, went for walks in the country, spent a couple of evenings with Edwin's parents and one with her own.

John was now quite taken with Edwin, being wounded made

all the difference, he could boast to his friends about his sister's boyfriend who was in the Navy and had been wounded in battle.

There had been only one anxious moment for Josie in the whole ten days' leave. Making their way to the Regent one evening, Josie was horrified to see Penny walking toward them accompanied by Buck and Mick. Curbing the desire to run in the opposite direction, Josie took Edwin's hand and bravely continued walking.

"Hi, Josie," said Buck.

"Hello," said Penny, realising that this could well be a very tricky meeting.

Josie was both surprised and relieved when Mick merely waved his hand as they passed by.

"Who's the Yank?" asked Edwin.

"Oh, that's Penny's boyfriend Buck."

Edwin chuckled. "Do you think he's named after Buck Jones?"

"Could be," said Josie smiling.

"You met him before?"

"Well, Penny introduced me when he took her home one night."

Soon it was time for Edwin to go back to his ship.

"I don't want you to come to the station Josie."

"Why not?"

"Well, firstly, you'll have to get time off from work and, secondly, I'd rather we said goodbyes tonight when we can do it in private."

Holding Josie as tightly as he could with his one good arm, he said, "Josie, do you think we could get engaged once you're eighteen?"

"Oh, that would be lovely!" sighed Josie without really thinking about it. Here was her hero home from the war and wanting to get engaged.

For the next month Josie was in a state of euphoria, dreaming of getting engaged and eventually married to Edwin. She refused all invitations to go dancing, even when Penny told her that Mick kept asking about her. Instead she stayed at home evenings in her room writing long letters to Edwin, drawing pictures of the house they would share when they were married.

At work, she found it difficult to concentrate for any length of time. Mr Simpson continually enquired if anything was wrong

191

when Josie lapsed into periods of silence. Never one to be too communicative, she now seemed to be even more preoccupied. Josie merely sighed and assured him that everything was fine.

Steadfastly writing to Edwin every other day, she was not in a position to know that mail-service to ships on active service was, to say the least of it, haphazard. Poor Edwin, receiving her letters in batches of dozens at a time was becoming the object of some mirth among his ship-mates. He was always followed by hoots and whistles as he tried to find somewhere to read Josie's letters in peace. He toyed with the idea of asking her to write less frequently but the thought of upsetting her made him put up with the ribald remarks.

Josie continued to write to Jimmy at regular intervals. After much soul searching she had stopped writing to Gerry. Much as she argued with herself that there was no harm in it, and after all he was a serviceman fighting for his country and it was up to everyone to give as much help as possible to the boys far from home, every time she came back to the thought that maybe Edwin wouldn't like it and now they were almost engaged this put a different complexion on the matter.

Gerry wrote a couple of times enquiring why she had stopped writing to him, was it anything he'd said or done? Josie felt that at least she owed him an explanation but didn't know how to put it into words. After a couple of letters unanswered Gerry had obviously got the message and Josie received no more letters, for which she was extremely thankful. This enabled her to put the whole matter out of her mind, Occasionally she had little niggling thoughts that she hadn't handled the situation very well.

Contenting herself with a couple of visits to the pictures each week and carefully avoiding the dance-hall, Josie settled into a routine. Penny still continued to meet Buck two or three times a week and had confided in Josie that she was a bit worried about Violet who seemed to have stopped going anywhere except out with Robert when he was off duty.

"I know you don't come to the dances any longer Josie but at least I see you when we go to the pictures, but Violet just seems to stay at home all the time - rum, don't you think?"

"Yes, it is a bit peculiar I'll grant you, maybe she's got something serious going with Robert so she doesn't want to risk getting involved with anyone else."

"Could be I suppose." Penny seemed to mull this over then she said, "Why don't you go round to see her? I'm not on visiting terms but you are, aren't you?"

"Well, yes, I suppose I could, after all she is a friend of long standing."

Josie realised that, with all her preoccupation with her own affairs, she hadn't even noticed this strange behaviour from Violet. She resolved to visit her as soon as possible.

In answer to her second knock, the door was opened by Jack's girlfriend who seemed to be at least twice the size she was last time Josie had seen her.

"Er . . ." said Josie, rather taken aback, "Is Violet in please?"

"Sure," said the blonde apparition. "Violet, your friend's here," she yelled.

Violet, manoeuvring herself around her brother's girlfriend who took up most of the doorway, looked surprised to see Josie.

"Oh, it's Josie, come in," she said as the large lady retreated into the hall.

Once inside, Jack's girlfriend having disappeared, Violet said quickly, "Hang on a minute Josie while I get my coat then we'll go out."

As they walked down the road Josie was chattering excitedly about getting engaged, when she suddenly remembered the reason for her visit.

"Penny's worried about you Violet, she says you don't go anywhere now, you just seem to stay at home. S'pose you go out with Robert though don't you?"

Josie was astounded to see tears well up in Violet's eyes. "Oh dear! Have you fallen out or something?" asked Josie, not quite knowing what to do about this show of emotion emanating from her friend.

"Josie, something awful's happened." The tears began to trickle down Violet's cheeks.

"Come on, it can't be that bad surely?"

"Oh yes it can," said Violet, wiping away her tears with the back of her hand. "Can't you guess what's wrong?"

"No," said Josie, "hanged if I can."

"I'm pregnant!"

"You're what?"

"Pregnant. I know it's awful Josie and you're the only person

193

j

I've told."

"Haven't you told Robert?"

"Yes, but he doesn't really want to know, he says he's too young to be saddled with a kid."

"It's a bit too late to take that attitude. Whatever is your mother going to say, first Jack and now you!"

"I know," said Violet, beginning to sob. "I don't know how I'm going to tell her." They were approaching Josie's house.

"Let's go indoors," said Josie. "Everyone's out, you look as if you could do with a cup of tea."

Having got Violet to sit down and told her to dry her tears, Josie busied herself making a cup of tea. What did one say? Josie had never been faced with a situation like this before, how did one broach the subject without upsetting Violet in the process?

When she returned with the tea-tray Violet looked more composed.

"Whatever am I to do?" she asked, taking the cup of tea from Josie.

"Well, you're certainly going to have to tell your mother."

"Oh, I couldn't," said Violet, beginning to look tearful again.

"Violet, it's no good crying," said Josie, putting a kindly hand on Violet's shivering shoulder. "Are you sure Robert doesn't want anything to do with it? That's pretty rotten of him."

Violet seemed to jump to his defence.

"Well, I suppose you can see his point of view, he's only nineteen, he can't take on a wife and child."

"But you're only seventeen and you've got to take on a child, surely he should take some of the responsibility?"

By the look on Violet's face Josie realised that it was futile to pursue this line of argument, she was simply making Violet even more upset. Obviously she still thought enough of Robert to rush to his defence when any criticism was levelled at him.

An uneasy silence settled on the two girls as they sipped their tea.

"Is there anything I can do to help?" said Josie somewhat despairingly.

"No one can help," said Violet sadly. "How can I tell my mother when she's already so upset about Jack, but at least they're getting married as soon as the baby's born."

In an effort to take Violet's mind off her own troubles, Josie asked, "When's it due?"

"In about three weeks, she's so enormous I think it might be twins," there was a hint of a smile on Violet's forlorn little face.

"You are sure about this aren't you, Violet?"

"Yes, I'm sure all right, it was confirmed by the doctor who said I must tell my mother."

"You don't think he'll tell her do you?"

"I shouldn't think so, he said he wouldn't anyway, he said it was up to me."

"Couldn't you tell your father?" asked Josie, trying to put herself in Violet's situation and knowing what she would do in the same circumstances.

"That would be even more difficult, I think I'd rather face my mother."

"You're going to have to do something."

"I know, I know."

"I'm not being much help am I?" said Josie.

"Yes, oh yes, it's a help to be able to tell someone."

"You're so young Violet, are you sure you want this baby?"

"No, not if I had a choice, but I haven't so that's all there is to it."

Josie had only a vague idea about abortion and no idea at all as to how one would organise it.

"If you're thinking of abortion, forget it, my mother's a Catholic," said Violet, correctly interpreting Josie's silence.

"Is she? I'd no idea."

"Well, I s'pose you could say she's not a practising Catholic but I know she would have a very Catholic outlook when it came to abortion. I know what she had to say about Jack." Although they were no nearer to any sort of solution at least Violet seemed a bit less agitated.

Saying a quick cheerio as Violet prepared to leave, following the return of her parents, Josie said, "Do you want to come round again tomorrow after work?"

"Come to tea if you like, Violet," said Mrs Brown, pleased that perhaps this might mean that Josie wouldn't spend all evening closeted in her room.

Next evening, after a fairly simple tea, which Mrs Brown had managed to stretch to cover an extra one, the girls went out for a walk.

As soon as they were on their own Violet said, "Don't ask Josie - no, I haven't told her yet."

"What can I say? It's up to you Violet."

"I'll think of something," said Violet without much conviction.

For the next couple of weeks, whenever possible, Josie spent her evenings with Violet.

Meeting Penny unexpectedly on her way home from work one day, she was faced with the inquisition of Penny wanting to know what was wrong with Violet.

"I think she's had a bit of a tiff with Robert, she's a bit down at the moment," Josie tried to be as non-committal as possible.

Josie steadfastly stuck to Violet during the weeks that followed, trying to persuade her to confide in her mother. Sometimes Violet, in desperation, promised Josie that she would but always when it came to facing her mother she backed down again.

Thus, the situation stayed exactly the same, until one evening when Josie was at home alone with John, there was a knock at the front door.

"Answer the door will you John?" Josie called from the bedroom where she was writing yet another letter to Edwin.

"Josie!" John called up the stairs. "There's an Air Force chap to see you."

"Oh, no!" said Josie, immediately thinking it must be Gerry come to ask why she wasn't writing to him as she had promised!

She came warily down the stairs wondering how she was going to explain this to John. She was completely taken by surprise because in the hall stood Robert, nervously clutching his cap in his hand.

"Hello Josie, may I speak to you for a moment please?"

"Come into the front room," said Josie, firmly shutting the door on John.

"Er - I wanted to talk to you about Vi. I daren't go round to her house in case her parents are there!"

"Yes, I can understand that," said Josie frostily.

"You know then do you, about me and Vi I mean?"

"I know about Violet, but you seem to have washed your hands of the whole affair."

"I'm sorry I said that but at the time I was completely floored, I've thought about it since and I can't leave Vi to face it on her own!"

"What do you intend to do about it then?"

"I don't know," he sounded desperate. "I love Vi and she loves me. I didn't mean to get her in this mess, but you know how it is."

Josie felt that she didn't know 'how it was' at all, she could only base her judgement on Edwin's behaviour toward her, but then she didn't see Edwin that often, maybe it was different if you saw each other all the time. Josie was trying hard to make allowances for Robert who looked completely miserable.

"What is it you want me to do?" she asked.

"I want to talk to Vi, I wondered if you could ask her to meet me."

"Would you like me to go and ask Violet to come up here? At least you can talk in private."

"What about your family?"

"They're all out and probably won't be back for at least another couple of hours."

Robert looked so worried that Josie felt her animosity towards him beginning to wane.

"You stay here then and I'll see if I can get her to come."

"Do you mind if I smoke?" Robert asked, fumbling for his cigarette case.

"You look as if you could do with one."

"You're a mate Josie, thanks."

As Josie walked towards her friend's house she wondered just what Robert intended to do. She thought that Violet would be overjoyed that he was trying to contact her again.

The door was answered by Violet's mother.

"Is Violet in?" asked Josie, searching Mrs Linsey's face for any sign that she knew Violet's awful secret, but she only smiled and said:

"I'm glad you've come Josie, try to persuade her to go out with you, she seems to do nothing but mope around the house and she doesn't get on very well with Joan - it's beginning to get on my nerves. Violet, Josie's here for you!"

Josie followed Mrs Linsey into the front room where Violet sat pretending to read a book.

"Hi Violet, I wondered if you'd like to come up to mine for the evening?"

"Anything to get out of here," said Violet under her breath as her mother disappeared down the corridor. "I'll get my coat."

It was not until they were well away from the house that Josie told her of Robert's visit and that he was waiting to see her. Violet stopped in her tracks.

"I thought you'd be pleased."

"What does he want?"

"He wants to talk to you, I think he's genuinely sorry."

"Fat lot of good that's going to do!"

"Oh, come on Violet," said Josie taking her arm, "don't say you're not coming to meet him."

"What about your Mum and Dad?"

"They're both out, so's John."

Josie pushed the reluctant Violet through the front door to where Robert, who had heard them approaching, was waiting.

"Oh Vi!" he said holding out his arms. A tearful Violet threw her arms around his neck.

"OK you two," said Josie, feeling like an intruder, "you can use the front room to sort out your troubles. Would you like me to make you a cup of tea?"

"Please," said Robert with his arm still around Violet, who was weeping quietly.

Josie made sure she took an age to make the tea, putting out some of her mother's shortcakes, which she knew she'd have to account for when her mother returned, but she'd think of an explanation by then. Carefully knocking on the door, after what she considered was long enough for all the making up to have taken place.

"Would you like your tea now?" she asked as she entered.

Violet was sitting in the armchair looking much happier. Robert sat on the arm of the chair with his arm around Violet's shoulders.

"Would you like me to go again?"

"No, no," they said together.

As Josie handed Violet a cup of tea, Robert said, "We've decided to face Vi's parents and see if they'll let us get married."

"I don't mind facing them if Robert's with me," said Violet.

"I'm pleased," said Josie. "What about your parents Robert?"

"I don't think they'll object, in fact I know they won't, they've always left me to make my own decisions. Anyway, I know they'll love Vi when they meet her. I have to get permission to

198

marry from my CO but I can't see any problem there. I'll explain the situation if I have to, that'll clinch things."

"Vi," said Robert after he had finished his tea, "shall we go and face your parents now?"

"We've got to do it sometime, so the sooner the better I suppose, I'm not looking forward to it, I think they'll go right up the wall."

"They may be more understanding than you think," said Josie encouragingly.

Josie was on tenterhooks for the remainder of the evening wondering how they were getting on. She felt she wouldn't dare go to Violet's house anymore, so she hoped that Violet would at least come round and let her know what had happened.

As she made her way home from work next day Violet was waiting at the bottom of the road, outside the telephone box which had been their favourite meeting place in the carefree days of their childhood.

"How'd it go?" she asked anxiously.

"They were furious, of course. I thought my father was going to thump Robert. Surprisingly, it was my mother who made him see sense. I thought she'd take it the hardest but she was quite understanding. I think she's grown to quite like Robert, suppose the fact that he wants to marry me carried a lot of weight with her. If he'd abandoned me, I think she'd probably have killed him."

"When are you getting married then?"

"As soon as we can arrange it. We're going to Robert's the weekend after next when he's got a weekend pass. He wants me to meet his family. Do you think they'll hate me Josie? They might think I've trapped him."

"Don't be silly Violet, I'm sure he wouldn't take you if he wasn't sure they'd accept you."

"I hope you're right, I'll be glad to get it over with. Provided there's no problems and Robert gets his CO's permission then we'll get married next month when Robert's got seven days' leave due. It'll be very quiet, just the parents I expect, but I hope you'll come Josie. Robert wants me to ask you."

"You've certainly got well ahead with your plans considering you didn't tell your parents till last night."

"Well, under the circumstances, there's no time to lose is there? I'd like to still look a reasonable shape when we go to the

Registrar's, I'd feel so ashamed if it was too obvious."

"I wouldn't get yourself too uptight about it Violet, it's a pretty common reason for getting married these days, it's nothing to be ashamed about. I'm glad it's working out so well for you."

"I'm very grateful to you Josie," Violet smiled. "If it's a girl I'll call it Josie."

"I'm flattered," laughed Josie, "but I expect Robert will want to call her Violet."

"Not Violet, I hate the name, I couldn't saddle my baby with it."

It seemed strange to hear Violet, who Josie had always looked on almost as a little sister, talking about her own child.

"You won't tell anyone will you Josie? Not Penny or anyone."

" 'Course I won't, your secret's safe with me."

The war seemed to have taken a back seat for a while, at least as far as Violet, Robert and Josie were concerned. So busy were they with various arrangements that they were only vaguely aware that in most war areas the tide seemed to be turning in favour of the Allied forces.

Edwin was very surprised when a letter from Josie gave more details of the forthcoming marriage of her friend Violet. He knew that Violet was even younger than Josie and, although he had never met Robert, he knew from Josie's information that Robert was younger than he was. 'They're a bit young for marriage,' he wrote in his reply to Josie's letter, 'I hope they don't live to regret it, so many hurried marriages seem to end in divorce.' He was not in a position to understand the reason for the haste and Josie, true to her promise to Violet, had not enlightened him.

Eventually the great day arrived. As the Registrar completed the simple service, Robert's mother was looking rather stony-faced. Oh dear! thought Josie, I don't think she's very happy with the arrangement. I hope this doesn't mean trouble for you, poor little Violet.

Back at Violet's house, the buffet, produced by Violet's mother, was quite impressive. Considering the shortages and rationing, it was nothing short of remarkable.

When next Josie ran into Penny, she wanted to know all about the wedding.

"Why didn't she ask any of her friends except you?" she asked.

"Well," Josie racked her brains for a plausible excuse, "they just wanted a quiet wedding and you know how difficult it is to arrange a reception with rationing and everything."

"Mm, who went then?"

"Just the parents, Robert's brother and me."

"What's his brother like?" asked Penny, never too hesitant at asking awkward questions.

"Very nice," said Josie, choosing her words carefully. "He's in the Air Force like Robert."

"Is there any reason they got married so quickly?" asked Penny, giving Josie a playful dig in the ribs.

"Not that I know of," lied Josie. "I think it's just the war and the possibility of Robert being sent abroad at any time."

Josie's self-imposed isolation from the opposite sex was beginning to wear a little thin, when something happened to justify an alteration in her attitude.

On a dull Saturday afternoon, when Josie was stuck at home feeling rather sorry for herself, all her friends being otherwise engaged (Penny had a date with Buck, the twins were working and Violet was not feeling very well), Josie gazed out of the window at the sparse display of confectionery in the shop window opposite wishing she hadn't already spent all her sweet coupons. She fancied a bar of nut chocolate, and the more she thought about it the more the longing for the taste of the chocolate grew. She wondered if she could borrow a couple of coupons from any of the family.

Having a sweet tooth and being a self-confessed pig when it came to chocolate, sweet rationing was, of all rationing, the one she found hardest to bear. When the war is over, thought Josie, I think I'll buy a sweet shop of my own. She had a mental picture of herself, safely married to Edwin, running a little sweet-shop together.

As she gazed idly out of the window an American serviceman walked past, he appeared to be looking at the house numbers and consulting a piece of paper he was carrying in his hand. Hesitating slightly, he pushed open the front gate to Josie's house. 'Heavens!' said Josie to herself, 'I wonder what he wants?'

He tramped down the gravel path and tapped smartly at the front door.

"I'll go," Josie called to her mother.

Standing on the step was a young American soldier wearing

rimless glasses and looking rather like Glenn Miller.

"Hi!" he said. "Are you Josie?"

"Yes," said Josie gazing at him mystified.

"I'd better explain," he said. "My name's Zigmund, I think we have a mutual pen-friend in Canada."

"Joan Garden," said Josie quickly.

"Sure, that's right, she's been my pen-pal since I was at school, yours too I guess. She gave me your address so's I could visit you."

"Do come in," said Josie. "What's your other name?"

"Grzybinski," he said, taking off his hat and entering the hallway. He laughed at Josie's surprised look, "It sure is a bit of a mouthful, my father's Polish you see."

Zigmund followed her into the living-room where her mother was busy sewing.

"You're Josie's Mum," he said, extending his hand, "I sure am pleased to meet you ma'am."

Josie explained the situation to her mother.

"How nice," said Mrs Brown. "It's as if we all know Joan, she's been corresponding with Josie for such a long time. Take your coat off and make yourself at home."

"Thanks ma'am," he said handing her his great coat.

From the pocket of his jacket he produced sweets and chewing gum.

"I thought you might like some candy bars and gum, seeing as how it's rationed here."

"How lovely," said Josie eyeing the confectionery hungrily.

The introductions were repeated as first Mr Brown and then John returned home.

"You'll stay for tea?" said Mrs Brown.

"That's most hospitable of you ma'am but are you sure, I mean with the rationing and everything?

"Oh, I think I can stretch to an extra one."

"Thanks then if you're sure, then maybe we could take in a movie Josie?"

"I'd like that," said Josie.

Over tea, Zigmund answered their questions about his home and his family. He charmed both Mr and Mrs Brown by calling them Ma'am and Sir. Mr Brown said later that he had never met such a polite young man.

"Which film would you like to see?" Josie asked as they walked down the road after tea.

"You choose Josie, you'll know which is the best movie."

"Well, I've already been to the Haymarket this week but there's quite a good film at the Regent and we can get there by bus."

Josie glanced at him shyly as they waited in the queue for the bus. He was quite handsome really and his eyes behind the unusual spectacles were blue and smiling.

This was the first of many dates Josie was to have with Zigmund. At the end of the evening after seeing her back home to her front gate he said, "Josie, before we say goodnight, I think I should tell you, I have a steady girlfriend in the States."

Relieved, Josie replied, "I've been trying to think of a way to tell you that I have a steady boyfriend."

Zigmund grinned.

"My girlfriend's named Ginny."

"My boyfriend's named Edwin, he's in the Navy."

"Good, now we've cleared the air about our commitments, I think we can be great buddies. When can I see you again?"

They began to have regular dates two or three times a week. Zigmund always arrived with his pockets full of sweets and chewing gum. At each visit he also brought Mr Brown a couple of cigars in aluminium cases which he purchased at the P.X. on the base. Mr Brown occasionally smoked one after dinner on Sunday but he saved most of them to have at Christmas.

For Josie, as well as much prized silk stockings, he usually brought a corsage of flowers in a small transparent box, something which Josie had never seen before and which she rather self-consciously pinned on the lapel of her coat.

After the first few dates Zigmund gently kissed her cheek as they said goodnight at the front gate.

"What will Ginny say?" Josie asked.

"Oh, she won't mind," said Zigmund, not very convincingly. "She appreciates the fact that I'm far away from home, guess she may be seeing other guys anyway."

Josie doubted whether Ginny would be very happy if she knew and she was certain Edwin wouldn't. She persuaded herself that, as long as it was limited to a goodnight kiss, perhaps it was permissible under the circumstances, after all there was a war on.

Anyway, she was at the moment quite glad of Zigmund's friendship.

Violet had obtained accommodation near Robert's base. She had called to tell Josie the news.

"It's not much, just a bed-sitter, but I think we can manage until I have the baby, then maybe we can get something bigger. I'll be glad to make the move anyway, whatever it is; since Joan's had her baby the house had been in turmoil, he cries most of the time, especially at night - thank God it wasn't twins! I hope mine's not going to be so much trouble."

"Has Jack married her yet?" asked Josie.

"Yes, last Saturday," said Violet. "I stayed at home to look after Bruce," she laughed. "What a name, I ask you?"

Josie waited to feel a pang at the news of the wonderful Jack's wedding but nothing happened, she just felt rather sorry for Joan and poor little Bruce.

Penny was now so wrapped up with Buck, she was talking about becoming a GI bride. The only friends available of late were the twins or, to be more precise one of the twins, as the other was going out with a Polish airman.

Ray was already expecting to be called up and was hoping to get into the RAF. Duncan had volunteered for the Army as soon as he was seventeen and a half, much to the consternation of his mother. He had already finished his basic training, home on seven days leave and, looking much more manly in his uniform, he invited Josie out for a date.

They chatted about old times when they were children. He told Josie that he had worshipped her from afar all the time they were at school. He laughed as he recalled the times she had stuck up for him when he got into any sort of trouble.

"The others used to call me 'Mother's boy' and I s'pose I was," he said. "That's one of the reasons I've volunteered, I need to get away from her."

"She's a bit overpowering I suppose but, with you being her only child and not having a husband, she has no one else to concentrate on. I think it'll be good for you to get away, pity there has to be a war to achieve it though."

Penny had somehow found out about Josie's dates with Zigmund.

"You're a sly one Josie, I thought you weren't going to have anything to do with Yanks in case Edwin disapproved," she said.

"This is a totally different situation," said Josie explaining how she had met Zigmund.

"Oh, I see," said Penny. "So have you told Edwin about him?"

"No, not yet," Josie confessed, "but I will when I get around to it."

Penny used all her powers of persuasion to try to get Josie to make up a foursome with her and Buck to go dancing.

"Ziggy's not keen on dancing," said Josie.

Penny had to admit that, fond as she was of Josie, when she thought about it, she rather enjoyed being on her own with Buck, he was very entertaining company.

The war dragged relentlessly on and, although things were now very much improved for the Allies, even the most optimistic of the population had to admit that they could see no end to it in the foreseeable future.

As a prelude to the invasion of Italy, the RAF were now daily bombing Italian rail junctions, these were reported to be out of action from Reggio to Naples. The following week, sitting next to Zigmund at the Odeon, there were amazing shots of the beginning of the naval bombardment in the Straits of Messina. Then came the report that Mussolini had been overthrown and his successor Marshal Bagadoglio was making overtures to the Allies for an armistice. By the following morning Italian forces were surrendering wholesale without even a token resistance.

In spite of Zigmund's assurance that he had told Ginny all about going out with her, Josie was not really convinced that this was the case. Her thinking was coloured by the fact that she had not yet told Edwin about Zigmund.

She was quite surprised, therefore, when in early December a parcel arrived bearing an American stamp. Rather mystified she tore off the brown paper wrapping only to find another wrapper covered in Christmas greetings, holly and the stars and stripes. Even more mystified, she removed this wrapping also. Inside was a gold coloured box tied with ribbon and, on opening this, Josie found an array of make-up such as she had not seen since before the war began.

"Coo! What have you got there?" asked John coming up behind her.

"Look at it, isn't it wonderful! But where has it come from?

Maybe Ziggy ordered it for me."

"There's a letter here," said John rummaging through the discarded wrappings. Hurriedly tearing open the envelope Josie searched for a signature at the bottom of the enclosed letter.

'Very best wishes for a Happy Yuletide, Love Ginny!'

"Who's Ginny?" asked John peering over her shoulder.

"A friend of Ziggy's, isn't it nice of her?" said Josie convinced at last that Ginny was aware of her existence.

Later in the evening she was showing Zigmund the gift.

"I didn't really believe you had told her about me, sorry Ziggy!" she grinned. "I have to admit I haven't told Edwin about you."

"Naughty Josie, do you think he'll be mad? Why should he be? Ginny was quite pleased I'd found you and your nice family, so I've got somewhere to visit when I can get off the base."

"Mm, give me time and I'll think of a way to tell him."

"I sure will be pleased when you do."

The war was almost forgotten, or at least was taking a back seat, as Josie found herself enjoying life more than she had since the war began. Zigmund became a regular visitor and had even been taken to visit Grandma who was just as charmed by him as her mother was.

The thing that Josie found most intriguing was the fact that she and Zigmund had become what she could only describe as mates or 'buddies' as Zigmund called it. Although they enjoyed each other's company, kissed each other on meeting and parting and often walked hand in hand, there was never any question of falling in love. The only explanation Josie could think of for this was that they were true to Ginny and Edwin in their own way.

As Christmas approached, Zigmund supplied many extras for the festivities, including a large fruit cake, sent to him by his mother.

"Thought you might like it ma'am," he said as he gave it to Mrs Brown.

"It's most kind of you, but if your mother sent it, I think you should keep it and share it with your friends."

"Shucks ma'am, we get plenty of cake at the base and I'm sure Mom would approve of you having it, she knows how hospitable you've been to me."

Mrs Brown did not need any further persuading, she accepted

with thanks. It was the most beautiful cake she had seen since the war started.

Zigmund would be on duty until late afternoon on Christmas Day. Mrs Brown had invited him for tea.

"Josie, do you think your Mom would mind if I bring my buddy, he's got nowhere to go, he doesn't know anyone in England, he's a nice guy, you'll like him."

"Of course she won't mind," said Josie, knowing without asking that her mother would never turn away a soldier.

Just before tea-time on Christmas Day Zigmund arrived at the front door. Josie ran to let him in.

"Merry Christmas Josie!" he said kissing her as he swung her off her feet. As he put her back on the ground, she was aware of a tall gangling young American still standing in the doorway. "This is my buddy Rex," he laughed. "Shut the door man and come on in."

The tall boy, blushing slightly, entered shutting the door behind him.

"This is Josie," said Zigmund by way of introduction.

"Pleased to meet you," said Rex, turning an even deeper red and shaking her hand. Golly, thought Josie, a shy American, I didn't think there was such a thing.

"I brought a couple of bottles of wine and a bourbon for your Dad," said Zigmund.

Rex stood awkwardly in the background.

'Come and meet the family," said Josie, trying to put him at e se.

"Thanks," he said politely, "It sure is kind of you to invite me."

"It's a pleasure," said Josie, relieving him of his great coat and cap.

Zigmund had already gone ahead and, opening the living-room door, shouted, "Happy Christmas Mom and Pop!"

"He's a great guy," said Rex, "I hope you don't mind me tagging along."

"Of course not, I'm glad you could come."

She studied Rex as she hung up his coat. He was much taller and thinner than Zigmund and he had soft brown eyes which crinkled up when he smiled.

"I've heard a lot about you from Zigmund," he said shyly.

When all the introductions had been completed and the wine

and whisky poured out, Ziggy raised his glass.

"Here's to a happy Christmas and an end to the war before the next one."

Sitting down to tea with the cake from Zigmund's mother in pride of place and an added festive touch provided by the crackers which Penny had obtained from her place of work, at last everyone pronounced themselves too full to eat another thing. Mr Brown made his usual announcement.

"Anyone care for a game of cards?"

He knew that they would all say yes, but it was part of the Christmas tradition to ask: "How about you young people?"

"Long as it's not whist," said Zigmund with a grin.

When they finally got seated to start their game of cards, Josie found herself sitting opposite Rex. As the game progressed, each time she looked up from her hand of cards, she found Rex gazing at her. As soon as she raised her eyes and met his, he immediately looked down at his cards, a faint pink flush covering his cheeks. Josie was already feeling strangely attracted to this shy awkward boy.

When a break for refreshments was announced, Zigmund said, "Let me help you ma'am," immediately got to his feet and followed Mrs Brown into the kitchen.

Everyone got up and moved around a bit admiring the Christmas decorations which, this year, were mostly hand-made by Josie.

Before she had time to start a conversation with Rex, he was collared by two of her uncles who wanted to know what life was like in the USA.

Rex was making a gallant effort to answer the questions being thrust at him but glanced anxiously at Josie as if imploring her to rescue him.

"Anyone like a cup of tea?" asked Josie.

"Oh, please," chorused Auntie Lil and Grandma.

"Rex, could you give me a hand with the tea?"

Rex thankfully disentangled himself and fled into the kitchen behind Josie. "I thought you needed rescuing," said Josie as she put the kettle on. "The cups and saucers are in the cupboard over there and the tray's on the table."

"Right," said Rex, making himself useful. Neither seemed to know what to say. Josie was racking her brains for something to say to prolong the tea-making as long as possible.

"Want any help?" said Zigmund cheerfully from the doorway and the spell was broken. "You all right buddy?" he asked.

"Sure, everything's fine."

The moment had passed. Ziggy, familiar with the kitchen layout, got the spoons and poured milk into a jug.

"I knew you'd like Josie, she sure is a great girl," said Zigmund.

Rex busied himself with the cups and didn't reply.

When the party eventually broke up and the grandparents, aunts and uncles had departed to catch the last bus home, Mr and Mrs Brown retired to the kitchen to clear up the debris.

"Can't face this in the morning Em," said Mr Brown. "Let's wash up and get it done with."

"Want any help ma'am?" enquired Zigmund.

"No thanks, all the same Zigmund, you take your friend and have a last drink with Josie before you have to go back to camp."

"Lovely fire, Josie," said Ziggy.

"Just like home," said Rex. "We had a coal fire in the parlour."

"I expect you miss your home," said Josie.

"Yes," Rex sighed, " 'specially at this time of the year. Oh, not that I haven't enjoyed visiting you," he finished lamely looking into her eyes pleading for understanding.

"I knew you'd like it here," said Zigmund cheerfully, unaware of Rex's confusion. "It's been a lovely Christmas Josie, thanks for having me," he laughed.

Josie poured the drinks and handed them round. The only illumination came from the twinkling lights on the Christmas tree and the warm glow from the fire. They sipped their drinks, each deep in thought.

"When will I see you again Josie?" asked Ziggy. "I'm off duty Monday afternoon."

"I've got the day off too on Monday," said Josie.

"Great then, when shall I call for you? Tell you what, do you have a girlfriend who'd make up a foursome? Then Rex could come too."

"Well, I think I've got one friend who won't be working," said Josie, praying that Maggie would agree to come.

"What do you want to do?"

Josie thought for a moment.

"There's the Christmas fair on at the Cattle Market, you might like that."

"Sounds great, what do you think?" he asked, turning to Rex.

"Are you sure it'll be all right Josie? I wouldn't want to intrude."

"You won't be intruding, I'd like you to come," said Josie.

"Fine then, I'd like that, the fair sounds great."

As they sat peacefully watching the last dying embers of the fire, the war forgotten, Josie thought this must be one of the happiest Christmases she had ever spent. She even forgot to feel guilty because she was obviously enjoying herself while poor Edwin was facing goodness knows what hardships at sea.

15

Rex

Maggie agreed to fall in with Josie's request to make up a foursome.

"I've nothing else to do," she said.

"Don't sound so enthusiastic," said Josie.

"What's he like, this friend of Zigmund's?"

"Well, he's nothing like Ziggy, he's rather quiet and a bit shy."

"Not a typical Yank then?"

'No, thought Josie, I suppose that's what I find attractive about him and he's really interesting to talk to if one takes the trouble to draw him out.' She was not, however, about to tell Maggie of her private opinion.

Although Monday was the 27th, it counted as Boxing Day as the 26th was a Sunday. The first good news of the day was of the sinking of the German Battleship *Scharnhorst*. The second good news was that the visit to the fair had gone even better than Josie had dreamed and she had to admit she had done a fair bit of dreaming since Christmas Day.

With what seemed like unlimited money supplied by Zigmund and Rex, they had visited almost all of the side-shows, tried their hand at every game of chance. Josie could not, however, overcome her dislike of the dodgem cars.

"Let's have a go on this," said Zigmund.

"I love the dodgems," said Maggie.

"I don't, I hate them," said Josie. "But you three go, I'll wait at the side."

"I'm not very keen," said Rex. "You and Ziggy go," he turned to Maggie.

"Do you mind, Josie?" asked Maggie.

"No, of course not."

"I'll stay with Josie," said Rex.

"Come on then, let's make with the action."

"Thank goodness for that," said Rex, greatly daring.

"Don't you like my friend?" asked Josie.

"Sure, she's OK, I just like you better."

Josie blushed and stammered.

"Do you think we should wait here until they finish their rides?"

"I'd like to go on the rifle range, maybe I can win you a teddy bear."

"Come on then, I expect they'll find us anyway."

Rex proved to be an excellent shot. They had wandered quite a way from the dodgems looking for a rifle range which had prizes. There were no teddy bears but there were little celluloid dolls with feathers stuck on their head.

"Kupie dolls," said Rex.

"I've never heard them called that before."

At the first try Rex was nowhere near the score required for a doll.

"I'll have another go," he whispered to Josie as he handed over the money for a second try. This time he scored four bull's-eyes and one near miss.

"Like a doll for your girl, soldier?" said the stall-holder.

Rex blushed and took the doll, handing it to Josie.

"Wish it was true," he said shyly, trying to get hold of Josie's hand as they were jostled by the crowd.

There was a shout of "Wait for us!" from Ziggy as he caught sight of the two of them.

"Gosh! that was some ride," said Ziggy. "What'll we do now?"

"The fair will close as soon as it's black-out time so how about finding somewhere for tea and then taking in a movie?" said Josie.

Ziggy moved to Josie's side taking her hand to battle his way through the crowds. Josie looked despairingly at Rex, trailing along behind with Maggie at his side. They managed to find somewhere for a cup of tea and a sandwich.

"I'm beginning to like tea," said Ziggy. "We drink mostly coffee in the States. I couldn't stand it at first though."

"I suppose it's an acquired taste," said Josie. "But we drink gallons of it, especially when we were getting air-raids every night. It's one rationed item that everyone finds hard to manage on, that and chocolate," she laughed. "Well, chocolate's not a problem since I met you," she said turning to Ziggy.

After the film they began walking home, they would have to pass Maggie's house on the way to Josie's. I hope, thought Josie, that we don't leave Rex to say goodnight to her while we continue home. She fretted all the way to Maggie's front gate, hardly taking in the conversation of the other three.

"So long Maggie," said Ziggy as she stood with her hand on the garden gate.

"Back to work tomorrow," said Josie, searching for something to say so that Rex wouldn't be left on his own with her friend.

"Me too," said Maggie. "I'm on late shift the rest of the week."

"I'll see you next week then, I'll come round," said Josie.

"Er . . . thanks for a pleasant day," said Rex. "I guess we'll meet again some time."

"S'pect so, goodnight all," said Maggie, moving toward her front door.

The two boys linked arms with Josie as they continued homewards.

"Great day," said Ziggy.

"Great," echoed Rex.

By Wednesday there was news of the sinking of three more German ships and a heavy night raid on Berlin. Zigmund had arrived early for their usual Wednesday night date. When Josie arrived home from work he was ensconced in the best armchair balancing a plate of Mrs Brown's home-made buns on one knee and a cup of tea in his hand.

"Hi, Josie!" he greeted her, attempting to rise.

"Sit down for heaven's sake," said Josie, "before you have an accident.

"I got off early," said Zigmund, then, looking at her sad face with some concern, he said, "Had a hard day, Josie?"

"Oh, much as usual."

Josie realised she was suddenly feeling sick with disappointment because Rex wasn't there.

As if sensing her mood, Zigmund said, "Rex is on duty tonight, we usually get the same rota but this month it's changed, so our duties alternate."

Josie looked even more depressed, did this mean that for a whole month Rex wouldn't be coming with Ziggy? She thought that she would rather put up with going out as a foursome than not see him at all.

When they returned home from their visit to the pictures, Zigmund, leaning on the front gate, his cap in his hand, said, "Josie, would you like me to arrange a date with Rex for you when he's off duty?"

Josie's first instinct was to say no, of course not, then she wondered just how often she had mentioned Rex in the course of the evening to bring Zigmund to this conclusion.

"Why do you say that?" she asked.

"Well, you seem to get on fine together and I know he'd like a date with you, and as we're on different duties, well," he finished rather lamely, "if you'd rather not."

"I didn't say I'd rather not," said Josie quickly.

Zigmund either didn't notice, or pretended not to notice, the eagerness of Josie's reply.

"You're sure he wouldn't rather have a date with Maggie?"

Zigmund grinned, "Yes, I'm sure about that, I don't think they hit it off too well together. He's off Saturday and I'm not, how does Saturday suit you?"

"Fine, I'm not doing anything Saturday."

Josie couldn't wait for Saturday to come, even old year's night enlivened by Zigmund's presence seemed to pale into insignificance when she thought of her forthcoming date with Rex.

On Friday night when there was a quiet moment during the festivities Zigmund whispered, "It's all arranged for tomorrow night. Rex'll meet you at the bottom of the road at six o'clock, he's a bit shy about picking you up from home."

"That's OK then," Josie tried not to sound too eager.

She wished she had been seeing the new year in with Rex instead of Zigmund, then immediately felt sorry for such thoughts, after all if it hadn't been for Zigmund, she'd never have met Rex in the first place.

As twelve o'clock chimed on the wireless everyone ran around kissing each other, she kissed Zigmund quite enthusiastically.

"Happy New Year Ziggy!" she whispered.

Josie got through Saturday morning in a kind of daze. When

the dinner-time whistle blew she left the factory thankful she didn't have to return until Monday morning.

The afternoon seemed to drag, she checked the clock every half an hour. To pass the time, she sorted out the clothes she would wear for her date with Rex, changed her mind three times, then went back to the outfit she had picked in the first place.

Promptly at six o'clock Josie made her way carefully through the darkness to the corner of the road where Rex was already waiting. She wasn't able to see if he was there until she was practically on top of him. Suddenly, she was able to distinguish a shadowy figure and a hand reached out to touch her.

"Hi, Josie," he said, not relinquishing her hand.

"Have you been here long?"

"Only a few minutes.

"Why didn't you come to the house? It's awfully cold out here."

"I didn't know if I ought to do that in case your parents imagined you were out with Ziggy."

"Next time, come to the house, it doesn't matter if they know I'm out with you, after all it's not as if they haven't met you."

"Right then, if you say so Josie, I'm glad you think there'll be a next time," he added still holding her hand, which he gave a comforting squeeze. "What would you like to do?"

"I don't mind, you choose."

"It's a bit cold for a walk, maybe we'd better go to the movies."

"We could walk to the Odeon, it's not far."

"Sounds like a good idea, that way we'll get a walk as well as a movie."

"This way then," said Josie leading the way. Rex tucked her hand through his arm as they walked in the soft darkness, not a chink of light could be seen anywhere. An air-raid warden passed patrolling his beat checking that all the black-out restrictions were being observed.

He called a cheery, "Evening, jolly cold night!" as he went past.

As they walked, their eyes became accustomed to the darkness and they found they were able to see better. Josie pointed out the spaces where houses had once stood and the flattened rubble strewn area that had once been her school.

215

For the next few weeks Rex dated Josie every time he was off duty. She found him much more interested in the cultural heritage of his temporary home town than Ziggy had ever been. Josie, always proud of her city, took great pleasure in showing Rex the cathedral, the castle and the numerous ancient churches.

One of the happiest days was spent visiting Elm Hill.

"Gee, it's so quaint, there's nothing like this in the States. I'm glad you're interested in your past history Josie, you've such a long one to look back on. In the States we just dream about this sort of thing, we imagine that one day when we're rich we might be able to afford to take a holiday in Europe and here I am getting it all for free; guess you might say that's one of the good things to come out of this war."

They sat for a little while on the wooden seat that surrounded the big elm tree, from which the street got its name.

The one thing that was causing Josie some heartache was when she thought of Edwin. She was surprised that Rex had never mentioned him, but eventually came to the conclusion that Ziggy was keeping mum on the subject and had not told his friend. Giving the matter some serious thought, she was forced to admit that her main worry was not that she was being untrue to Edwin but that Rex might find out about him.

She still saw Ziggy, although less frequently. He teased her about Rex.

"He's really fallen for you Josie, I always looked on him as a big slow loveable guy, he always says he's not very good with girls, but he seems to hit it off with you all right."

It was on the tip of Josie's tongue to ask Ziggy not to mention Edwin but she thought better of it. If he hadn't mentioned him up to now, chances were he had no intention of doing so.

As the weather grew slightly warmer they abandoned churches in favour of parks. After a couple of weeks Rex knew the location of every park in Norwich.

One evening, sitting under cover in the pavilion in Wensum Park, Rex, looking very serious, said, "Josie, would you like me to bring you flowers?"

"Flowers, why flowers?"

"Well, I know Ziggy does."

Josie tried to stifle a giggle without much success.

"Oh, that's it, Ziggy does, well promise you won't tell him, but

I find his corsages a bit of an embarrassment."

"Do you? It seems to be the practice where he came from when a guy is taking out a girl."

"Maybe if we were going to a dance then it would be quite nice to wear flowers, but pinning them on my coat when we're going to the pictures seems to me to look a bit ostentatious."

Rex laughed.

"Thank heaven for that, I'd be a bit embarrassed in a flower shop and I think I'd die carrying them through the streets. Doesn't seem to bother Ziggy though. When are you seeing him again?"

"Not until Saturday, you don't mind do you?"

"What if I did? Mind I mean?"

"Guess I'd stop seeing him," said Josie without hesitation.

"Would you? Would you do that for me?"

"If that was what you wanted."

"Gee," said Rex, "I wouldn't want that though, I know you're just friends and he's told you all about his girlfriend Ginny."

"Yes, and he's told her about me, and I guess she doesn't mind 'cos she sent me a Christmas present."

With some trepidation, Josie waited for any mention of Edwin; it had occurred to her that this might be what Rex was leading up to, but the moment passed and Rex said with a sigh, taking her hand.

"Gee, Josie, I've never met a girl like you before."

"Didn't you have a girl back home?"

"I knew one or two girls but no one special, I never really felt very much at ease with girls."

"Why not?"

"Well, I'm kind of awkward and clumsy and I get tongue tied when I get anywhere near a female."

"You don't with me, well, maybe you did at first but it's only because you're shy."

"I suppose so, I know I never felt so much at home with a girl before, I wrote and told my Mom about you, you don't mind do you Josie?"

Josie began to feel that things were perhaps moving a bit too fast, she was beginning to get overwhelmed by the devotion being shown by Rex. She knew that she liked him a lot, loved him maybe, but she needed time to get things in proportion and, at the back of her mind, there was always the nagging problem of what

217

k

to do about Edwin. She felt she needed to be very sure before she actually did anything at all about him. She tried to recall the happy times spent with Edwin, but the only thing which registered was Rex holding her hand and looking at her with such devotion in his eyes. She found it hard to even remember what Edwin looked like. They walked home hand in hand, the moon was bright and everything looked so peaceful it was hard to believe there was a war on.

Declining the offer to come in when they reached Josie's house, they stood for a few moments at the front gate arranging their next date.

"There's a good film on at the Odeon, Bob Hope in 'Let's Face It'. Do you like Bob Hope?" asked Josie.

"Sure, he's OK, good for a laugh. I can't get off till six on Thursday."

"We could meet outside the Odeon, it'll save some time if you don't come to collect me."

"Well, if you don't mind, that would be great, let's say six-thirty outside the Odeon."

Rex bent to kiss her goodnight.

"You won't bring me flowers will you?"

"How about candy bars?"

"Ah, candy bars, that's different."

"In that case, I shall woo you with candy bars."

With another kiss they parted. "Until Thursday!" he whispered in her ear, then he was gone. Josie watched him disappear out of sight as he turned the corner.

Still feeling slightly confused, she entered the house.

Josie decided to take a packed tea to work with her on Thursday afternoon, there really wouldn't be time to get home and back to the Odeon by six-thirty.

She ate her tea in the fire-watchers' hut sharing their pot of tea. Having tidied up and put on fresh lipstick, she said her farewells to the two duty fire-watchers and made her way to the Odeon.

Standing outside the swing doors she waited for Rex. Six-thirty became six-forty, she looked inside in case he was waiting there. A couple of servicemen leaned against the wall obviously waiting for their dates, but of Rex there was no sign. Going outside into the chill of the night air, she searched again as her eyes grew accustomed to the darkness, but there was no sign of him. 'Maybe he's got held up, or had to do extra duty. I'll wait until seven and see if he turns up,' she thought.

At seven she decided to wait until quarter-past seven then till half-past seven. At half-past seven she decided that he wasn't coming and she'd better go home.

Not keen on walking in the dark she waited for a bus. Sitting sadly in the dim interior she brooded about what had happened. Maybe there was a straightforward explanation for Rex's absence. If he had been unable to leave the base there was probably no way he could have let her know. She couldn't believe there could be any reason why he didn't want to meet her. She thought of their last meeting, of his shy hand clasp and his voice saying, 'I've never met a girl like you before'. So, she felt certain it was nothing she had said or done. A horrible thought occurred to her, supposing Zigmund had told him about Edwin?

"We're here Miss," said the conductor.

"Thanks," said Josie, rising quickly from her seat.

Josie spent an even more miserable day on Friday wondering why she had still heard nothing from Rex, surely if something unavoidable had happened last night he'd try to get in touch today. Day turned into night, Josie stayed at home just in case Rex called.

She spent a restless night, twisting and turning while she racked her brain to think of a reason for Rex's behaviour, sleep finally overcame her in the early hours of the morning.

The following day Josie had a date with Ziggy who was calling for her at 5.30. She had placed tea things on a tray ready for when Ziggy arrived, but by six o'clock he had still not arrived.

Putting on the wireless, the strains of the introduction music for 'In Town Tonight' greeted her. As usual there was a sudden stop and the announcer's voice said, "Once more, we stop the roar of London's traffic to introduce some of the interesting people who are 'In Town Tonight'. Lost in thought, Josie paid scant heed to all these interesting people who were saying their piece on the wireless. "Where the heck is he? Don't say he's not coming either," Josie muttered despairingly to herself.

By the time it reached seven-thirty Josie was forced to make the reluctant conclusion that indeed he wasn't coming. Maybe, she thought, he's told Rex about Edwin, so Rex doesn't want to see me anymore and he's decided to do the same. But why would he do that, she reasoned? After all, he's known all along that I hadn't told Rex about Edwin and I presume neither had he, so why should he do so now. There must be some other explanation. Perhaps the fact that Ziggy hadn't turned up was quite a good omen really, maybe they were confined to the base for some reason.

The days passed and there was no news of either Rex or Ziggy, they just seemed to have vanished. Josie had never really been sure of exactly where they were stationed and felt she would be too proud to go looking for them even if she had. She decided to stop thinking about them, it seemed the only way.

Edwin received a sudden shower of letters all in one batch. Strange, rather formal letters, not at all like Josie's usual effervescent style. Why, he wondered, had she suddenly written so many when previously she had slowed down the flow to a trickle, much to his relief. But Josie was salving her conscience and at the same time trying to blot out her feelings of being rejected.

After a few weeks, Josie had resigned herself to never hearing from her American friends again. She wished she could be like Penny, when her romance with Buck had ended, she had simply reiterated her belief that in war-time romances seldom lasted. Josie wondered all the same whether Penny was quite as blasé about it as she would have everyone believe, after all, it wasn't long ago that she had been considering becoming a GI bride.

The two girls, both hiding the truth and refusing to admit that they felt very let down by the Yanks, joined forces and decided to start going out together again.

"Let's not get involved with anyone, let's just enjoy ourselves," said Penny.

"Suits me," said Josie, "I've got to think of Edwin anyway."

But even as she said it, she wondered if she really wanted to think about him, or if she wasn't just turning her attention back to him because she was upset about Rex. How would she ever solve the dilemma? She didn't know if she really wanted to go back to staying at home writing letters to Edwin but knew in her heart of hearts that she didn't.

Firmly putting all thoughts of Ziggy, Rex and Buck out of their minds, the girls began once again to enjoy each other's company. They limited their activities to the cinema, walks, bike rides and visiting each other's houses, carefully steering clear of the dance-hall. They had vowed that they wouldn't allow themselves to be tempted in any further liaisons with the male sex. When not with Penny, Josie still had time to brood on her apparent abandonment by Rex.

Returning home for a hurried dinner one day, Josie's mother greeted her with the words:

"Letter for you, Josie, on the hall-stand."

"Oh," said Josie, not terribly interested, assuming it was from either Edwin or Jimmy. "What's for dinner?"

Casually picking up the letter, she didn't recognise the handwriting - certainly not Edwin, Jimmy or her pen-friend Joan. She tore open the letter, 'Dear Josie' it read. Josie's heart began to thump, as she turned over the page to find the signature, the letter ended, 'Your ever loving, Rex.'

Rex had written to her, she hadn't been jilted after all. She turned back to the beginning of the letter hoping that his strange disappearance would be explained. 'We've been moved, as I expect you've guessed by now. I'm not allowed to tell you where but you can write to me c/o C351 Engineer Regt. APO 872. Please write to me Josie, it would cheer me up no end. Just when everything was beginning to work out for us, I have to go and get posted. There was no way I could let you know, I kept thinking of you waiting for me at the Odeon.' Still clutching the letter, Josie sat down on the stairs, her legs seemed no longer able to support her.

"Dinner's ready," called her mother. "Who's the letter from?"

Josie was still gazing at it, slightly stunned.

"Rex, it's from Rex, he's been moved, he can't say where."

"Ziggy too?" enquired John.

"Well, I don't know for sure about Ziggy but it would seem likely that he's been posted too."

That evening Josie excused herself from going to the pictures with Penny, pleading a headache. After Penny had left looking somewhat disappointed Josie retired to her room to write to Rex. She told him of her anguish when he had failed to turn up for their date, of how she just couldn't imagine what had gone wrong. She started the letter and tore it up three times before finally being satisfied that the message she wanted to convey had been transferred to paper.

16

D Day

From Italy the news was good. Cassino had fallen after more than five months of ferocious fighting, during which time British, American Indians and French on the one hand and Germans on the other, fought and died in thousands.

The little ancient town was shadowed by 'Monastery Hill' which was crowned by the famous Benedictine Abbey. In the town itself the Germans had turned every house into a fortress.

As May gave way to June and the weather improved there seemed to be a general air of anticipation as if waiting for something momentous to happen.

Shortly before midnight of June 5th there was the familiar drone of aircraft on their way to bomb targets in France, only tonight the noise was louder than ever before. Many of the sleeping citizens who, hardened by the events of the past few years, usually slept through most noises, were awakened and gazed at the sky listening to the drone of what appeared to be hundreds of aircraft.

By dinner-time on the 6th the whole nation were made aware of the invasion of France by Anglo-American forces.

"At six o'clock this morning Allied troops once again set foot on French soil," said the dramatic announcement. "Airborne troops had landed two hours earlier."

Bulletins throughout the day continued to repeat the announcement. Sea-borne troops and supplies continued to land. "Troops were making good progress," said a later report.

It had dawned on Josie as soon as she heard the first reports that perhaps this explained the mysterious departure of Rex and Ziggy and the secrecy surrounding their whereabouts.

Within a couple of days the Allied troops had advanced from the beaches and captured the town of Bayeux, a name known to most British schoolchildren because of the Bayeux tapestry. The French population were reported to be mad with joy. Further reports stated that more troops were still landing but German resistance was hardening. However, enough advance had been made to enable Spitfires to touch down on emergency landing strips, Liberators and Fortresses continued to hammer away at enemy fortifications.

Details were beginning to filter through about a wonderful British invention named the Mulberry Harbour, this was a prefabricated harbour which had been towed by tugs across the Channel to facilitate the landing of men and supplies. The Luftwaffe made repeated attacks but were, in most cases, driven off by gunfire and fighters. Later reports said some damage had been sustained but the harbourage continued to protect Allied shipping.

There had been no communication from any of the boys for almost a month, which seemed to suggest that they were indeed now in France, after the first few days of Allied slow progress and German counter-attack.

The news reports stated that American forces, under the command of Lieutenant General Omar Bradley, had occupied the head of Seine Bay and the small port of Carentan. They badly needed to establish a permanent port on the French coast, thus relieving the situation for the supplies being landed on the temporary Mulberry Harbour.

The newsreels at the cinemas were once again showing long lines of dejected German prisoners being ushered into wire compounds by surprisingly few well-armed British and American guards.

On June 22nd waves of bombers plastered the German lines.

As the weeks went by the reports were all of advances by British, American and Canadian forces. One of the most difficult battles took place at Caen, where the Canadians had to fight against German suicide squads of Nazi snipers who lurked in the ruins.

On July 9th it was announced that fighting in Caen had ended and the Canadians were now in complete control. Though the town was a wreck the newsreels showed the inhabitants welcoming their liberators with a fervour, which was quite surprising in view of their frequent losses. It was reported that, throughout the battle, they had sheltered in the old abbey and its cloisters.

Amid the euphoria at the way the war was progressing in France, the population of London were once again propelled into the front line. On July 15th the Germans started launching a new weapon of mass destruction on the capital, called VIs. These projectiles were soon dubbed 'Doodle-bugs'. The true description was a Pilotless Aerial Torpedo. The contraption was jet-propelled with a ton of explosives in its war head. They could be heard rushing through the air at an alarming rate, then suddenly the engine cut out, the noise ceased, and there was an uncomfortable silence while everyone ran for cover, then a terrific explosion as it hit the ground.

The citizens of the battered capital seemed to meet this new challenge as stoically as they had endured the earlier blitz, if the news reports were anything to go by. Josie, watching in a comfortable seat at the Odeon, felt that, as with the blitz, this cheerful attitude was being somewhat exaggerated. The thought of actually knowing something was about to drop from the sky made Josie go cold with fear.

During the next month the state of things in London took precedent over even the progress of the war in France. The newsreel pictures were horrifying; often the camera caught a 'doodle-bug' in its lens, recording its rapid decent once the noise stopped, then the terrible impact as it hit the ground, destroying everything around it.

These projectiles were fired at random, very few hitting military targets, but damage to property, hospitals, churches and even Buckingham Palace and Westminster Hall was considerable.

As the war progressed with almost every day a good day, as far as the Allies were concerned, the defeat of Hitler was looking a distinct possibility.

Out of the blue came a letter saying simply, 'Josie, please write to Rex at this address - Comp 'C' 351 Engineers, 4317 Hospital Plant, U.S. Army.' Josie had pounced joyously on the letter almost before it was through the letter-box, but her heart sank as she read the message and the signature, 'Love Ziggy.' What did it mean? Obviously Rex was in hospital, or could he just be attached to the hospital for some reason? But in that case surely he would have written himself.

Seeing her stricken look her mother asked, "Is it bad news from Ziggy?"

"He says Rex is in hospital," said Josie.

"Oh, dear, did Ziggy say if he was wounded?"

"He didn't say anything except would I write to him and he gave me the address."

By tea-time Josie had completed her letter to Rex. She had finally settled to keeping things on a rather formal basis. Once she had heard officially from Rex, things might be different but she felt it was up to him to determine the nature of their relationship.

She had also written a short note to Ziggy, hoping he was safe and thanking him for letting her know about Rex. She found it much easier to compose this letter as there was no conflict of emotion involved in her friendship with Ziggy.

She had arranged to meet Penny and go to the pictures in the evening. Though her heart was not really in it, Josie felt that she couldn't let Penny down, so, after eating what her mother called a 'proper tea' and assuring her father that she was now much better, Josie hurried down the road to meet Penny.

"The bus is about due," said Penny as they reached the stop. They were the only ones waiting.

"Rex is in hospital," said Josie dramatically.

"Golly, is he wounded then?"

"I don't really know for sure but I suppose he must be, I can't imagine that he could be attached to a hospital, he's in the Engineers so it doesn't seem very likely does it?"

"I s'pose not, how awful Josie, how did you find out he was in hospital?"

"Ziggy wrote to me to ask me to write to Rex."

It was on the tip of Penny's tongue to say 'that doesn't sound too good,' but she stopped in time as she looked at Josie's worried face. Instead, she said, "It might not be anything serious. Josie, how are you going to find out?"

"I've written to him and posted it on the way to meet you, now I can only wait."

"You're fond of him aren't you?"

"Yes, I like him a lot I suppose."

225

"What about Edwin?"

"I'm a bit worried about that, 'cos he wants us to get engaged next time he gets leave."

Josie had also received a letter from Violet informing her of the birth of a daughter. Robert was delighted, Violet had written, because he wanted a girl. The relationship with both sets of parents had improved greatly since the birth of their grandchild.

In her anxiety over Ziggy's letter she had almost forgotten that Violet had asked her if she would be a god parent to Elizabeth Violet, as the baby was to be called.

"Robert and I would be so pleased if you would and we'll be coming back to Mum's for the christening."

As they settled into their seats in the bus, Josie told Penny of Violet's request.

"Are you going to oblige?" asked Penny.

"I think I will, it would be rather nice, wouldn't it?"

"Considering how well you kept their secret, even from your best friend," said Penny, "I reckon it's only right for them to ask you."

"Doesn't seem possible does it, Violet a mother?"

A few days later Josie was still anxiously waiting for a message from Rex when something happened which momentarily took her mind off her worries about him: Edwin arrived home on leave unexpectedly.

Not having time to write a letter, Edwin had sent telegrams to his parents and to Josie, without realising the trauma a telegram could cause. The telegraph boy knocked at the door, which Josie answered.

"Telegram for Miss Josie Brown," he said.

Josie felt her heart turn over, telegrams always meant bad news. Her hands trembled so much she had difficulty in opening the small buff envelope. It couldn't be news of Jimmy because the telegram would be for her parents. It must be either Edwin or Rex. 'Home late afternoon, Love Edwin,' she read.

"Any answer?" said the boy.

"No thanks," said Josie in a shaking voice.

He turned smartly and marched back down the path. Josie watched him mount his red bicycle and ride away, although she was still in a daze.

"Who was that?" asked John. "Lord! a telegram!" he said as he caught sight of the printed form. "Not bad news, Josie?" he put an arm around his sister's shoulder.

Josie pulled herself together.

"No, no, not bad news, Edwin's coming home on leave."

"When?"

"Late today."

"That's good, isn't it?"

"Yes, that's good." Then with more enthusiasm because her brother seemed to expect it, "Of course it's good, it'll be great to see him again."

"Seems a long time since he was home." As his father appeared from the garden John called excitedly, "Edwin's coming home this afternoon Dad."

"Is he?" he looked at his daughter with some concern, wondering how she was taking the news.

Sensing that he was trying to weigh up her reaction, Josie tried to look suitably excited.

"Be lovely to see him again and it's so unexpected, I suppose he can't have had much warning himself or he would have written instead of sending a telegram."

"The telegram scared Josie, she went as white as a sheet," said John.

"I wonder if he sent one to his parents, I bet his mother nearly had heart failure if he did," said Josie.

Mr Brown thought Josie was rather overdoing the cheerful enthusiasm about Edwin and he wondered how much of her heart now belonged to the shy gangling American he had welcomed into his home. Although she had tried hard not to show it, he knew she had been devastated by the news that Rex was in hospital.

"I'll have to let Penny know that I won't be going to the movies tonight."

The quite unconscious use of the American word for a visit to the cinema instead of the English 'pictures' proved to her father just how much she was still thinking of the American.

For the rest of the afternoon Josie wrestled with her conscience. Should she tell Edwin about her friendship with Rex and Ziggy? Supposing he still wants to get engaged, did she really want to get engaged to Edwin? By tea-time she was almost dreading Edwin's knock at the door.

Her confusion did not escape her father's shrewd glance as she picked fretfully at her tea.

"Aren't you excited Josie?" enquired her mother. "It seems ages since Edwin came home."

"Yes, of course," she said without looking up and continuing to push the food around on her plate.

"Is he coming round tonight?"

"Depends what time he gets home I suppose, so I'll stay at home in case he comes."

By the time her parents returned from their visit to the pub, Josie was asleep in a comfortable armchair, the book she had been reading on the floor beside her. She stirred herself at the sound of a key in the door and went to greet her parents.

"Well, he hasn't come, perhaps he's not home yet."

"Possibly not, he didn't give any time on the telegram did he?"

"No, he probably didn't know, it's difficult to account for hold-ups when you're travelling these days."

"I think we'll go to bed Josie, are you intending to wait up?"

"Maybe I'll stay downstairs till midnight, if he's not here by then, well, I wouldn't think he'll come until tomorrow."

Going to work next morning, still having heard nothing from Edwin, Josie found herself getting a bit worried about his failure to turn up. Perhaps he would arrive home sometime today, or perhaps he may have arrived very late last night. In spite of herself, Josie was beginning to feel that her apprehension at the prospect of seeing Edwin again had probably been due to his long absence rather than her guilty feeling about keeping him in the dark about Zigmund and Rex.

By the time work finished for the dinner-time break, Josie was out of the door ahead of everyone, scanning the entrance for a sight of Edwin. Half way across the yard she could see his familiar navy clad figure, his sailor's cap on the back of his head and the quiff of hair that refused to stay put over his forehead.

"Josie!" he shouted, waving his hand.

Josie ran the rest of the way and was enveloped in his arms.

"It's so good to see you," he kissed her firmly on the lips.

"Not here," said Josie as a couple of boys passing by whistled.

By the second day's leave, they seemed to fall as naturally into their old relationship as if their separation had never happened. Later on, Josie came to wonder if it would have been quite so easy if there had been news from Rex. However, whilst Edwin was on leave, there was no communication whatsoever from Rex and Josie, on the odd occasion when she thought of him, was rapidly coming to the conclusion that maybe she never would hear from him again. She hoped her attitude to Edwin was not in any way coloured by this, it would be very unfair to Edwin if it was.

One evening, after a visit to the theatre and a leisurely drink in the theatre bar, they made their way to the bus stop.

"Let's walk home," said Edwin. "It's such a beautiful night, it seems a shame to be cooped up in a stuffy bus."

The moon cast a silver glow on buildings and bomb-sites alike, even the most devastated areas looked less forbidding in the moonlight.

"I think the civilians in Norwich have had as tough a time as anyone in the forces," said Edwin as they passed yet another pile of rubble, which had once been a thriving shopping centre. His hand tightened on Josie's.

"I don't know what I'd do if anything happened to you," he put his arms around her and kissed her tenderly.

They continued their walk in companionable silence for a little while, then Edwin stopped.

"Josie, if I can find somewhere romantic before we reach home, I want to ask you a question. I don't think I'm very good at this romantic stuff, but you know how I feel about you, don't you? I know everyone thought that because you were so young, once the war started and we were separated, we were bound to drift apart." Encircling her with his arms and kissing her cheek he continued, "They don't know you Josie, I never had any doubts that you'd be true to me."

Josie felt something inside her knot up. How could he be so trusting? She blinked away a tear, keeping her face pressed into the rough blue serge of his uniform.

"Let's get engaged Josie, we talked about it ages ago," he said as he stroked her hair.

"I - I don't know," muttered Josie.

"You mean you don't want to get engaged to me?"

"Yes, yes, I do," said Josie, reluctant to hurt his feelings. "It's just, well, getting engaged is a big step isn't it?"

"How do you mean?" He held her at arm's length.

229

"Well," said Josie floundering, "getting engaged usually means you're on the point of getting married."

"Not always, specially not in war-time. I mean, we don't have any idea how long the war will last and I wouldn't want to get married till it's over. I wouldn't want to leave you a widow before you'd got used to being a bride. Anyway," he finished, "I know you're too young to get married."

"That's all right then," said Josie, putting her arms around his neck and kissing him.

"There isn't any other reason is there, Josie? I mean you haven't found someone else or anything?"

"Of course not," Josie crossed her fingers as she lied.

As they started walking again, this time with their arms around each other, Edwin sighed.

"I'd always thought I'd propose to you on a summer's day in a field full of buttercups and daisies, or maybe lying on the sand dunes at Horsey Mere listening to the sound of the sea, instead of halfway over a bomb site."

Josie laughed.

"It's what you said and the way you said it that matters, not where you said it."

"You deserve better."

"Stop worrying, it's not always like it is in films you know."

Edwin grinned, kissed the top of her head, then said seriously, "What about the ring, when are you going to choose it? Perhaps I can make that a bit more romantic."

"I suppose it'll have to be Saturday afternoon, unless I ask for time off from work."

"Saturday afternoon is OK with me if it suits you. My mother wants to give a little engagement party for us. She could organise that for the evening, then I'll still have a couple of days before I have to go back."

"Does your Mum know you were going to ask me to get engaged then?"

"Well, yes, I told her and my Dad, they thoroughly approve, Josie."

Josie felt a bit put out by this bit of information. Their engagement had been discussed with his parents before he had even asked her. What, she wondered, would have happened if they hadn't approved, would Edwin then not have asked her?

It struck her as somewhat immature of him to feel he had to get their approval first, surely most men would have got engaged and then announced it to their parents. But then Edwin wasn't most men, in fact, thought Josie, he's really still a boy. One would have thought being in the Navy would have made him grow up a bit. In her mind, Josie began comparing him unfavourably with the other men of her acquaintance; she was sure none of them would feel obliged to seek their parents' approval before getting engaged.

By the time they reached home, she was in a turmoil of indecision.

"Let's tell your parents," said Edwin.

Reluctantly Josie walked down the front path and tried the front door. It was unlocked, a sure sign that her parents were in.

"Edwin wants to talk to you," she said, wondering if he would do the 'I want to ask for your daughter's hand in marriage' bit. Surely not, thought Josie, feeling very embarrassed. She didn't know why she felt so reluctant to actually announce that she was getting engaged to Edwin, after all she knew they were very fond of him.

"We thought we'd get engaged," stammered Edwin.

Her father looked up from his paper.

"Engaged?" he echoed.

"That's lovely!" said her mother enthusiastically, "I always hoped you'd marry Edwin."

I don't think that's true, thought Josie, I think you always hoped it'd be Ziggy.

Mr Brown shook hands with Edwin and kissed Josie.

"I hope you'll both be very happy."

"We're going to pick the ring on Saturday afternoon and my mother wants to give a little party in the evening, just you and Josie and me and John, of course, if he wants to come, that is."

Blimey, thought Josie, it's all arranged, right down to who's invited. Wonder what would have happened if I'd said no?

On Saturday Josie decided to put all thoughts of Rex, from whom she had still had no message, out of her mind. Dressed in her best clothes, a lavender coloured dress with a lace collar, she waited for Edwin to arrive to select the ring.

"You look nice," said John being unusually complimentary.

"Thanks," said Josie without looking up from the book she was

231

reading.

"Josie, you're sure you really want to get engaged?"

"Of course I'm sure, there could never be anyone as devoted as Edwin has been."

"I don't think that's a very good reason for getting engaged, I mean you can't say you've been all that devoted to him can you?"

"Oh shut up John and if you dare to mention anything about Ziggy or Rex I'll kill you!"

"Don't worry, I shan't shop you, I'm not coming to your silly old party anyway, I've got other things to do."

There was no time for any further arguments as Edwin, after knocking at the door, opened it and called, "Josie, are you ready?"

"Ready and waiting," said Josie. "Let's be off. 'bye Mum!"

"You coming tonight John?" asked Edwin as they prepared to leave.

"Can't I'm afraid, I've made other arrangements. I'm sorry Edwin," said John politely.

Josie found that the visit to the jewellers was the nicest thing about being engaged. When the jeweller got out tray after tray of beautiful rings, she found it very difficult to decide.

As he watched her carefully checking the prices, Edwin whispered, "It's all right Josie, stop worrying about the price and pick the one you like best."

Finally selecting a solitaire diamond, Edwin placed it carefully on her engagement finger.

"Congratulations!" said the jeweller smiling on, yet another happy pair, war or no war, life goes on, he thought.

The engagement party was not a roaring success. Josie seemed slightly withdrawn. At one point his mother asked Edwin if Josie was all right. Josie's father had already decided that she was not all right and he wondered if she was already regretting the engagement.

Getting her on her own, Edwin put his arms around her and asked, "What's up Josie? You don't seem very happy."

"I'm all right, it's just that I'm not very good at parties, your mother's very kind but I'm not sure she thinks I'm the right girl for you."

"Is that all?" laughed Edwin. "Haven't you noticed, my mother wouldn't think any girl is good enough for me, it's a pity she didn't have more children then maybe she wouldn't be so possessive." After a pause to gaze into Josie's eyes he said, "I was getting worried, I thought you might have changed your mind or something."

"Don't be silly," said Josie, trying to reassure him, she couldn't bear to see him looking so forlorn.

They were locked in each other's arms when a discreet cough interrupted their embrace.

"Your mother's made a special cake," said Edwin's father from the doorway. "She wants you and Josie to come and cut it."

"What a lovely party," said Mrs Brown when they arrived back home again. "Edwin's mother had gone to such a lot of trouble. You're a lucky girl to be getting such a nice mother-in-law."

Josie turned a bit pale at the thought of Mrs Tuttle as a mother-in-law.

For the rest of his leave, Edwin was in blissful ignorance of his fiancée's confused state of mind. Whenever she lapsed into a brooding silence, he found he could jolly her out of it. So jolly had their every encounter become that Josie was beginning to feel slightly nauseated by it all and longed for the peace of being her own person and not half of a pair. Though she wouldn't admit it even to herself, she was quite relieved when Edwin returned to his ship.

On the same day that Edwin left, Josie received a letter from Rex, 'My dear Josie,' he wrote, 'Thanks for writing to me, I can't tell you how much it meant to me to receive your letter. I'm not wounded, it's just that I've had a bad bout of pneumonia, caused I suppose by getting soaking wet when we landed on the beach. We had to wade in with the sea nearly up to our necks. Our clothes eventually just dried on us, which probably didn't help. We advanced inland quite quickly but after four days I was rushed into the field hospital, where I have been ever since. It seems to have been a long job but I think I'm beginning to feel a bit better now. Maybe, when I'm recovered, I'll see some action, I'd hate to have to tell my children when they ask "What did you do in the war, Pop?" that I landed in France and got pneumonia!

'I've lost track of Zigmund, our company are miles inland now. I don't quite know what will happen to me once I get fit again. Please write to me again Josie and I'm longing to hear from you. If my address changes, I'll let you know straight away. As I lie here, I keep thinking of all the fun we had together. I'll never forget you Josie. All my love, Rex.'

No one else had been in the house when the letter arrived, so Josie was able to hide it away in her bedroom until she could answer it in private. Before she had an opportunity to do this, she had read it thoroughly at least half a dozen times.

If only she had received it before deciding to get engaged to Edwin! The more she thought about it the more she wondered if she had done the right thing, but she admitted that there was really no way of refusing Edwin short of finishing with him altogether, and she wasn't really sure she would want to do that. Josie was beginning to get a bad headache with the worry of it all.

The first person outside the family to be told about the engagement was her friend Penny.

"Golly, what a lovely ring," said Penny admiringly. "Bet it was expensive."

"It was, I was a bit worried about that 'cos sailors don't get paid much do they? But Edwin says that while he's at sea there's nothing to spend his money on."

"I'm glad you finally made up your mind Josie."

"The day Edwin went back to his ship I got a letter from Rex."

"You going to tell him you're engaged?"

"I can't. He's in hospital with pneumonia, so I can't do that, can I?" she pleaded, hoping for Penny's approval.

"I suppose not under the circumstances but you'll have to tell him eventually won't you?" Looking at Josie's worried face she added, "I don't think you're really sure which one you like best, are you?"

"No," said Josie unhappily. "If only I'd got Rex's letter before Edwin came home!"

"Would you have refused to get engaged?"

"I don't suppose so, if I'm honest."

"Don't you think it would be best if you didn't answer the letter?"

"I couldn't do that," said Josie quickly. "Not while he's ill and saying he's longing for a letter, I just couldn't."

Nevertheless, Josie took Penny's advice to heart and for more than a week debated on the advisability or otherwise of replying to the letter. So many times had she read and re-read the flimsy air mail sheet that it was beginning to fall apart. Each time she got to the words, 'I'm longing to hear from you' she remembered the deep voice murmuring, 'I've never met a girl like you before Josie.' She smiled at the memory of the tall gangling boy who seemed to be all arms and legs.

Finally, she decided that, engaged or not, she couldn't just ignore his plea. She started her letter, 'My dear Rex' and ended it with 'All my love, Josie' and in between enquired how he was feeling, what he was doing, whether he had any news of Ziggy; anything, in fact, that she could think of until the air mail form was full and she had no room to tell him of her engagement to Edwin.

Baby Elizabeth's christening in July went off without a hitch. The baby herself was so good, not even crying when the vicar made the sign of the cross in cold water from the font on her forehead. Violet's parents had prepared a small feast to celebrate after the christening was complete.

As they sat around the table Josie was impressed with how much Violet had matured since she last saw her. She looked after the baby as if she had been doing it all her life.

Robert looked every inch the proud father, taking his turn at holding the baby, who gurgled happily each time he picked her up.

Towards the end of July there were rumours that there had been an attempt to assassinate Hitler. Later the rumours were confirmed, although several officers present at Hitler's headquarters were severely injured, the Fuehrer had a miraculous escape. Those responsible were tried and shot within the hour.

As the warm sunny days of July passed into even warmer August days, Josie found time to catch her breath from what had been a very busy period, time to read the papers and listen to the wireless. The battle for France was still occupying all the front pages.

By the middle of August the talk was all of the 'Falaise Pocket'. The closure of this pocket of resistance would complete the disaster of the German armies in France. The German forces south and south-east of Caen had hung on too long. General von Kluge, who had replaced Runstedt, decided to pull out but it was too late to escape. The German columns clogging up every road to the East were easy targets for Allied bombers and artillery.

On August 16th the Falaise Pocket was six miles wide, two days later it had narrowed to two miles, on the 19th of August it was finally closed.

Meanwhile, von Kluge's retreating forces, with ten of their generals dead, were still reeling back towards the Seine when the Allies struck another blow. An armada of ships landed British, American and Free French troops at Frejus and several other small Mediterranean ports between Cannes and Toulon.

The German forces were hopelessly scattered and within ten days the American 79th Army under Lieutenant-General Patch was in Grenoble.

In those same ten days Paris was liberated by the French Forces of the Interior. General Patton was threatening Verdan, General Hodges was on the Meuses and General Montgomery had brought his forces to the Somme.

The newsreels at the cinema were becoming so exciting that the previously quiet, reticent audiences were standing up and cheering.

There was no news from either Jimmy or Ziggy, which suggested that they might be in the thick of the fighting. How lucky, thought Josie, that Rex was being spared all this by being confined to hospital, although his last letter suggested he was now 'chomping at the bit' in his anxiety to join his buddies. How strange men were in their apparent enjoyment of conflict, even her gentle Rex seemed unable to resign himself to being out of the war.

Next week the pictures from the Russian front added to the impression that the war for the Allies was, at last, going according to plan. Marshal Stalin's strategy of attacking Germany through Poland into Prussia and through Rumania and Hungary into Austria and Czechoslovakia, seemed to be working.

For the next few weeks it was worth the admission price at the cinema just to watch the newsreels. General De Gaulle was pictured entering Paris in triumph. A few days later Montgomery's men entered Brussels. Flags, which must have been carefully hidden for the whole of the German occupation, were draped from every building. Belgian citizens sang 'Tipperary' as tanks and armoured cars, followed by marching troops, passed through.

On September 17th a great aerial armada streamed out of airfields in Britain with planes towing enormous gliders containing jeeps, guns and small tanks and more paratroopers than had

236

ever been seen before in one airborne operation.

There was a wireless bulletin stating that the paratroopers had landed and pretty soon there was news of the capture of Eindhoven, and then the town of Nijmegen was captured after a sharp struggle. Simultaneously the ground troops moved forward; the whole point of the scheme was for the ground forces and airborne forces to link up. This was accomplished on the following day.

On the 20th another huge force of planes towing gliders landed reinforcements and equipment. The contingent of paratroopers landed at Arnhem had succeeded in capturing the bridge, together with an area about two miles square.

The bulletins now reported frantic enemy counter-attacks by day and night on the troops of Arnhem. On the 23rd thousands of British and American glider-borne troops were dropped in an effort to relieve the Arnhem men.

The news was beginning to get less inspiring, there was now a great deal of anxiety about the paratroops at Arnhem. The Germans, recovering from their first shock, rushed up tanks and guns. Eventually, came the sad news that the air-borne troops had now been split into small groups, still fighting but with the enemy ring around them slowly tightening.

By the 25th it was becoming obvious, even from the limited amount of information being broadcast, that the bid had failed, there was no longer any hope that the main army could link up with the troops at Arnhem.

During darkness on the 25th and 26th survivors slipped through the enemy lines and were taken back in boats. It was not until sometime later that the world became aware of the full cost of the Arnhem bridgehead. Although many troops escaped, the wounded, who numbered thousands, had to be left behind.

People in England had no sooner congratulated themselves on being rid of the VI flying bombs menace when a new terror confronted them. The Germans now had a second secret weapon, a device known as the rocket bomb or V2.

The missile was more ingenious and deadly than the flying bomb. It's flight could not be intercepted, it made a hole of 30ft deep and usually shattered everything where it fell. Once again, Pathé News, first on the scene, brought graphic pictures of the devastation in London where most of the missiles were landing.

But as time went by it became obvious that this weapon was far less accurate than the Vl and there were incidents of them dropping anywhere between Southend and Reading.

As Christmas approached, preparations had to be started much earlier. Parcels were despatched to Jimmy, Rex, Ziggy and Duncan, who was now somewhere on the Western front.

By the end of November letters from Jimmy confirmed his parcel had been received and a letter from Rex told Josie that he was still in hospital and had received her parcel on Thanksgiving Day.

By mid-January the British in the North and the Americans in the South had hurled the Germans back to their original positions.

On February 23rd a further dramatic announcement raised spirits even higher. British, Canadian and American troops, using a typical Montgomery technique of smoke-screens, a devastating artillery barrage and a heavy air umbrella, opened a general attack from Nijmegen to Venlo. General Eisenhower's stirring words echoed around the free world.

"We are going," he said, "to destroy every German west of the Rhine."

This was no idle threat, the Americans, swarming across the Ruhr, had taken München-Gladbach and were shelling Cologne. The British and Canadians were also advancing on all fronts. The Siegfried Line had been breached.

Everywhere battle was joined and advancing Allied troops were forcing the Germans to the Rhine, broken and bewildered, many of the German troops were drowned, others tamely gave in.

The pictures from the Russian front were equally encouraging, featuring the annihilation of the German garrison at Budapest.

With the news for all theatres of war becoming more than satisfactory, it seemed to add an extra poignancy to the news brought by Duncan's very distressed mother.

On returning from a visit to the city with Penny and the twins, Josie's mother, looking very upset, met her at the door.

"Oh Josie, it's awful," she blurted out. "Duncan's Mum has had a telegram to say he's missing, believed killed."

Josie felt her knees suddenly give way. Not Duncan, inoffensive little Duncan, somehow he was the last person one could associate with violent death.

"His mother is terribly upset. I felt awful, I know how I'd feel if it had been Jimmy."

Josie felt too stunned to reply as the tears began to prick her eyes. Her mother put an arm around her shoulder.

"I'm all right," said Josie, who still felt unable to move or grasp the enormity of the news.

Memories came flooding back, Duncan as a small boy with a funny accent, no father and a very protective mother. Duncan struggling to wean himself from his possessive mother. Duncan at school latching on to her whenever he was in any sort of trouble and Duncan grown tall and strong and so proud to be in the Army. It can't be true, thought Josie, not just when he was becoming independent and starting to enjoy life.

"I suppose I should go next door and see Duncan's Mum."

"If you feel you should and it's not going to upset you too much."

"It'll upset me 'cos you don't know what to say at times like this, but I think Duncan would expect me to keep an eye on his mother - in fact he asked me to do that when he joined up."

However, it was several hours before Josie could pluck up the courage to go next door to visit the distraught woman.

Knocking rather timidly on the door, she hoped for one minute that perhaps Mrs Scott would be out. In her heart, she knew that this was extremely unlikely as Mrs Scott seldom left the house, and certainly wouldn't do so at a time like this. Josie braced herself as the door opened a few inches.

"Oh it's you Josie, come in," Mrs Scott was red-eyed from weeping.

As Josie entered the darkened room where all the curtains were drawn tightly across the windows, she stammered, "I'm so sorry to hear about Duncan."

Mrs Scott began to wail uncontrollably, she sat down and rocked to and fro in her distress.

"Is there anything I can do?" Josie asked, feeling helpless, not quite knowing what to do in this sort of situation.

"He's all I've got," murmured Mrs Scott between sobs.

"I know," said Josie. "It's a terrible thing, but sometimes you know when men are reported missing, they are eventually found alive."

She had been comforting herself with this thought ever since her mother had given her the sad news. Now she tried to instill

239

some hope into the older woman.

"I don't know what I'll do."

"Have you had anything to eat since you got the telegram?"

"I couldn't eat."

"But you must, you can't go on like this, you'll be ill."

"I don't care. If Duncan's gone, what is there to live for?"

"Now come on," said Josie, "let's draw the curtains and let a little light in."

"No," protested Mrs Scott, but Josie carried on and carefully drew back the curtains.

"I'll make you some tea and a sandwich."

Returning to the living-room, she was glad to find the wailing had stopped, but Mrs Scott was sitting staring into space.

Shaking her gently, Josie said, "Come on now, try to eat something and have a cup of tea."

Still protesting, Mrs Scott drank the tea and took a few bites out of the sandwich before pushing the tray away.

"I don't think you should be here alone."

"I've been alone ever since Duncan joined the Army."

"I know, but I don't think you should be alone at this time. Would you like to stay with us for a bit? We've got Jimmy's bedroom."

"Would your mother mind?"

"No, I'm sure she wouldn't."

"You wouldn't consider sleeping here for a few nights I suppose Josie? You're right, I would appreciate some company."

"If you'd rather I did that than you come to stay with us, of course I'll come."

"I'd still have to come back wouldn't I and - face things."

"Well, I see your point, perhaps it would be harder that way, but you'd get more company at our's. I mean, I have to go to work and I often go out in the evening."

"I'd rather you come here," said Mrs Scott pathetically. "I want to be here in case I get another telegram." Josie realised that this was what Mrs Scott pinned her hopes on, which seemed a better alternative than giving up in despair.

"All right," said Josie, patting her shoulder and hoping that the wailing wouldn't start again, "I'll get some things and tell my Mum I'm staying with you for a bit."

The next day, being Sunday, Josie had not planned to go out so she was able to spend the day with Mrs Scott, cooking a dinner and pleading with her to eat it, chatting incessantly to try to take her mind off the loss of Duncan.

Although her father had not been very keen on the arrangement for her to stay with Mrs Scott, Josie felt that perhaps it was helping her as much as Mrs Scott, somehow they had both to come to terms with what had happened. Mrs Scott had no wireless and scarcely looked at the newspapers, being so swamped with her own grief as to not be interested in the progress of the war. What did it matter if we won if Duncan wouldn't be coming home?

Soon after her return home, Josie made her usual rush to the front door at the sound of the postman. Gathering a couple of letters addressed to her father, she looked at the last one lying on the doormat, it was addressed to her in Rex's spidery writing. In her anxiety to open the envelope, she failed to notice the address on the back.

Rushing up to her room for a bit of privacy with the letter still in her hand, she sat down on her bed to read it.

'Dearest Josie, you will see by my address that I have been invalided home.' Smoothing out the envelope which had been torn in her anxiety to get it open, she saw it had an address in Texas, USA.

As she read further Rex explained that the hospital authorities had decided that his pneumonia was not responding to treatment and he was certainly not fit enough to rejoin his unit, so he had been flown home. 'It's great to be back home even though I'm going to have a further period in hospital, but at least my folks can come and see me. I wish you could come Josie, I miss you. I was hoping that maybe when the war was won, as it looks like it will be quite soon, that the unit might return to England before being shipped home and I'd be able to see you again, but I guess this was not meant to be. Josie, will you send me a photo so I can keep it on my locker? The only one I've got is the snap taken by Ziggy of us both in the park. I'd like a proper photo to remind me of you, not that I need reminding. I've told my Mom about you, she hopes you will be able to come to the States when the war is over.'

Josie felt her heart beating fast. What exactly did he mean about visiting the States? It was so inconclusive.

1

The news from all war zones during the chilly weather of March brought an unexpected glow to the cold, pinched faces of the British population, it helped them to put up with shortages of both fuel and food.

There was news now from Burma where Allied troops were facing the crafty Japanese jungle fighters. Events in Burma had been somewhat overshadowed by events in Europe.

The news from the European front continued to report advances, all the time the Allied troops were getting nearer to Germany.

There was now immense pressure on the German forces on all fronts. Added to this, when April brought brilliant sunshine, Allied bombers pounded away at the enemy columns. The Luftwaffe appeared to be grounded; it was later disclosed that they had very little petrol left. In the air as well as on the ground, the game was up for Germany, the end of the war seemed to be in sight.

Also advancing ever nearer to Berlin, the Soviet Army had taken the Austrian capital Vienna.

Though she had told nobody, Josie was becoming alarmed at the state of melancholy which Mrs Scott seemed to be in, it seemed to get worse week by week. Another thing she found upsetting was the way the house was gradually being turned into a shrine to the memory of Duncan. The large framed photograph of him in his Army uniform stood in the middle of the sideboard, a vase of fresh flowers on either side.

It was now that a second tragedy struck. Everyone had been aware for some time that some of the bloodiest battles were being waged against the Japanese in the Far East.

Another of the dreaded telegrams had been delivered, this time further down the road to the parents of Ray. It was not, however, concerning Ray, but his elder brother Len, who had been a life-long friend of Jimmy. This time the telegram stated - 'Regret to inform you that your son Corporal Leonard Anderson has been killed in action'.

It was several days before Ray's mother felt up to telling anyone else about the loss of her son, preferring to keep her grief to herself. When, eventually, the news seeped out, the Brown family were once again devastated. Should they write and tell Jimmy of the death of his friend, or would it be better to keep the news from him until he eventually came home?

Josie didn't have quite the same feeling of despair as she had about Duncan. Len had been Jimmy's friend and had never really had much time for either his young brother or Josie. In any case, Josie was finding something nearer to home to worry about.

Though she had never said anything, Josie knew that her very superstitious mother was thinking 'Two telegrams, sure to be a third, would it be Jimmy?' When Josie carefully broached the subject, her mother hurriedly denied that she was thinking any such thing. Josie remained unconvinced as she watched her mother's reaction to every unexpected knock at the door.

On April 12th there was sad news from America. The death of President Roosevelt was announced.

He was succeeded by Vice President Truman, the quiet man who had always been at Roosevelt's side. For a while it seemed impossible to believe that, with the end of the war so near, one of the 'Big Three' would not be there to enjoy it. President Truman would have a long way to go to achieve the popularity of his predecessor.

The Russians and the Western Allies continued to advance on all fronts, each day further progress was reported, there were no longer any German counter-attacks. The Allies were now well into Germany. Every bulletin and newsreel showed the two forces drawing closer to each other. There seemed no way that the Germans could avoid defeat.

On April 26th an unknown town called Torgau in the very heart of Germany ensured its place in history, as the place where the American and Russian advance patrols met. Newsreels showed American and Russian soldiers leaping from their tanks and embracing each other.

The usually grim-faced Russian troops were laughing and shaking hands with every American they encountered. The pictures in the papers had headlines like 'Comrades in arms meet'.

There was much rejoicing in the whole of the western world. At home, every work place and pub celebrated the latest advances. Everyone thought dreamily of peace, no more bombs, the boys back home again. Except that is for the many families like Mrs Scott to whom the promise of peace now meant very little.

There was astonishing news from Italy on April 28th. The 'Duce' Benito Mussolini had been executed by Italian partisans. There were pictures of the Duce and his mistress hanging upside down in the city of Milan, where a jeering, jostling crowd had gathered. Dreadful as the pictures were, it was hard to feel any sympathy for the deposed enemy who had aligned himself with Hitler.

On the following Sunday the 'Sunday Pictorial', as well as reporting the utter collapse of the Germans, had news of an offer made by Himmler to surrender to Britain and America only. It further stated that Himmler had been given until Thursday night to offer unconditional surrender to all three Allied governments.

The back page carrying the late news stated, 'Allied officials confident that Germany will speedily consent to unconditional surrender to Russia too'. Going back to the front page, Josie noticed the words 'Where is Hitler? - see back page.'

"Listen to this," said Josie. "Mystery of Hitler, dead or captive. Hitler is dead, dying or a prisoner, in any case he no longer counts, so much is obvious from reports from inside Germany which reached the outside world after the Himmler peace offer. Himmler is reported to have told the Allies via Stockholm that Hitler is not very well."

"Not very well," chuckled John, "I should think he's as sick as a toad."

Josie continued, "Hitler may have only twenty-four hours to live and there has been a report from Switzerland that both Hitler and Goebbels were shot three days ago."

"Well, what do you make of that?" asked Mrs Brown.

The Allied forces continued to advance on all fronts. On May 5th the news-reader at the BBC, usually so calm and matter of fact, couldn't keep the excitement out of his voice as he announced:

"The whole German force occupying Holland, Denmark and Germany has surrendered to Field Marshal Montgomery unconditionally at Lüneburg. Nearly a million Germans have been taken prisoner."

The newsreel pictures of the prisoners penned up in makeshift enclosures made everyone realise just how vast was the area needed to contain them. Each day still more men came to surrender from generals to privates. Each new influx placed a further strain on Allied administration.

On May 6th 250,000 more surrendered to the Americans. Nothing remained of the Third Reich but a few fighting fragments, the ruins of their towns, the bodies of their dead and the lasting shame of their evil deeds.

What little sympathy there might have been for the suffering of the German population had quickly evaporated on the discovery of the Nazi concentration camps of Buchenwald, Dachau and Belsen.

When the stomach-churning pictures from inside the camps were released there was an outcry from all civilised nations. Millions of Jews had been put to death and those who were still alive were like skeletons. Piles of dead bodies were everywhere. No one had appreciated to what lengths the Germans had gone in their persecution of the Jews.

17

VE Day

On May 7th newspaper headlines announced, 'Germany offers surrender to Soviet, British and US'. Underneath in slightly smaller print, 'Terms give Nazis bad jolt but we won't budge'. After that, followed further details of a delegation from the German General Staff arriving at Russian Army headquarters to learn the terms on which the United Nations would accept their surrender. British and American Generals were also present.

'When the Germans sign and the state of their forces is such that it is not likely to be delayed for more than twelve hours - the war in Europe will be at an end and VE Day will be proclaimed. At a later date, there will be a formal public surrender in the ruins of Berlin.'

The German delegates appeared to be thunderstruck by the conditions laid down in the Instrument of Surrender, the paper reported, but they were informed on behalf of the three Powers that there could be no modifications.

'The surrender up to now by Commanders in the field will be superseded by the general Instrument of Surrender imposed on behalf of the Allied Powers and applicable to Germany and the German Armed Forces as a whole.

'The Prime Minister will make only a brief announcement of VE Day on the wireless, leaving the main speech to be made by the King at 9.00 p.m.

'Should the announcement come today, it is not likely to come before the afternoon. It will take at least that time to make arrangements with Moscow and Washington for simultaneous release of the news so that all countries can celebrate together.'

Most of the population were able to read these glad tidings before leaving for work. Understandably, there was less work than usual done that day, everyone was intent on discussing whether VE Day would be declared in time for a day off on the following day.

It seemed impossible that after nearly six long years, it would all be over, although celebrations would still be slightly overshadowed by the need to continue fighting the Japanese, and so many family members would still be absent. Most families, in common with the Brown household, were saving the biggest celebrations of all for when all the boys returned home.

In the evening the 'Eastern Evening News' carried on from where the morning papers had finished, 'Doenitz orders surrender' said the bold headline, 'German radio announcement, senseless to go on' in slightly smaller print.

There was a Reuters report on how the German population had received the news. 'The announcement,' it said, 'Was made by Count Schwerin Von Krosick, German Foreign Minister, over the German Flensburg Radio today - after a heroic fight of almost six years of incomparable hardness. Germany has succumbed to the overwhelming power of her enemies; to continue the war would only mean senseless bloodshed and a futile disintegration.'

Glancing from the page Josie chuckled at the advert for the 'Samson and Hercules' - 'Dancing to the music of Gerry Hoey and his band' - then in large print - 'VE Day, irrespective of any other announcement or advertisement already issued, the following arrangements have been made for VE Day whenever it is officially announced:

VE Day - 3.30 to 5.30 - 2/-
At night - 7.30 to midnight - 3/6'

The following day's prices were the same as VE Day. It had now been stated that two days of national holiday would be granted for VE victory celebrations.

"Trust the 'Samson' to beat everyone else to the punch," said Josie. "I wonder if Penny will want to go?"

"Better keep the wireless on until they close down in case there're any further announcements," suggested Mrs Brown.

"I can't bear to leave it to go out," said Josie, "in case I miss anything."

"Well, I'm off, we're going to the pictures," said John, departing to pick up his girlfriend.

Although it had been intended that VE Day would not be declared until the Prime Minister had spoken, it was almost midnight before there was an announcement that VE Day would be tomorrow. It took a little while for the significance of the statement to sink in.

"There will be a two day official holiday, tomorrow and the following day. Thousands have been thronging the streets in London waiting for an official announcement," said the news-reader. "At one stage they were told that there would be no announcement until the following day but the crowd had thinned very little, the majority hoping that there would soon be something to cheer about. And now there certainly is," said the news-reader, fading into an outside broadcast of the noise from the crowds in the street.

Members of the public interviewed seemed either incoherent or too emotional to say much. "Mr Churchill," the broadcast continued, "Will announce the official end of the war in the House of Commons before his 3.00 p.m. broadcast tomorrow."

The Brown family hugged each other. Mrs Brown shed a few tears, Josie felt a lump in her throat and was glad when her father brought out the glasses and the port.

"VE Day!" said her father lifting his glass.

"Public holiday!" said John. "No school for a couple of days, what shall we do to celebrate?"

"It's now time on this historic day for us to close down," said the announcer. "We would like to wish everyone a joyous VE Day."

"I don't feel in the least like going to bed," said Josie.

"Nor me," replied John.

"All the same, I think it's a good idea to go to bed now so that we can be up by the time they come back on the air."

Josie was quite surprised when she actually got a good night's sleep, she had felt she was far too excited to sleep. It was not until there were signs of movement in the household, taps running and the kettle whistling, that Josie finally surfaced. As she leapt out of bed, convinced she would be late for work, she remembered suddenly that there was no work, only a day of rejoicing.

John appeared from the bathroom looking bleary eyed.

"Didn't sleep much," he informed Josie.

"I did, I don't remember much after thinking thank God it's over."

As the family sat down to breakfast there was a sound of sprinting footsteps on the gravel path and the *Daily Mirror* shot through the letter box.

"Crumbs, he's in a hurry this morning," said John. "I bags first look at the paper."

But his father had beaten them to the door.

"What's it say?" enquired Josie, drinking her second cup of tea.

"VE Day, Public Holiday today and tomorrow," said her father. "Be worth keeping this, one day it might have some historical value."

Mr Brown settled down to scanning through the paper.

"Listen to this," he said, "Goebbels and his family are found poisoned, it says that the bodies of Dr Goebbels, his wife and six children have been found by the Russians. Hitler's body has not been discovered, neither has the body of Goering. There is now some speculation as to whether, after all, the Fuehrer and Goering may not have fled to a place of hiding."

"Wonder if we'll ever really know what happened to them?"

"It says the Prime Minister will broadcast at 3.00 p.m. and it's probable that later in the afternoon General Eisenhower, Field Marshal Montgomery and Field Marshal Alexander will also speak over the radio to the Allied world. At 9.00 p.m. the King will broadcast to the nation."

Breakfast over, John left to contact his girlfriend. When he had left her last night they hadn't known for sure that this would be VE Day.

Josie settled down to read the paper and listen to the wireless. The whole paper was obviously taken up with the news of the end of the war.

Finally, Josie turned the page to her favourite cartoon strips, Buck Ryan in the battle field proclaiming he had found something for a toast to the European Armistice.

Beelzebub Jones had one single picture taking up the space usually allotted to four or five; joyous characters in cowboy hats firing six guns were shouting, 'Yippee!'

Belinda took four pictures to tell her friend Des that the war was over and he wouldn't have to fight, to which he raised his fists and declared, 'Cor! I wanter fight B'linder'. In the next picture Belinda explained that he could fight poverty, bad health, mean houses, mean people until we've made the world a better place for decent folks to live in.

"I think I'll go and check what Penny is up to," said Josie, having worked her way through the newspaper. At the door, Penny greeted her.

"Hello Josie, what are we going to do to celebrate?" she paused. "How about going to the 'Samson' tonight?"

"OK if that's what you'd like to do, we've got to do something special haven't we?"

"You staying for a cup of tea, Josie?" enquired Penny's mother.

"We're listening to the wireless, they seem to be going mad in London."

"Not surprising is it? I mean it's been bad enough here but at least we didn't have any doodle-bugs to contend with."

Later that day, as the family waited for Mr Churchill to begin the victory speech, Josie glanced idly at the paper again. One very small column at the foot of the page brought a smile to her lips, it was headed - 'No coupons for red, white and blue'. It continued, 'Until the end of May you will not have to give coupons for cotton bunting provided it is in red, white and blue and does not cost more than 1s 3d per square yard.

There was a sudden hush as the Prime Minister began his speech. In his usual slow, deliberate and dramatic way of speaking, which held everybody spellbound, he began:

"Yesterday morning at 2.41 a.m. at General Eisenhower's HQ General Jodl the representative of the German High Command and Grand Admiral Denitz the designated Head of the German State, signed the Act of Unconditional Surrender of all of German land, sea and air forces in Europe to the Allied Expeditionary Force and simultaneously to the Soviet High Command.

"The German representatives will be Field Marshal Keitel, Commander in Chief of the German Army, Navy and Air Forces."

After announcing the hour of the formal 'Cease Fire', the Premier went on to say that, "The Germans are still resisting the Russian troops in places but should they continue to do so after midnight they will, of course, deprive themselves of the protection of the laws of war and will be attacked from all quarters by

Allied troops."

After explaining the situation in further detail he said, "This does not prevent us from celebrating today and tomorrow as Victory in Europe Days."

There was one of Mr Churchill's dramatic pauses then he said in ringing tones, "Today, perhaps, we shall think mostly of ourselves. Tomorrow, we shall pay a particular tribute to our Russian comrades."

Mr Churchill continued to praise all of the Allied countries and those over-run by Germany, who were now free nations again. After another pause he said, "We may allow ourselves a brief period of rejoicing, but let us not forget for a moment the toil and efforts that lie ahead. Japan, with all her treachery and greed, remains unsubdued. We must now devote all our strength and resources to the completion of our task both at home and abroad."

Drawing to the end of his speech, Mr Churchill finished with the words:

"Advance Britannia. Long live the cause of freedom. God save the King!"

This was followed immediately by the ceremonial sounding of the end of the war in Europe by the buglers of the Scots Guards, and outside the church bells began to ring for the first time since war had been declared.

Josie felt tears of emotion in her eyes, feeling slightly embarrassed she brushed them away until she noticed that even her father looked tearful.

Shortly after Penny appeared, looking at Josie's red eyes she said, "You've been listening to Mr Churchill, so have we and we had a bit of a cry as well, doesn't seem possible it's all over. We'll be able to go back to living normally. It's hard to remember what living normally means. Are we still going to the 'Samson' tonight?" she asked Josie.

"We said we would didn't we?"

"The buses seem to be few and far between," Penny remarked.

"S'pose the drivers and conductors are joining in the celebrations along the route."

"We can't walk all the way, not in high heels, it'd be murder."

"Why not invest in a taxi?" said Mr Brown. "After all, it is a special occasion."

"We could pay half each," said Josie.

"Brilliant idea Mr Brown," laughed Penny. "Let's go in style, Josie, it's time we pushed the boat out, if you can't spread yourself a bit after six years of austerity, when can you, I ask?"

Penny decided not to stay for tea, knowing that it would take her a good couple of hours to get ready for the night out.

At seven o'clock there was a hoot from the taxi's horn.

"Bye, Mum!" said Josie, hurriedly descending the stairs.

"You look very nice Josie," said her father. "Mind what you get up to, don't get too carried away by tonight, remember you've got the rest of your life to live!"

As Josie and Penny made their way to the 'Samson', Josie said, "Wonder who'll be there. I've heard that British Servicemen have been asked to stay in their barracks."

"Where'd you hear that?"

"On the wireless last night."

"That's rotten, why can't they celebrate the same as everyone else?"

"It did say they were being asked, not ordered."

"Oh well, that's different, I can't see many of them doing what they're asked, can you?"

"Not really."

"Anyway, I bet the place will be flooded with Yanks."

As they stepped elegantly from the taxi they found they had to join the end of a long queue waiting for the doors to open.

"Hope I'm not going to have to stand here too long, my feet are killing me already."

A couple of GIs standing in front of the girls turned round.

"Sorry about your feet," said one with a grin.

Penny blushed at being overheard.

"What's your name?" asked the GI.

"I'm Penny and my friend's Josie."

"Well, hello Penny and Josie, I'm Joe and my friend's Mac, how about us making a foursome?"

Although this was not what the girls had in mind, it seemed difficult to refuse without causing a bit of a stir and there were so many people standing around.

"OK then," said Penny as the queue began to edge forward.

"Four please," said the GI called Joe.

"No, we can pay for ourselves," said Josie.

"Wouldn't hear of it," replied Joe.

"See you later then girls," said Mac as the girls made for the cloakroom.

"Oh dear, we fell for that didn't we?" said Josie.

"Yes, I s'pose so, now they've paid for us to come in we're sort of stuck with them, aren't we?"

"They seem quite nice though, so perhaps it won't be so bad."

"At least we'll probably get free drinks all night."

The cloakroom was filled to capacity, it was hopeless trying to get near a mirror and there were others waiting to get in so the girls wasted no time going into the ballroom.

Their partners, now minus caps and great coats, were waiting at the bar. Both had regulation short back and sides haircuts. Joe's blond hair refused to lie flat despite the haircut. Mac, with very straight red hair, had no such problem; in the bright lights of the ballroom the freckles on his nose and cheeks became more prominent.

"Bags I the blond one!" laughed Penny.

"OK, I'm not fussy," replied Josie. "Don't suppose we'll ever see them again after tonight anyway. I think the ginger one's rather sweet."

As the band began the first number both GIs said, "How about it girls?"

Gerry Hoey had never sounded so good, all the musicians seemed inspired by the occasion. With few exceptions they danced every dance, changing partners regularly between the four of them but not dancing with anyone else. Occasionally they stopped for a drink and became part of an enormous group of girls and G.I.s all in high spirits.

Shortly before midnight a group of slightly drunk British servicemen made a noisy entrance.

"Who's coming to the market?" shouted one during a break in the music.

"There's thousands up there," shouted another.

"Thousands," echoed a very drunk sailor.

"Where's the market?" asked Joe.

"Up near the Town Hall," replied Penny.

"Let's go, shall we?" said Joe with his hand on Mac's shoulder.

"We'll be late getting back," said Mac.

"Heck! So what! Surely no one's going to bother over much if we're an hour or two late on a night like this."

"How'll we get back to base?"

"If there's no transport around, we'll get a cab."

"Great idea," said Mac, downing his beer in a flash and beginning to look a little bleary-eyed.

Penny looked at Josie, trying to suss out how she was feeling about all this.

"OK by me," said Josie.

"Great, let's get our coats before the rush starts."

But the rush had started, whether inspired by the drunken sailor's ramblings or the desire to carry on celebrating somewhere else, no one was quite sure. All they knew was the group seemed to get larger and larger, all apparently making for the market.

The sailor had been right, there were literally thousands of people packed into the market square, all singing and shouting, the din was unbelievable. It seemed impossible that any more could be squeezed in but, nevertheless, the dozens approaching from every direction were somehow accommodated.

Unable to move for the crowds, the girls and the new GI friends joined in the singing, on the fringes of the crowd people were attempting to dance.

Everyone seemed to be kissing everyone else. Encouraged by this, Joe and Mac took advantage of the situation by kissing Josie and Penny.

Glancing at her friend when she managed to get close enough to her, Josie recognised the tell-tale signs: Penny was falling in love again. Maybe she'll still end up a GI bride, thought Josie. For her own part, she certainly liked the red headed boy who had rather shyly kissed her, 'But I'm not getting involved,' Josie told herself severely, 'I've got problems enough as it is.'

The crowd were still singing and dancing at midnight, when Josie said, "Come on Penny, I think we'd better start thinking of going home in case we find we've got to walk all the way."

Penny and Joe were locked in a farewell embrace.

"It's been nice meeting you Mac, this is a night we'll all remember for ever," said Josie.

"I hope I'll see you again," said Mac.

"Do you think you can prise your friend away from Penny so you can get back to camp?"

"Come on Joe, we've got to find a cab somehow," said Mac as

they approached the entwined pair.

"OK, I s'pose you're right," said Joe, reluctantly releasing Penny, "Now don't forget what I told you," he said as he hurried over to Mac's side. "So long girls, see you soon."

"Take care," said Penny.

"Come on, let's go," said Josie as the two GIs disappeared from sight.

"Isn't he lovely?" sighed Penny.

"Penny, you've only just met him, how can you possibly know if he's lovely, he might be horrible when you get to know him."

"No, I'm sure he won't be, sometimes you know about these things even when you've only known someone a few hours."

"Love at first sight!"

"Well, it's possible, isn't it? It does happen sometimes you know."

"I s'pose so, mostly in films though."

"I arranged to go to the 'Samson' tomorrow night with him, will you come? Joe said Mac would probably be there."

"Look Penny, it's been a lovely VE night, one we'll remember when we're old and grey, we'll probably tell our grandchildren about it, but that's as far as it goes with me. Mac's a very nice boy but I don't want to see him again and it's no good telling me we could just be friends 'cause it doesn't work out that way, does it? I've got problems enough deciding between Edwin and Rex, no way do I want to complicate it even more. You go ahead Penny, maybe this GI Joe will prove to be the right one for you, but remember what you've told me in the past, there's a lot of things to consider if you're thinking of marrying a Yank."

As the girls walked home they encountered several groups of singing, shouting, slightly drunk citizens, but they managed to avoid getting entangled with them.

When finally they came to the parting of the way, Josie said, "It's been great Penny, one of your better ideas going to the 'Samson'. You go tomorrow, I'd like to come with you but I'm not going to, I've made up my mind."

"What are you going to do then?"

"Oh, I guess I'll probably write a letter to Rex and Edwin. There's such a lot to say, I wonder what they did to celebrate?"

"I don't think I'd tell them what you did."

"Why not, it was all quite innocent wasn't it? But maybe

you're right, I think I'll forget to mention Mac and Joe."

"Anyway Josie, you're going to have to decide between them, you can't just keep putting it off, perhaps tomorrow would be a good day to make your momentous decision."

It had been some time since Josie had received any news of Edwin but she was not unduly worried as there had been no mention of his ship being in any sort of action.

When she had time to dwell on the subject, which wasn't often, Josie wondered how things would work out when Edwin eventually returned home for good. On the other hand he might decide to stay in the Navy and make a career of it. Either way, Josie knew she would soon be obliged to make some sort of decision about how she really felt about him.

Her whole thinking was now coloured by the letters she was receiving with greater frequency from Rex, each getting bolder and more intimate. The letter she had received a couple of weeks ago had begun, 'My dearest Josie, It looks as if the war will soon be over, thank God. I'm hoping you'll come to visit the States sometime in the future. My Mom and Pop are very anxious to meet you.' The letter ended, 'When it's all over Josie, promise me you'll come. I'll mail the money for your fare, but if you're not able to do so, then I'll come to England. I can't think of anything else at the moment except meeting you again.'

Josie was, at first, stunned by the letter. She read it and re-read it. After it had time to sink in, she realised that she felt quite elated, wasn't this what deep down she had always hoped for? But where did this leave her engagement to Edwin? What would her parents say? What would Edwin's parents say? Josie went from being elated to being confused and then depressed.

Josie sat in her bedroom on the second night of the VE celebrations trying to write a letter to Edwin and to Rex, having steadfastly refused to go out with Penny to meet Joe and Mac.

Josie's note-paper remained blank, she had been trying for hours to decide between them, but had reluctantly come to the conclusion that she couldn't hurt either of them. After trying unsuccessfully to compose a letter to each of them, she leaned back with a sigh. "I'm beginning to wish I'd gone to the 'Samson' with Penny. Wonder how she's getting on with Joe? Wonder if Mac was disappointed because I didn't go?"

"Josie, we're going out to celebrate, why don't you come?" her mother yelled from the bottom of the stairs.

"No thanks, I'll be all right."

"I don't think you should be spending tonight on your own, you should be out enjoying yourself."

"I'm perfectly OK, I'm writing a letter. You go out, don't worry about me."

The closing of the door announced the departure of her parents. Why was life always so complicated? she mused, refusing to accept Penny's summing up that most of her present problem was of her own making. Reaching into her handbag she found the letter from Rex and read it once again.

Then, to adhere to her policy of fair play, she read through the last letter she had received from Edwin. She was no nearer coming to a decision as she leaned back on her pillow; a letter in each hand, she closed her eyes. Why, oh why, with the dawn of a new era of peace and tranquillity, was her life in such a state of turmoil?

Still clutching the letters, Josie did her usual trick of postponing any decision till a future date and, with a smile on her face, she drifted into a peaceful sleep.

Epilogue

Before Peace was a month old, Josie had made two momentous decisions. Having faced the fact that marriage to Edwin, completely dominated by his mother, just didn't bear thinking about, she had turned her attention to life with Rex. Her father was already saying that America was the other side of the world and mournfully stating that they might never see her again.

Coupled with this, the description Rex had given of his home on his father's ranch where the nearest neighbour was thirty miles away, now seemed somehow much less desirable.

Josie's only knowledge of cowboys had come from her frequent visits to the cinema. However, when Rex described weeks spent on the trail at round-up time, it somehow seemed much less romantic. She imagined herself left with Rex's mother, whilst Rex and his father rode away into the sunset to round up their stray cattle. Suppose she didn't get on with his mother, who would she turn to?

Thus, after a month of indecision, Josie decided that neither way of life would really suit her.

Anyway, what better way to celebrate PEACE than to make a completely fresh start . . .